D0212434

The Politics
of Narration

THE POLITICS
OF NARRATION

James Joyce,
William Faulkner,
and Virginia Woolf

RICHARD PEARCE

RUTGERS UNIVERSITY PRESS
New Brunswick and London

Library of Congress Cataloging-in-Publication Data
Pearce, Richard, 1932–
    The politics of narration : James Joyce, William Faulkner, and
Virginia Woolf / Richard Pearce.
        p.   cm.
    Includes bibliographical references and index.
    ISBN 0-8135-1656-0
    1. English fiction—20th century—History and criticism.
2. Joyce, James, 1882–1941—Technique. 3. Faulkner, William,
1897–1962—Technique. 4. Woolf, Virginia, 1882–1941—Technique.
5. Politics and literature. 6. Modernism (Literature) 7. Narration
(Rhetoric) I. Title.
PR888.P6P43 1991
823′.91209358—dc20   90-8977
                                                            CIP

British Cataloging-in-Publication information available

Dedicated to my colleagues and students at Wheaton College in our last years as a woman's college— when we helped each other learn the new scholarship on women and cultural diversity. Also to my wife, Jean, and daughters, Karin and Emily, who never let me get off the intellectual or emotional hook at home. And again to Jean for helping me see what I needed to clarify at many stages of this project.

Contents

Acknowledgments

I am indebted to The National Endowment for the Humanities for a fellowship that helped initiate this project six years ago. I would also like to thank Bernard Benstock for his commentary and encouragement on an early draft of the Joyce section, Susan Bazargan for her sensitive and scholarly reading of a later version, Fritz Senn for keeping me centered on Joyce's language, Don Bialostosky for his help on Bakhtin, Linda Kauffman and Judith Wittenberg for their very helpful comments as feminist Faulknerians, Jane Lilienfeld for her tough criticism and warm support as I ventured into the world of Virginia Woolf. And I want to thank Bernard Duyfhuizen, John Duvall, Blanche Gelfant, Phillip Herring, Toni Oliviero, Thomas Schaub, Bonnie Kime Scott, Brook Thomas, Florence Walzl, James Watson, and Alan Wilde for their careful readings of my manuscript in its different stages, their thoughtful suggestions, their encouragement, and their support. James Kenneally was extremely helpful in bringing the role of American nuns from the margin to the center of my thoughts. Eva Stehle and Dorthea Wender gave me valuable advice on classical literature and history. And I am grateful for the sharp eyes of Pamela Hardman in proofreading with such care and under such pressure.

I would especially like to thank Morris Beja for his thorough and incisive criticism of what I thought was the final manuscript, Garry Leonard for the perspective he gave me as I tried to tie the final knots together, and my editor Leslie Mitchner for asking the hard questions as well as providing enthusiastic support.

Early versions of this book appeared in "Voices, Stories, (W)holes: The Politics of Narration," *New Alliances in Joyce Studies,* ed. Bonnie Kime Scott, University of Delaware Press, 1988; "The Politics of Narration: Can a Woman Tell Her Story in Yoknapatawpha County—Even with All Those Yarns," *Narrative Poetics: Innovations, Limits, Challenges,* ed. James Phelan, Center for Comparative Studies in Humanities, Ohio State University, 1987; and "Virginia Woolf's Struggle With Author-ity," *Works and Days* (special issue on "Image and Ideology"), Spring–Fall 1988. I am grateful to the University of Delaware, The Ohio State University, and *Works and Days* for permission to use this material.

Introduction

Voices, Stories, (W)holes

Marlow sits on the deck of the *Nellie* in the company of a lawyer, an accountant, the Director of the Companies, and an admiring young sailor—who becomes *our* storyteller, or narrator, and who therefore brings us into Marlow's community of listeners. Marlow's yarn is not like the yarns of ordinary seamen—or ordinary storytellers. The meaning is not inside, like a kernel. Indeed, the kernel is absent. But there is a set of meanings, nonetheless, which relates to the absence, and these meanings are embodied the shape of his story. Joseph Conrad's *Heart of Darkness* is a prototypical modern story in the way it gives shape to "dark" experiences that are beyond consciousness and beyond language—and in the way it makes absence a felt presence.

A very different kind of tale is told by the old, coffee-brown, black-veiled woman who makes her living telling stories by the ancient city gate in Isak Dinesen's "The Blank Page." Transforming the blank space on Marlow's map of Africa into the blank page of a snow-white wedding sheet, she generates a radically different experience of what is beyond consciousness and language, and of what is absent. She also leads us to see that storytelling is a political act: a way of addressing, in fact defining, a community of listeners, and perpetuating or subverting the values of those in author-ity—of those who have taught us how to listen, read, and tell stories, as well as those who govern businesses, countries, and empires. And she prepares us to understand the rebellious modernist strategies of James Joyce, William Faulkner, and especially Virginia Woolf.

Heart of Darkness is shaped into the form of a quest, a journey of discovery. The story includes Marlow as both hero and story-teller, and it includes its storytelling context: the community of listeners. Marlow is a seaman, an adventurer, and an explorer, but he is also a ship's captain who is at ease in the company of the lawyer, the accountant, the Director of the Companies, and the man who will become *our* storyteller. We know nothing about this man except that, like the other listeners, he no longer follows the sea, and, more important, that he shares their social status. But he is different from the other listeners in that he stays awake. He is an active listener, who identifies with Marlow, shares his experience vicariously, depicts his hero and transcribes his speech with reverence, and shapes his story to reflect the experience that singled Marlow out from ordinary men. The reader who shares this experience becomes part of Marlow's community of listeners.

A successful storyteller must share the views and values of his listeners. What Marlow shares with the other men on deck are the values of men who have not only "followed the sea," but succeeded in business and in building the British Empire. *Our* narrator begins with a naive grasp of colonialist values, expressing his enthusiasm for "the dreams of men, the seed of commonwealths, the germs of empires" (5). As a result of his active listening, his vicarious participation in Marlow's story, he comes to understand that the dreams are also nightmares. But we should wonder how much Marlow was changed by his experience—despite his reaction to "the horror!" and despite his despair at having to lie to Kurtz's "Intended." We might also wonder whether *our* narrator has changed, despite his seeing that England's "venerable stream" no longer leads romantically to the "uttermost ends of the earth" but (just as romantically) into "the heart of darkness." And we might wonder whether readers who stay awake, become active participants, and identify with the storytellers, are changed—unless, to use Judith Fetterly's term, we become "resisting readers."

When Marlow was a "little chap," he had a passion for maps; what aroused him most were the blank spaces. It was "the biggest, the most blank, so to speak—that I had a hankering after" (8). Although he came to see this blank space as the heart of darkness, his story is shaped to fulfill, or at least to recapture, the same desire. Actually, Marlow's journey is motivated less by the desire to encounter the blank space than it is to reach Kurtz. And I want to make two points about this desire. First, when considered within the communal framework aboard the *Nellie*, it illustrates what Eve Kosofsky Sedgwick defines as the homosocial attraction, or the network of male relationships (friendship, mentorship, entitlement, rivalry, and homosexuality) that grounded male power in nineteenth-century English society and literature. Second, the "heart of darkness" is not just an unknown, or "uncivilized," space. It is also an unknown, or "uncivilized" man—or, since Kurtz is never individualized, "civilized man's" capacity for evil. But the logic, the shape of the story, the politics of narration lead us to conclude that the unknown and "uncivilized" African interior is responsible: it causes the civilized man to lose control. The story shifts the blame from the "civilized" to the "uncivilized"—that is, from the colonizers to the colonized, from the known to the unknown, from the intruder to the victim.

Control is stopping within "civilized" limits. It may also be manipulating for advantage. And it may be suppressing what threatens. Marlow's story may express the inexpressible through its palpable absence, but it also silences, suppresses, or controls, what threatens "civilized" consciousness. The difference between Kurtz's excesses and the kind of business conducted by men who—after three years at the station still wore high starched collars, neckties, white cuffs, and kept their books "in apple-pie order," men who had "backbone" and had "verily accomplished something" (18)—is a difference only of degree.

Marlow also identifies the "heart of darkness" with Kurtz's "savage" mistress. "The immense wilderness, the colossal body of the fecund and mysterious life seemed to look at her, pensive, as though it had been looking at the image of its own tenebrous and passionate soul" (62). That is, he also shifts the blame for Kurtz's rapacity onto the woman who is his captive, or victim, however independent Marlow makes her appear. An unknown land, a black society, and a black woman's sexuality combine into the ultimate, inexpressible threat to civilized (and now we see that "civilized" is identified with "man's") values.

Well, not quite the ultimate threat. For Kurtz's Intended—though no more than a "pale head, floating towards [Marlow] in the dusk" (75)—is even more threatening. He describes the black woman's "barbarous" sensuality at length, but the "civilized" Intended has a claim on him, and is so menacing that he suppresses her actual body. Both descriptions are forms of idealization, manipulation, suppression—ways Marlow has learned to control his desire and a reality he cannot face. The blank space, the dark world through which he navigates, Kurtz's mistress, and Kurtz's Intended are denied their own names, voices, bodies—their own physical, social, and political identities—to fit into a story of exploration, discovery, conquest, empire. It is important that the lie Marlow tells the Intended out of compassion makes *him* a tragic hero. She is denied a name, a body, knowledge of her beloved, a story of her own; he takes on the white man's burden. By turning her into a character in his story, he establishes the relationship among patriarchy, imperialism, and a dominant kind of storytelling.

I do not mean to underestimate Marlow's sensitivity to the horror of imperialism. And I do not want to depreciate his courage in telling his story, in trying to understand his decision to lie, in exposing himself to judgment. What I want to show is how the values of patriarchy and imperialism are inscribed in the traditional (male) quest story, how this story governed Marlow's imagination, and, as I will later develop, how the quest story maintains its power despite the successful strategies of male and female modernists to subvert it. The romance of the quest aroused Marlow as a "little chap" to hanker after the blank spaces on the map. It drove him in search of Kurtz. It motivated a decision, compelled by the experience and logic of his journey, to lie to Kurtz's Intended. And it provided the shape in which to tell his story, to understand his action to judge himself in a way that leads *our* narrator to canonize him as a tragic hero.

For, while Marlow embodies the values of imperialism, patriarchy, and its kind of storytelling, his companion, the listener who becomes *our* storyteller, sanctifies and perpetuates them in the minds of a public beyond the small community on the deck of the *Nellie*. He amplifies Marlow's authorial voice. And he gives Marlow's story the shape of a hero's journey—a linear story, the logic of which leads to the tragic knowledge and a form of action that single out the hero from ordinary people. If Marlow suppresses what threatens "civilized" consciousness, *our* narrator transforms and appropriates these threats to *his* story's logic and goal.

Marlow's story not only reflects his community of listeners, it requires their collaboration. There would have been no story had all the listeners in the story fallen asleep. The nameless narrator functions as a bridge between Marlow and the reader. But, while it may seem easy to identify with him because he lacks a distinct identity, anonymity is not the same as universality. The community on the deck of the *Nellie* could not have included Kurtz's Intended or his mistress, or any woman, or any African. And the wide-awake reader may ask whether she or he is included, or wants to be. Nina Pelikan Straus convincingly argues that traditional critics have evaded this question, thereby engendering either false consciousness or alienation in the woman reader—and contributing to the authority of this kind of story in a way I will soon explain.

Isak Dinesen's storyteller is too wise to have thought herself a part of Conrad's community. She would have been alienated not only by class but by gender, by race—and by being virtually colonized. "The Blank Page" was part of an uncompleted collection of stories to be set in the Kingdom of Naples in the 1830s (a kingdom that had been exploited by Spain for three hundred years). But Dinesen does not name the ancient city in this story. And all we know about her nameless storyteller is that she is indigent, old, coffee-brown, black-veiled, and sitting by the city gate. Despite Dinesen's conservative views, she implicitly identifies the situation of women with that of colonized people and intuitively foreshadows the arguments of Simone de Beauvoir about the way women, minorities, and colonized people are made "other." Dinesen's storyteller makes her living by telling stories to tourists. That is, she tells stories from the vantage of those who have been denied their names, their social and political identities, by the very class of those who pay to hear her. Moreover, the old storyteller is not a hero, and *our* narrator does not depict herself as a listener in the frame story. The old storyteller is addressing her customers: "You want a tale, sweet lady and gentleman?" (99). So, while *our* storyteller is part of her mentor's community, the listeners are not. They do not share the same experience, social position, or language. The tourist couple would never address the ancient storyteller as "sweet lady"; this ingratiating language, which masks its irony and disdain, is the language of the colonized and the serving class. Nor would she expect the couple to grasp her ironies or understand her tale.

At least not the sweet gentleman. For the ancient woman has learned to tell a different kind of tale than those "when I first let young men tell me, myself, tales of a red rose, two smooth lily buds, and four silky, supple, deadly entwining snakes" (99)—or, we might add, like the stories Marlow told the Intended. The wily storyteller intrigues the tourists, though, for they pay her well, and, having gained a dominant position, she continues in good spirits. She even patronizes the wealthy couple, telling them that "we . . . the old women who tell stories" are averse to telling the story of the blank page, "for it might well, among the uninitiated, weaken our own credit. All the same, I am going to make an exception with you, my sweet and pretty lady and gentleman of the generous hearts. I shall tell it to you" (100).

The old woman's story also contains a journey, or quest, but of a very different shape and purpose from that of Marlow's. Most of her story focuses on a convent, high up in the mountains of Portugal, which still took pride in growing the finest flax and manufacturing the most exquisite linen in the land. The quality of the linen was due to the linseed that had been brought by a crusader from the Holy Land. It was, therefore, used for the royal bridal sheets and the "venerable custom" that the storyteller goes on to describe. On the morning after a princess was married, the chamberlain or high steward would hang the sheet from a balcony of the palace and "solemnly proclaim: *Virginem eam tenemus*—'we declare her to have been a virgin' " (102–103). The center of the snow-white sheet was then cut out, framed, adorned with her royal name plate, and hung in the main wing of the convent.

The ritual of marriage and the "venerable custom" of hanging out the bridal sheet were forms of imperialism: men's ways of imposing an identity on women, of fitting them into their kinds of stories. Indeed, the medium that sanctified their stories was made of flax from the Holy Land; the seed had been a souvenir of the man who journeyed into a barbarous land to subdue the infidels. But, as Susan Gubar points out, the *texts* of the women's stories were their own—literally and physically—for they were composed of the women's own bodies, and they could be read only by those initiated into their language (248).

The journey or quest, which is central to her story in such a different way from Marlow's, is a journey of the initiated: a "long, stately, richly colored procession . . . of princesses of Portugal, who were now queens or queen dowagers of foreign countries, Archduchesses, or Electresses, with their splendid retinues . . . on a pilgrimage which was by nature both sacred and gay" (103), winding its way through the mountains and the flax field to the convent and then past the frames within which their stories were inscribed. One sheet commands particular attention. "The frame . . . is as fine and as heavy as any, and as proudly as any carries the gold plate with the royal crown. But on this one plate no name is inscribed, and the linen within the frame is snow-white from corner to corner, a blank page. . . . It is in front of this piece of pure white linen that the old princesses of Portugal—worldly wise, dutiful, long-suffering queens, wives, mothers—and their noble old playmates, bridesmaids and maids-of-honor have most often stood still. It is in front of the blank page that old and young nuns, with the Mother Abbess herself, sink into deepest thought" (104–105).

The story ends with a community of women, gathered in a space of their own to read the stories of their lives and to ponder the story of a woman, who lacks both a name and a stain. For the male community, this double lack, or double negation, reflects the woman's "failure" to achieve the "identity" of the virgin who becomes her husband's physical possession, which is another double negation. Indeed, whatever form the male story takes—whether or not the bride was a virgin, whether or not she refused to consummate the marriage—it denies her the possibility of having made a deliberate choice. But the women's ritual subverts the ritual of marriage and the male story by giving value to what has been negated. It brings together a community to share a language and read a story that could not be told and that they will not share with the community of men in power.

So it cannot be shared by the sweet gentleman whom the old storyteller ingratiatingly addresses. It could be understood by the "sweet lady," though we may expect her to be listening with ears still tuned by the young man. But what about us? *Our* storyteller reflects a community with a wider range of classes—from queens to indigent old storytellers—but, she does not function as a bridge between the old storyteller and the reader. Our bridge is the sweet couple with generous hearts. In leading us to identify with them, *our* storyteller puts us in the uncomfortable position of those excluded from the story's community. The woman reader can enter the community through an active kind of listening or reading quite different from the one Marlow inspires. The male reader can gain some understanding, but at the cost of experiencing our own exclusion and powerlessness.

Martin Green defines "empire" primarily as "a country possessing colonies." But, he insists, "the word is also appropriate to some other political systems, in which one group is dominant over others whom it regards as alien and inferior. And in such systems—which are to be found in all large states—the arts, sciences, and ideas, become charged with the same energies as the politics, and can be called in some sense imperial" (3–4). I am introducing my study of the politics of narration in Joyce, Faulkner, and Woolf with a comparison of Conrad and Dinesen to establish a connection between the dominant form of storytelling and the dominant culture, even when, at the brink of modernism, writers were breaking with the old forms. The quest is the epitome of linear, goal-oriented storytelling—a way of colonizing and dominating the "other," who is constructed as inferior and alien. Indeed, as Green shows, it was the basis of the popular adventure story that formed "the energizing myth of English imperialism," and that reflected the American drive into the frontier (3 and 129ff.).

My comparison of these two modern frame stories is also designed to distinguish three components of the politics of narration—voices, stories, and (w)holes.

Voices. In both stories, the voice of the central storyteller is enhanced by a nameless narrator, who echoes it with reverence. The nameless narrator also brings the community of listeners into the field of each story. When he acts as a bridge between the community of listeners and the community of readers, as he does in *Heart of Darkness*, he establishes and draws us in to what I will call a presupposed narrative community.

The actual narrative community—the lawyer, the accountant, the Director of the Companies, our narrator, and Marlow as he describes the ritual journey that bonded him to Kurtz—is white, male, and established. This homosocial narrative community reflects the male network that Eve Sedgwick shows as having secured and perpetuated its power in English political, social, and literary institutions. Sedgwick focuses on eighteenth- and nineteenth-century literature. When we apply her argument to the twentieth-century fiction that undermined traditional forms of character and plot, we discover that this hegemony was inscribed not just in forms of representation, but in a more elemental level of narration—in the authorial voice as it forms and draws us into a presupposed narrative community that will continue to retain a residual power.

But let me call attention to a problematic use of "us" and "we" in parts of this book. Some female colleagues who read or heard drafts of my manuscript objected, for they—along with large number of readers who had learned to resist the powers of convention, view authority figures with skepticism, and attend to the voices and stories that have been neglected or suppressed— were not drawn into the presupposed narrative community. And I was often not describing their reading. I decided to retain my use of "we" and "us," nonetheless, for two reasons. First, to represent most people, including myself and many female feminist colleagues, who accepted traditional author-ity and were drawn into the presupposed narrative community up to some point in our educations. And, second, to dramatize the power of traditional author-ity over the majority of readers, scholars, critics, and teachers—for to ignore this power is to ignore textual, cultural, and historical context.

Joyce will mock the hegemonic narrative community in the "Cyclops" episode of *Ulysses* by representing it as a group of narrow-minded, mean-spirited, aggressive, and chauvinistic Dublin drinkers. But he will recuperate it in "Oxen of the Sun," where Bloom joins Stephen and his (male) friends in the maternity hospital, and the narrative voice traces the gestation of English literature by echoing the style of one great (male) author after another, and the (male) characters get drunk—while Mrs. Purefoy gives birth offstage. Faulkner will tell his stories through a cast of character-narrators that range in race and class as well as gender, shifting from one viewpoint to another and never allowing us any certainty; but it is the white males who carry the

most weight. And Virginia Woolf will create a new, female authorial voice, but it will struggle against a male narrative hegemony.

Conrad's narrator leads us to see, but Dinesen's narrator leads
us to understand, the power structure that gives the authorial voice
its author-ity. Dinesen's narrator also leads us to understand why a
storyteller trying to speak in a voice of her own needs to subvert
the traditional authorial voice. And she also leads us to understand
the difficulties.

There is only one other voice in the old storyteller's story, that of
the chamberlain or high steward, who solemnly proclaims: "*Virginem eam tenemus*—'we declare her to have been a virgin.' " The
king's servant-spokesman declares the princess's past-perfect and
in so doing author-izes her future identity. The ritual declaration is
a speech act. The performative "we declare" is both an utterance
and an act; it publicly defines her as a clean slate and a valued
possession.

The "we" makes no pretense of extending to those beyond the
throne. Latin—the language of the Church used to sanction declara-
tions of the king—is the language of men in power. It is not the
language of princesses or of those who listen beneath the palace
wall. Nor can the powerless find voices of their own by speaking in
the vernacular, for the common language will always be rooted in
the language of the fathers, governed by a similar logic and "symbol-
izing" a similar reality. The women, officially identified with their
bodies, can reappropriate and share what is not only their own, but
what is feared by men in power. Their "texts" have the power to
express the wild, threatening, joyous, fluid, polyvalent experience
that transgresses syntax and denotation. This is what Julia Kristeva
calls the "semiotic" (as opposed to the "symbolic")—which develops in the pre-Oedipal and prelinguistic stage of development, when
we find our source of pleasure, security, and value in the mother's
body.

Related to the semiotic is what Kristeva calls the "*chora*," from
the Greek word for enclosed space, or womb. To Plato the chora
was "an invisible and formless being which receives all things and
in some mysterious way partakes of the intelligible, and is most
incomprehensible" (Roudiez, 6). The woman's body, especially her
womb, was mysterious and incomprehensible to Plato—and suppressed by the Church and king—because it was "other," contradictory, uncontrollable, and could not be fixed in language. It is
significant that Conrad pictured the threatening heart of darkness
as "the immense wilderness, the colossal body of the fecund and
mysterious life," and that he ultimately associated it with Kurtz's

"savage" mistress, a woman he cannot name. For Freud reflected the same bias and fear when he referred to the sexual life of women as a "dark continent" (212). It is also significant that the quest of Dinesen's women leads to a blank page, that the text of the woman's body is silent, and that the woman's story can only be told through the voice of a devious and subversive storyteller.

Stories. Conrad's storyteller speaks in an authorial voice, which gains its author-ity from a canon of literature that reflects the values of a privileged, homosocial, governing community, and defines *its* experience as natural and universal. Epitomizing this canon is the quest story, the logic of which leads a hero to achieve understanding, power, and, therefore, an identity limited to those who are in control. As a modernist, Conrad breaks new ground, delving into an ambiguous and threatening unconscious. But he does not delve into the universal unconscious, as many critics claim, for he reflects an experience shaped by the unconscious desires and fears of men in power at a particular moment of history. And he recuperates the imperialist ideology he seems to attack by foregrounding the shape of the quest, which valorizes conquest in the guises of heroic adventure, exploration, and rational control.

Dinesen's story, while focusing on a journey, has no hero and is not linear. It is an example of what Nancy Miller calls an erotic, as opposed to an ambitious text, valorizing the woman's body and relationship. It does not separate out an individual but leads to the formation of a community of the powerless, and hence to a different kind of power: an empowerment by sharing what has been devalued and suppressed—made unconscious—by those who controlled their lives and language, or author-ized their stories. The women at the end are neither telling nor listening to stories of heroism, but looking at the blank page, sunk "in deepest thought."

(W)holes. While the stories and voices of Conrad and Dinesen are clearly opposed, they are distinctively modern: they evoke the darkness we experience at the heart of darkness and the blankness we encounter in the blank page. Both Conrad and Dinesen focus on absences or holes, which in different ways and for different reasons are beyond the power of language, knowledge, and imagination—but which nonetheless become powerful presences. Let me digress for a moment to bring this distinctly modern characteristic into focus—and in doing so break down one of the major distinctions between modernism and postmodernism.

From classical times to the beginning of the twentieth century, the basic impulse of the Western, rational, humanist tradition was to see the world as potentially knowable—as full, continuous, amenable to logic, and explicable in terms of cause and effect. Even Freud, who may have contributed most to the breakdown of rationalism, was driven by its impetus: he demonstrated that the greatest part of human thought was irrational, prelinguistic, suppressed, disguised, by definition unknowable—a noetic hole—but he then proceeded to fill it up, describe its special language, explain it rationally. The modern impulse, on the other hand, is toward a realization, both terrifying and exhilarating, that holes—discontinuities, disruptions, fragmentation, silences—help form the very fabric of our material and mental worlds. And that an acceptance of *holes* leads to a sense of the *(w)hole*, ironically denied by the rational, humanist tradition.

I am using the term "(w)hole" to denote what is all-inclusive. The (w)hole includes what is not valued, what is suppressed, absent, changing, and potential. The inclusive "whole" (which I will sometimes spell conventionally) is opposed to the closed world, which is all there, complete, fixed in the view of an omniscient narrator, or limited by the imaginations of a class that defines itself as universal. The subject of Conrad's story is the heart of darkness, and its form is designed to make us feel the presence of what we cannot see or say or think. But he totalized "human experience" by implying that we could all be part of the community of listeners on the deck of the *Nellie*, or by excluding the experience of the "other." If Conrad embodies what civilized man has suppressed, Dinesen illuminates the forces of suppression from the perspective of the underside, and liberates, at least for a moment, the suppressed body-text.

"Holocaust" is an expression of modern Western consciousness in its most terrifying form. We have lived through the holocaust of the Jews under Hitler and with the threat of nuclear war, and we now live with the threat to our entire ecosystem. Holocaust literally means "burnt whole" but carries the awful pun of "burnt hole." On the one hand it implies the destruction of an order that transcends the human imagination, an annihilation of a whole people—a whole way of life, or the whole world. On the other hand it leaves a hole: there is an inexplicable gap in human history, human psychology, human language; there is nothing left. To understand the impact of the holocaust, or to approach such an understanding, we must accept the reality of this gap.

After World War II, Jean Paul Sartre reflected the reality of what he called "nothingness" as opposed to "being." And Martin Heidegger defined man as "being-toward-death," or total absence, which the Catholic Unamuno characterized as more frightening than any hell that had been imagined. Nothingness, total absence, would be not only imagined but made palpable on the stage as Samuel Beckett, in *Waiting for Godot* and *Endgame*, evoked the modern situation through his imaginative use of silence and empty space. And recently Jacques Derrida, Jacques Lacan, Kristeva, and others have brought us to an understanding of the metaphysical, epistemological, linguistic, and psychological consequences of absence.

If modern consciousness began to be fully realized after the experience of World War II, we can trace its beginning back further. Nor is it arbitrary to start at the turn of the century when Conrad wrote *Heart of Darkness* and Henry Adams declared that the continuity of history snapped, unleashing forces that would be impossible to control. Indeed, in *The Education of Henry Adams*, he articulated the discontinuity on an individual level by speaking of himself in the third person.

Moreover, by turning back to this point we can see that words like "nothingness" and "discontinuity" are not just metaphoric and are rooted in modernism as well as postmodernism. In 1900 Max Planck demonstrated that physical reality itself was discontinuous. Planck was working on the problem of black body radiation, trying to find a mathematical way to explain how something like a piece of charcoal turns from red to white as the fire gets hotter. For years he tried to find an explanation within the classical theory. But he finally had to conclude that light does not flow in a continuous stream: it flows in bursts, discontinuous packets, quanta, whole integers rather than one fraction at a time. (Physicist Alan Friedman explained this to me by picturing a child going to bed 5′ 3″ and waking up a full inch taller—*never* being 5′ 3 1/4″ or 5′ 3 1/2″.) In 1913 Niels Bohr proved that electrons jumped discontinuously from one orbit or energy level to another. They did not pass through a series of intervening points; indeed, nothing could account for their existence in between.

The classical view was of a material world that was full, where each point in space and time could be potentially accounted for. But this view led to very basic problems in accounting for the behavior of physical matter and energy. By denying this view, by accepting the reality of holes in space and time, modern scientists gained a greater sense of the material (w)hole, or that the material world is not a plenum but includes gaps.

James Joyce, like Planck, began as an advocate of the classical view of a full and continuous world, though he was attracted toward the gnomon (a parallelogram with a corner missing) in the very first story of *Dubliners*. In *Ulysses* he wanted "to give a picture of Dublin so complete that if the city one day suddenly disappeared from the earth it could be reconstructed out of my book" (Budgen, 67–68). He had an incredible memory and could outdo an old friend who just came from Dublin to Paris by recalling every shop for a mile along O'Connell Street, as well as the name of each owner. He mined *Thom's Directory* to situate other stores and minor characters in his novel. He absorbed facts from the Dublin newspapers. He asked his Aunt Josephine to see if it were possible "for an ordinary person to climb over the area railings of no 7 Eccles street . . . lower himself down from the lowest part of the railings till his feet were within 2 feet or 3 of the ground and drop unhurt" (Ellmann, 519). His sense of time was so accurate that Clive Hart could walk through Dublin with a stopwatch and verify the movements of the many characters in "Wandering Rocks." In 641 pages he takes us through almost every minute of the day Bloom wandered through Dublin to avoid the scene of Molly making love to Blazes Boylan. Yet he omits that crucial scene. He shows us how Bloom admires a young woman's "moving hams" on the way back from the butcher's; how he carries on a secret correspondence with Martha Clifford and a vicarious affair with Gerty MacDowell as she leans back to watch the long Roman candle rise into the evening sky and reveals "the secrets of [her] bottom drawer" (361); how he continually thinks of women, though his mind always returns to the voluptuous Molly, who for 30 pages tells us how much she enjoys making love. He even shows us Bloom climbing into bed and kissing "the plump mellow yellow smellow melons of her rump" (604). Yet nowhere does he tell us why Molly and Bloom have not had sexual intercourse for ten years, five months, and eighteen days. He implies that Bloom becomes assertive as a result of his experience during the long day, and Molly's monologue is generated by his singular request for breakfast in bed. But, though the Ithaca chapter is noted for its overwhelming quantity of detail—right up to the moment Bloom falls asleep—it omits the passage where he makes this request and, thereby, denies us the opportunity to judge the consequences of all we have been through with him. Moreover, the novel disrupts and undermines the continuity of the plotline, leaps from perspective to perspective, from one stylistic prism to another, and the style is so opaque in places that it obscures what we are most anxious to see.

Ulysses may be both the most densely packed reflection of "reality" in literature and the most radically discontinuous, or filled with holes. And just because of the holes in its fabric, it is one of the most complete experiences of a (w)hole. Bloom becomes the "allaroundman" Joyce wanted not because of his resemblance to Ulysses, but because the very notion of "manhood" is interrogated and undermined, and because of the enigmas in his story. If the novel generates an experience of authentic social and historical breadth (rather than universality), it is because we are so uncertain of the links between Bloom's story and its many mythic allusions. We feel the experiences of multiplicity, simultaneity, and parallax because of the discontinuities in perspective and style.

Modernism is often defined by its faith in a language that can connect what has been fragmented in modern experience, and postmodernism by its insistence on the gap between signifier and signified. But this is to mistake ways of reading for ways of writing in the early twentieth century. It is also to perpetuate readings that, while historically necessary, are limited. Revolutionary writers had to be recuperated, or read in a conservative way, for them to be read at all. Joyce was denounced for saying what should not be said in *Dubliners*. He disturbed the readers of *A Portrait* with its breaks in continuity and leaps through time and space. He chose *not* to title the chapters of *Ulysses* and to dismantle, indeed deconstruct, the Homeric superstructure he needed when he began. But T. S. Eliot and Edmund Wilson needed the superstructure to get hold of his revolutionary novel. So of course did writers and readers who could not approach the imaginative daring of *The Waste Land* poet or the boldness of one of the world's most accomplished critics. And for almost half a century everyone needed Stuart Gilbert's Homeric guide.

Modernism became the way people learned to read the daring and disturbing texts of Joyce and Woolf and Faulkner. It also became the second-rate writing such reading inspired. The misreading of modernism was perpetuated in the New Criticism after World War II, when higher education was expanding, when English Literature was coming into its own, and indeed when, as Richard Poirier points out, many students who would become influential teachers were being empowered as vigorous and openminded readers by professors who were more dedicated to teaching than publication. But the New Critics, whose influence was more widespread just because they published, considered themselves custodians of modernist culture, which they identified with their notion of organic form and their values of unity, wholeness, and balance.[1] In an important study called *Creating Faulkner's Reputation*, Lawrence H. Schwartz shows how these values were not only shaped by the Cold War ideology but supported by the

Rockefeller Foundation. The misreading of the New Critics domesticated, naturalized, appropriated what was new and distinctive in modernism: the unbridgeable gaps, the intransigent obscurities, the intolerable contradictions, the dizzying leaps in perspective.[2]

The distinction between modernism and postmodernism, then, diminishes the radical achievement of the writers like Joyce, Faulkner, and Woolf. Joyce leads us to see that an acceptance of holes generates a sense of all-inclusive (w)holeness, because our experience comes to include the gaps. But he also shows us how some experiences do not fit into stories traditionally told, and how some characters—like Eveline, Maria, Gretta, E—C—, Gerty MacDowell, and, up to a point, Stephen Dedalus—are denied not only the means to enact, but the voices to articulate, and indeed the language in which to imagine stories that would be truly their own. Therefore, he leads us to understand that some holes result from the failure to recognize or the need to suppress stories and voices that are not valued or might be threatening, that is, the voices and stories of women, the colonized, the poor, and other disenfranchised or exploited groups.

Which leads back to my comparison of Conrad's *Heart of Darkness* and Dinesen's "The Blank Page," for I want to focus on the politics of narration. Conrad's storyteller creates a hole to realize a greater sense of the whole, but for a community restricted to those who share his authority, privileges, and values. He may illuminate the nightmare upon which his authority rests, but he perpetuates the authority, privileges, and values, nonetheless. By appearing to address those excluded from power as members of the presupposed narrative community—or positioning them as sympathetic and collaborative listeners—he limits our imaginative horizons and discourages the potential of an alternative community.

Dinesen's storyteller is a model for the alternative, subversive, and revolutionary voices in the novels I will discuss. She creates a hole that subverts the traditional storyline. Her storyline (which is not actually a line) does not lead to the initiation of a hero or the realization of power but to relationship, in the forming of an alternative community. She also subverts the authorial voice by telling a story, the very center of which is excluded from those who have the power not only to listen but to tell—and impose—traditional stories. Her subversive narrative strategy reverses the relations of power.

But not quite. For she gains her power by ingratiating her listeners. She pretends that her adversaries will understand, or that she serves the same ends as the traditional storyteller. She speaks in a double voice, then, one that is authorial and one that ironically undermines it. But—since the authorial voice has gained and maintained its power through author-ized conventions, canon, and modes of reading—it exercises an author-ity that, even when undermined, remains potent.

To use the language of Mikhail Bakhtin, Conrad's story is monologic; Dinesen's is dialogic. In the monologic story the authorial voice dominates. In the dialogic story the authorial voice contends—or establishes a dialogue with—the independent voice or voices of his characters. The ultimate dialogic or polyphonic story is like a carnival, where the authorial voice is only one among many voices that speak, argue, harangue, cajole, mock, and take joy in their contradictoriness. Julia Kristeva adds a psychological dimension to Bakhtin by seeing the monologic voice as regulatory, linguistic, and "symbolic," acquired when the child learned to accept his or her father, and the energy of the carnival as "semiotic," connected to the pre-Oedipal stage when the mother's body is the source of multiple and contradictory desires, pleasures, and values. For Bakhtin the novel is revolutionary because of the variety of voices that contend ideologically with the authorial voice. For Kristeva the novel can become a polylogue, where "words come to mind, but they are fuzzy, signifying nothing, more throbbing than meaning, and their stream goes to our breasts, genitals, and iridescent skin" (*Desire,* 163).

Bakhtin understands the power of "the unitary language" and talks about "the politics of style." And Kristeva insists that the symbolic and the semiotic are always interconnected, that the semiotic chora is constrained or regulated by family and social structure. But they do not deal systematically with the fact that some voices have more power than others—or with the ways they maintain their author-ity. For their author-ity derives from tradition, or a canon and way of reading, established by the class whose authority the authorial voice reflects and perpetuates when it addresses (or inscribes) its readers as members of his presupposed narrative community. And although this power may be undermined, it cannot lose its force.

Let me give a graphic example of the power of the authorial voice from an experience I had at a Chagall exhibit. Chagall had belonged to Bakhtin's circle in the mid-twenties. And I discovered what Bakhtin would call the carnival and polyphony or heteroglossia of his paintings: the many different individuals and classes of people engaged in different kinds of activities, evoking laughter, lyricism, sadness, anger, reverie, and nightmare—all at the same time. Unfortunately, I made the mistake of going early in the morning, when groups of public school children are bussed in. It was impossible to find a moment of peace and quiet or to have a picture all to myself; the noisy and heterogenous flocks roared into Chagall's carnival.

At one point I was standing in front of a cubist painting called *The Garden of Eden,* in which there is no dominant image, but a rich variety of forms fractured into geometrical facets. All of a sudden a group of children swarmed around. The teacher asked "What do you see?" and several voices responded "Everything." Then the teacher asked "Who can find Adam and Eve?" There was a moment of silence. Then a little boy said "There's Adam," and a little girl followed "I see Eve." The painting changed before my eyes. Suddenly, the figures of Adam and Eve were dominant, their heads on top, the allegorical motifs all in place.

Later I returned to look at the picture alone, but soon a few of the same children came back. This time they were silent and smirking. One pointed to what looked like a penis, another pointed to a breast, another to a goat-like figure. One found an artist's palette. They giggled. Then a mother came up with two little girls in tow. "Who can see Adam and Eve?"

The children not only turned the museum into a carnival by their playfulness, noise, and covert rebellion; they insisted on the polyphony of Chagall's paintings. But the teachers and parents had the power to author-ize one among the many voices in the painting, silence others, and turn the carnival back into a museum.

It is important to recall that carnival was traditionally licensed by authority. The Roman Saturnalia, the Kalends of January, the Feast of Fools were legitimized ways to release pent-up energies; they were situated outside of normal time. But, at a predetermined moment in time, order would be restored. Moreover, carnival often perpetuated repression. For, as Victor Turner points out, marginal groups were considered especially dangerous in a world where anything could happen. Indeed, Emmanuel Ladurie adds, Jews were stoned and women raped during carnival activities.

Which is not to say that carnival is devoid of revolutionary potential. According to Natalie Davis, it also provided models for women, opened new options for behavior, and even sanctioned political disobedience and riot for both men and women in a repressive society.[3] Nor do I mean to imply that the authorial voice cannot be undermined, disrupted, subverted, or reduced to one among the many voices that argue with one another as independent subjects. I will show how Joyce developed a "revolutionary voice" that expresses itself directly through the *body* of the text and finally in the persona of Molly Bloom, how the dead body of Faulkner's Addie Bundren violated the laws of logic and verisimilitude to tell a story of motherhood that no one in the community could tolerate hearing, how Virginia Woolf could subvert not only the plotline but the very basis of character and the source of voice. But I want to recognize the residual power of the authorial voice, describe the power relations, distinguish the absence of disruption from the absence of suppression, and show how the voices line up.

Lining up the voices will be one goal of *The Politics of Narration*. I will show how the authorial voice employs traditional conventions to make power relations seem natural, speaks through other narrative voices, co-opts or lends its authority to voices that would seem to challenge it. I will also show how the authorial voice is challenged, disrupted, and subverted by rebellious voices. Another goal will be to illuminate the different kinds of stories and describe the rebellious narrative strategies. This is especially challenging when we turn to Joyce, Faulkner, and Woolf, who created novels where the polyphony is far more obvious and disorienting and where the gaps are far more disrupting than anything I have been able to suggest in my brief comparison of Conrad's and Dinesen's stories, or in those more traditional novels Bakhtin considered. They challenged the authorial voice, disrupted the traditional storyline, and developed alternative voices; they expanded the carnival, tested the limits of narrative author-ity, and discovered ways to tell stories that could not previously have been told.

Of course, the authorial voice remains intransigent, asserts its power in unpredictable ways, and co-opts some rebellious strategies in these dialogic or polyphonic novels. Moreover, all three writers were deeply ambiguous about the authority of Western culture. So I will be describing the struggle of three modern novelists against author-ity. But it is important to recognize that their struggles were not the same.

Joyce struggled against the authority of Catholic Church, the British Empire—and the author-ity of the literary canon that denied him an authentic voice. He undermined this authority through various forms of disruption and parody. But in doing so he requires his readers to recall or more often learn the canonical works he was disrupting and parodying, put them to active use in our reading, and even teach them to a new generation of readers. And he requires that we admire the way he parodies and undermines canonical writers and thereby recuperates them.

Faulkner developed an American version of Joyce's modernism.

He vented his outrage against the biblical and classical legacy, and the inflated rhetoric of the South—whether because it was inherently destructive, cynically or innocently appropriated, or simply misused. And he followed Joyce in the ways he undermined the traditional author-ial voice. But the authorial voice—echoing in his privileged storytellers like Quentin and his father, Darl, and Gavin Stevens—admires and author-izes the legacy and rhetoric. Moreover, Faulkner builds his novels largely on the tall-tale—a frontier version of the adventure story that became the energizing myth of English imperialism, and the myth of success. Thomas Sutpen may be the American version of Conrad's Kurtz. Like Marlow's, Faulkner's tale implies a false sense of community among his powerless characters, and, as we will see, particularly excludes women and blacks from author-ized achievement. And his pronouncements on literature and life, at least from the time of his Nobel Prize speech, echo with the rhetoric of a canonized author.

I do not mean to imply that Joyce and Faulkner were dominated by the canon they repudiated. Or that they did not find ways to author-ize voices and stories of the powerless. Only that they were not alienated from the canon—or that they could have found their places aboard the *Nellie*. But Virginia Woolf could not have taken her place aboard the *Nellie* and was alienated from the canon—just because she was a woman. And she came to articulate the political implications of her struggle against author-ity.

Although she continually argued against the political novel, Woolf wrote political essays that illuminated the power of traditional author-ity, exposed the ideology upon which "great literature" is based, and established a theory upon which an alternative tradition could be built. She recognized that language is largely shaped by cultural forces or institutions, by those who have the power to govern, preach, teach, rule the family, report the news, and publish what we accept as important or interesting. And she recognized that those who have such power are men. Inevitably language—the very structure of sentences—was shaped to reflect men's values and suit their needs. Moreover, language—and the way words were "laid end to end" to form stories—came to reflect not only the values but the posture of those in power. In *A Room of One's Own* and *Three Guineas* Woolf shows how the language of the fathers is hierarchical, exclusive, and oriented toward goals and mastery—indeed, toward imperialism and fascism.

Woolf become more self-consciously political, or aware of her relationship to traditional author-ity, as she became more aware of women's historical repression. And she established a line of modern fiction that struggles against the male narrative hegemony and the imperial thrust of the traditional storyline, as well as against the hegemony of male modernists.

I hope to establish that telling stories is a form of political action and to set forth a model for exploring the politics of narration, especially in works of modern fiction that rebel against totalizing conventions. While I will argue that the traditional story—in fact the plotline—is a form of repression, I should admit that I love a good story. I feel that *Ulysses* should be first read for its plot, that Faulkner's distinction is in developing the form of the tall-tale, that Woolf's disruptions are effective just because her storylines are so engaging. So I feel the pulls of the dialogic. And I believe, as Robert Scholes has put it in the very title of *Textual Power*, that readers should submit to the power of the text before taking stock and taking a stand—or asserting our power over it.

Moreover, while this study is informed, indeed inspired, by much reading and thinking about theory, I am drawn to the original meaning of "theory," which was "to see." Jolanta Wawrzycka points out that the original theorists were chosen by the polis to witness an event.[4] And I want to bear witness to the literary imaginations of James Joyce, William Faulkner, and Virginia Woolf: to the ways these writers gave voice to traditionally voiceless characters and shape to experiences traditionally neglected or suppressed, to the ways they dealt with author-ial constraints, and to the ways they sometimes broke through them. Of course, one bears witness from a position, constructed on a theoretical base. I have begun to build this base and will continue to do so, developing my theory in relation to my readings, which I hope will be fresh and provocative.

I will begin with James Joyce, but will stop short of *Finnegans Wake*, for I want to focus on works where the break from traditional realism and the struggle against traditional forms of authority are still clear. After Joyce I will skip chronologically to William Faulkner, because he extends Joyce's struggle into American culture and deals with a wider range of social classes, because he is more conservative on many issues and shows us different ways the authorial voice maintains its power—but mostly because he continues in the male line of modern fiction. And I will conclude with Virginia Woolf because she established a line of fiction that is significantly independent from that of Joyce's and Faulkner's, and because she leads us to become more fully aware of the politics of narration.

Three important books have recently appeared, which complement or supplement my study of Joyce in very different ways, and which I have only begun to assimilate: Vicki Mahaffey's *Reauthor-izing Joyce*, Patrick McGee's *Paperspace: Style as Ideology in Joyce's Ulysses*, and R. B. Kershner's *Joyce, Bakhtin, and Popular Culture: Chronicles of Disorder*. Also, I would have gained a great deal of sophistication in working with Faulkner had I had time to master the analytical tools developed by Stephen Ross in *Fiction's Inexhaustible Voice: Speech and Writing in Faulkner*. And I would have learned much about reading Faulkner's women had I time to assimilate Minrose Gwin's *The Feminine and Faulkner*.

In dealing with the politics of narration, I am aware that I am limiting my range to the three major figures of high modernism, which is by definition elitist, which is limited by its middle-class perspective and values, and which in the case of Virginia Woolf, its most politically conscious writer, is limited even in its range of sympathies. I am also aware of the difference between what Judith Fetterly calls the "resisting reader" and what Barbara Harlow—who reaches out into literature of what we designate as the third world—calls "resistance literature," one of the goals of which is to resist formalism altogether and engage itself in more direct revolutionary activity. Joyce, Faulkner, and Woolf are limited to the arena of the thought and discourse of the ruling class, as well as the readership that might be affected—but these readers also have the power to attack the author-ity that is challenged and valorize the alternative voices, stories, and (w)holes.

What do I hope the reader will take away from *The Politics of Narration*? Not necessarily a re-vision of three pivotal modern writers, or totally new readings of their novels—though important parts of my readings will be new. But a new way of reading these novels—or engaging the interrelationships in a shifting field of narrative forces—which, in turn, may be applied to novels that are both more traditional and more revolutionary. The new way of reading will sustain the disruptive energy of subversive and rebellious voices, keep the holes open, and generate or nourish the urge toward a radically inclusive whole. It will also illuminate the holes in the modern novel, not as something to fill in or avoid or expose as a mark of artistic failure or ideological contradiction or disconnection between language and "reality," but as a source of power. It will distinguish holes from absences, the power of rebellion and subversion from the power of coercion and repression. And it will resist the authorial voice in order to tune in voices and highlight stories that have been marginalized or suppressed. Resisting reading is, of course, being practiced today by many critics, teachers, and students, especially feminists and those engaged in cultural studies. But it creates an empowering corrective at the expense of the dialogic context and the residual power of traditional authority.

What makes my approach distinctive is its insistence that we understand the power of the authorial voice: the many ways it ignores, marginalizes, suppresses, and co-opts voices that are other and that oppose it. Even more important, my approach insists that we do not ignore or suppress its impact, as so many strong readings do, that we keep the authorial voice in our field of critical attention. For to ignore the authority of the authorial voice, the way the quest has become inscribed in the traditional plotline, the attraction of the adventure story, the momentum of the chase, the power of the ambitious text, the lure of the linear plot, the inescapability of causal logic—no matter how they are undermined, parodied, marginalized, or subverted—is to ignore the context of text, culture, and history. It is to ignore the full play of narrative forces and interrelated conflicts. It is to ignore the forces in our culture—especially the authorial voices of scholars and teachers—that have empowered the authorial voice in the novel. Moreover these forces must be given full recognition in order to affect the power of traditional author-ity as well as understand the value and realize the power of alternative stories—where the authorial voice gives way to a body-text and various forms of the ambitious storyline give way to a field of shifting relationships.

I will begin to develop this argument at the end of my section on Joyce—after I define my terms, trace the struggle between the rebellious and the authorial voice, and reveal some of the ways Joyce changes the shape of the narrative field—by refocusing the power of traditional author-ity. Then I will develop to its extreme an argument that Caddy's story in *The Sound and The Fury* is excluded from the four interwoven narratives, that chronological disruption gives way to an equally coercive narrative pattern, that the authorial voice turns us into accomplices by requiring us to reconstruct the chronology and the language of cause and effect, and that Caddy becomes the first cause of the family's destruction. I will return Rosa Coldfield to the center of *Absalom, Absalom!* , but I will also illuminate the narrative hegemony and authorial dynamics that marginalize and co-opt her. And I will insist that, despite Woolf's success in stretching the male sentence and shattering the plotline of *Mrs. Dalloway*, Peter Walsh completes a powerful courtship plot by having the last word, that Lily Briscoe must complete the men's story in *To The Lighthouse* before completing her own, and that in *The Waves* Bernard imposes his story on all the others and co-opts "the woman writing," or Woolf's power-fully realized female authorial voice.

That is, after illuminating the different ways Joyce, Faulkner, and Woolf interrogate, undermine, subvert, and find alternatives to the traditional authorial voice, I will re-authorize and re-empower it. And I will do so to restore the context, to help us understand the forces against which Caddy had to contend, why Rosa could not be heard, how Woolf struggled with author-ity—and how, in their different ways and toward different ends, Joyce, Faulkner and Woolf gave full expression to the dialogic of power relations.

Which leads to a further problem. For one of my aims, like that of many theorists and critics today, has been to attend to the heterogeneity of voices, identify the multiplicity of positions, maintain openness, and avoid dualisms that derive from and perpetuate traditional hierarchies. But I end by reducing the carnival to an agon, heterogeneity to polarization, multiplicity to dualism. And this is because the authorial voice is imperialistic—which is one reason why I introduced *The Politics of Narration* with "Heart of Darkness" and "The Blank Page." It is exploitative. It strives for power, control, homogeneity, conversion, and closure. Its orientation is toward a goal. Its mode is purposeful and aggressive. And it therefore polarizes the field.

Bakhtin, who defined the carnival and illuminated the hetero-glossia, was seduced by his prolific metaphor. He failed to recognize that the carnival too has a hierarchy, that all the positions are not equally central, that all the voices not equally potent, and that—since its hierarchy is an inversion of society's—traditional forces maintain their potency. Nor does he account for their strategies of seduction and co-optation, the way authorized reading has become canonized and "natural," and the way it is perpetuated in traditional scholarship, interpretation, and teaching.

The dialogic, then, is a struggle for author-ity. Traditional criticism, pedagogy, and reading had valorized the authorial voice. Therefore it became necessary to resist it and attempt to escape its power through strong readings that moved marginalized characters, events, problems, and strategies into the center. Now it is necessary to bring the authorial voice back into the field, identify its sources of power, and explore the interconnected conflicts among the voices, stories, and (w)holes.

James Joyce

1

Holes and (W)holeness in *Dubliners*

It's hard to decide which of Joyce's "two gallants" is more despicable and, finally, more reprehensible—the cocky Corley who exploits a poor, young housemaid not only for her sexual favors but for seven weeks of her wages, or the sycophant Lenehan, who flatters Corley, eggs him on, and anticipates his exploit so shamelessly. But this kind of uncertainty pales beside the enigma of the climactic scene.

Having paid his two pence for a plate of peas, Lenehan makes his way to Merrion Square. He leans against the lamppost, keeping his gaze fixed on the point where he expects to see Corley return with the young woman. He strains his eyes as each tram stops at the far corner. Suddenly he sees them coming and follows them down Baggot Street, taking the other path, and stopping when they stop.

They talked for a few moments and then the young woman went down the steps into the area of a house. Corley remained standing at the edge of the path, a little distance from the front steps. Some minutes passed. Then the hall-door was opened slowly and cautiously. A woman came running down the front steps and coughed. Corley turned and went towards her. His broad figure hid hers from view for a few seconds and then she reappeared running up the steps. The door closed on her and Corley began to walk swiftly towards Stephen's Green.

"Did it come off?" Lenehan asks as Corley walks past him. Corley keeps him in suspense, then extends his hand with a grave gesture "and, smiling, opened it slowly to the gaze of his disciple. A small gold coin shone in the palm" (59–60).

The description of Corley and the woman is designed so that we see no more than Lenehan could, straining his eyes from across the way. We cannot expect to know what Corley and the woman said to each other, or what actually happened in the few seconds she was hidden by his broad figure. But how are we to account for what we do see? Why does she go *down* into the area and return from the main entrance *above*? And why does *the young woman* we've seen with Corley lose her identity to become *a woman* when she comes out of the house? According to Warren Beck, the housemaid could have gone down into the servants' entrance, then upstairs to steal a half-pound gold coin from her mistress, and taken the quickest way out—as she might have done earlier that evening when she rewarded her lover with "two bloody fine cigars . . . that the old fellow used to smoke" (Beck, 144). Or she might have asked her mistress for a six-week advance on her wages, and then become so flustered as to run right out the front door. It might not even have been the housemaid but the mistress herself who ran out to Corley, which would account for the switch from definite to indefinite article and from youth to adulthood.

This, of course, is becoming far-fetched. Upon reading a draft of my manuscript, Florence Walzl admonished that my explanations "are incredible," given "the strictness of the rules and regimen imposed on servants at the turn of the century in Ireland." The point I want to make is that in the climactic description of "Two Gallants," key details can never be accounted for. What actually happened in the house on Baggot Street is unrecoverable. There will always be something about the characters and the story that is beyond our grasp. For at the very center of the story is a hole.

Nor should this hole be confused with the ellipsis we find in the climactic scene of Henry James's *Ambassadors*, published only a few years earlier, where Lambert Strether watches a small boat come into view and complete the picture that had been taking shape in his mind all day. There are holes in James's leisurely and finely detailed description. We never know what the happy couple say to each other. Nor will we ever know exactly what went on between Chad and Madame de Vionnet in the past ten chapters where, like Strether, we had been blind to their relationship. But we soon come to know enough to feel confident, if not certain. And from the perspective of the novel's end, the ellipsis becomes conventional: whatever specifics are missing, the reader can supply the general meaning. The narrator and the reader are now sufficiently close, we now have enough in common that we are like old friends who can nod to one another without having to finish a sentence. James's ellipsis is designed to make us feel that, like Strether, we can always learn more—not that there will always be a missing piece.

The hole in Joyce's "Two Gallants" is not a conventional ellipsis; it remains a hole. Indeed, it is the source of the story's power. It generates the unspeakable nature of Corley's act (what happened when Corley and the housemaid were out of sight?), of Lenahan's vicarious enjoyment, and of the young woman's identity as a victim. Moreover, it isolates us as readers. That is, it denies us our expected link with author-ity, or our privileged position in the storyteller's community. But as our experience comes to include the hole—or absolute discontinuity, absence, silence—the story becomes inclusive, or (w)hole. For the hole derives from or reflects the mediation of language, the materiality of the text, our separation from what was supposed to have happened, the limitations of subjectivity, and the fact that we cannot fully know the subjectivity of the "other." To affirm not only the necessity but the value of holes is to affirm the value of difference.

A closer look at the hole in "Two Gallants," though, may lead us to challenge these assumptions. For while the young woman (who is also a member of the serving class) is effectively characterized by her absence, she is also denied a voice of her own. Her story is not told or is silenced. Holes in the storyline, then, may reflect the narrator's failure to recognize or need to suppress stories that are not valued or might be threatening: the stories of women, servants, the colonized, and other disenfranchised or exploited groups.

As in *Heart of Darkness*, these holes evoke the silence; they textually embody the threatening "other." But Joyce takes a different posture toward his subject. He mocks the idea of gallant heroism, and the hole in the story shows the woman to be more of a victim than a threat. For he was sensitive to the experience of absence, or exclusion. And in this brief discussion of *Dubliners* I want to show how he was exploring ways to embody this absence, as well as the presence of social forces that limit the imagination. He was also beginning to undermine the presupposed narrative community, challenge habits of reading, and discover the power of disruption. That is, he was becoming sensitive to the politics of storytelling.

Joyce began experimenting with holes in the very first story of *Dubliners*, where the key word, as Phillip Herring points out, is gnomon—a parallelogram with a small parallelogram missing, that is, with a hole in the right hand corner. "The Sisters" is told from the viewpoint of a young boy, whose mentor, a paralytic priest, has just died. So missing from the story right off is the enigmatic character whose death causes such confused feelings of attraction, repulsion, identification, guilt, and liberation in the young boy's mind. What helps create the confusion, Herring illuminates, is the gnomic nature of the adults' language. There are mysterious allusions to the priest's character, but in addition there are holes in the text. "No, I wouldn't say he was exactly . . . but there was something queer . . . there was something uncanny about him," says Old Cotter. "I'll tell you my opinion . . ."(9–10). There are also significant silences, hollow phrases, and misused words. And, finally, there is the open ending, the enigma of the final image, which is accentuated by ellipses and the accelerated indefiniteness in Eliza's speech. One night, she tells the aunt and the young protagonist, the priest was discovered sitting in his dark confession-box, "wide-awake and laughing-like to himself. . . . So then, of course, when they saw that, that made them think that there was something gone wrong with him . . ."(18).

Are these actual holes in the text, or only conventional ellipses? Colin MacCabe helps us with an answer. He compares the opening of the early and late versions of "The Sisters" to show Joyce departing from the kind of text in which uncertainty is only a theme. In the early version, we do not know to what the young boy is referring when he tells us that "three nights in succession I had found myself in Great Britain Street . . . had raised my eyes to that lighted square of window and speculated. I seemed to understand that it would occur at night" (MacCabe, 33; ellipsis mine). But our uncertainty is short-lived, for we will soon learn that "it" was the priest's death. The "realist" text situates us in a privileged position, where we see and finally understand all that has happened. It also uses a language that suppresses the fact that it is a language—the very nature of which is to stand for objects and experiences that are absent from words. In the revised version "paralysis," "simony," and especially "gnomon" have an excess of meaning, which the text will never fully explain. They call attention to themselves as words, signifiers—and to a "gap" between the signifier and the signified. Under the influence of Lacan, MacCabe goes even further. Lacan points out that children learn language at the very age they recognize the absence of a desired mother or penis and the power of masculine authority. That is, language is associated with the Oedipus complex, absence, desire, and the patriarchy. And MacCabe goes on to reveal what we might call the presence of the "absent Father" in "The Sisters," connecting the protagonist's absent father, the dead priest, the Church, and the language of adults. For the Lacanian, holes contain what is suppressed but what can still be recovered by applying neo-Freudian concepts. Ironically, then, the system designed to ensure openness becomes a "totalizing" determinant. Which may be why the reading of much postmodernist criticism, however illuminating and important, often generates a feeling of solipsism.

Nonetheless, MacCabe leads us to see that in revising his first story Joyce began to develop beyond psychological realism. His language is no longer designed to be invisible; it is beginning to call attention to itself. Nor is it designed to reflect what a character cannot know but what we—from our privileged relation to an authoritative narrator, and with our authoritative sense of language—can fill in. We may go even further. In the revised version Joyce has added ellipses and transformed the dashes to dots to define empty space, especially in the conclusion. He was beginning to discover the power of disruption and the power of absence-as-presence in a text that calls attention to its own physical reality.

In "Eveline" the ellipsis is more dramatic. The story opens with the protagonist sitting at the window. An older daughter who works in the Stores and takes care of her widowed father and two young children, she is contemplating her barren life and anticipating her flight from Ireland to Buenos Ayres. Eveline thinks of the Saturday nights, when she had to "squabble" over her hard-earned marketing money before her father would get "fairly bad." She contrasts her squalid life with the romance that began with Frank taking her to see *The Bohemian Girl* and that would end in a new home in "a distant unknown country," where she, Eveline, would be married. Nor would she be treated like her mother, or any longer feel "herself in danger of her father's violence." She thinks of her mother's sacrifices and final madness, and stands up "in a sudden impulse of terror. . . . She had a right to happiness. Frank would take her in his arms, fold her in his arms. He would save her."

A series of dots defines an empty space in the text.

And then comes the final scene where she is paralyzed at the gangplank. "All the seas of the world tumbled about her heart . . . he would drown her. She gripped with both hands at the iron railing." Frank cries for her to come, rushes beyond the barrier, calls again. "She set her white face to him, passive, like a helpless animal. Her eyes gave him no sign of love or farewell or recognition" (38–41).

The space in the text is usually considered a conventional ellipsis. Time passes, and there is no need for the narrator to fill in all the details as Eveline leaves home and travels to the pier. The ellipsis might be like that in "The Boarding House," the reticence of which contrasts with what we might imagine Mrs. Mooney saying to her future son-in-law, while upstairs Polly dips the end of a towel in a water jug and refreshes her eyes with cool water (68). But it is also possible that the ellipsis signals a leap not in the story's action but in Eveline's *thoughts*, that the final scene takes place in her mind—that Eveline never moves from the window. She is so paralyzed she cannot move, and will remain trapped in the house for the rest of her life. The imagery evokes a nightmare of paralysis: with the final shift in perspective she is looking into her own face.

Granted, it may make no ultimate difference, either way Eveline misses the boat. But the story changes as we encounter the lacuna. The hole in Eveline's story does not result—as it did in the other stories—from what the narrator, having chosen a limited perspective, cannot see. Nor is the absence one of meaning or of what happens. Missing here is a passage, a sign, to tell us how to read the story. We have lost not only a narrative but a linguistic community. Moreover, the hole is physically embodied: a blank space on the page, highlighted by the row of dots. It leads us to become aware of the physicality of the text, which we encounter as the hole opens in Eveline's story.

While our awareness of print on a white page may lead to a greater critical consciousness, it need not detract from our emotional response. To shift from fiction to film for a moment, let me recall one of the most powerful moments in Ingmar Bergman's *Persona*. Anna, the nurse whose life and profession have required control, is aroused to uncontrollable anger when she learns that her patient Elizabeth, who may only be playing mute, has been toying with her. We feel her rage when the camera cuts from her face, looking through a window, to a hole burning in the very film that has been recording her. And Bergman goes even farther, as if impelled by the logic of his choice. As the hole continues to burn, we see a series of disconnected cartoon shots and shots from Bergman's earlier films. Included, then, in an experience of Anna's white-hot rage, is the very material upon which it was represented—a physical strip of film, which has both a cultural and personal history. Anna's story is disrupted. We are disturbed by the disruption—and by the intrusion of the physical medium into an experience that, however disturbing, is secured by realistic conventions. Though breaking the conventions of mimesis, the disruption contributes to the mimetic experience. But, it goes beyond mimesis. For the strip of film calls attention to the physical reality of the medium and the cultural substratum of Anna's story, which are denied by realistic storytelling.

So we may look for the cultural subtext of the holes in *Dubliners*—which are identified with guilt and sexuality. In "The Sisters" part of the young protagonist's guilt derives from his difference from other boys—his not learning "to box his corner" (11) and his association with the old priest about whom there was "something queer" (10). What makes him feel guilty is the language of adults, who despite their patriotic talk have internalized their colonized status, and despite their powerlessness perpetuate the language of power. For this language turns difference into queerness and what ultimately is unspeakable.

In "An Encounter" the protagonist, having learned the language of adults, has become the narrator. But, as we see in his series of false starts—or in the discontinuities of the opening—he has great difficulty in coming to grips with his experience. The story opens with a declaration that "it was Joe Dillon who introduced the Wild West to us" (19). But Joe Dillon drops out of the picture after the second sentence. Joe's brother Leo, introduced almost parenthetically, becomes central for the first third of the story—until he fails to show up for the day's adventure. Then Mahony, introduced in the same offhand way as Leo, becomes the center of the narrator's attention, and it is Mahony who saves him from the dark man who arouses such ambivalent feelings of kinship and guilt.

The false starts, or narrative discontinuities, reflect the crisis of the young protagonist. His anticipation of an adventure and his rebellion against authority lead to an experience of inadequacy and guilt—or identification with "the queer old josser" who "described . . . how he would whip . . . a boy as if he were unfolding some elaborate mystery"(27), his identification, that is, with an unmanly pervert rather than the sailors and Mahony. The narrative discontinuities also reflect the situation of the narrator, who has had to learn the language of authority to write stories of his youth. For the language of authority rejects, suppresses, or transforms what is different or other. In the world of boys' schools, adventures of the "Wild West," and fantasies of sailing to mysterious ports, to be different is to be identified with girls, or worse, with sexual perverts.

The language of authority perpetuates sexual stereotyping and the resulting dualism. It cannot be used to tell an alternative male story. Nor, as the hole in Eveline's story reflects, can a woman's story be told or her identity expressed in the language of author-ity. Indeed, it prevents her and the other women in *Dubliners* from thinking of alternative stories for themselves. If the hole in Eveline's story reflects her fear of sexuality, it also reflects her difficulty in finishing—in acting, or even imagining out—her own story in the language that dominates her consciousness. And the difficulty results from the fact that her story is modeled after stories where sailors fall on their feet in Buenos Ayres and girls get married. These are, as many critics have pointed out, men's stories even when written by women. That is, they are stories written in the language of the patriarchy that limit the possibilities as well as the imaginations of women.

In "Clay" Maria's tiny voice quavers as she omits the verse where "suitors sought my hand" from the hit tune of *The Bohemian Girl.* Gretta's recollection of Michael Furey is shaped by the language of romance. Mrs. Mooney may think in a more aggressive dialect than Eveline, but she fits her daughter into the marriage plot and she is presented as a two-dimensional character who "dealt with moral problems as a cleaver deals with meat" (63). And Mrs. Kearney might have insisted that the concert committee "wouldn't have dared to have treated her like that if she had been a man" and "would see that her daughter got her rights" (148), but she could do no more than rage, while her daughter—who never figures in the story at all—can only follow "her mother meekly" (149).

In "The Dead" the power of the dominant language takes on more explicit political dimensions. Here we begin by focusing on the housemaid. "Lily, the caretaker's daughter, was literally run off her feet" (175). But Lily disappears from the story, or the narrator shifts his point of view from her to Gabriel, right after Gabriel fails to see her as a full, separate person. "I suppose we'll be going to your wedding one of these fine days with your young man, eh?" Lily responds bitterly with another cliché, "The men that is now is only all palaver and what they can get out of you" (178). But there is a difference between the two kinds of clichés. Gabriel's cliché reveals him as well-meaning but insensitive; when we discover that he is writer and speaker who identifies with the language of authority, we may intimate how this language keeps serving girls in their place. Lily's cliché is an expression of futility. There is no other language available to her when she tries to choose an identity different from the one Gabriel imposes on her. And there is no other way for her to say what turns out to be true. Gabriel is full of palaver when he fails to see Lily as an independent person. He is full of palaver when he gives his after-dinner speech. And he is full of palaver when, seeing his own wife standing on the stairs, he transforms her into a romantic symbol.

We discover that he has never fully seen Gretta or known about the "real" love she shared with a consumptive boy who was "in the gas works." Ironically, when Gabriel sees her as a symbol and thinks of painting her in a picture entitled *Distant Music,* she is remembering Michael Furey, who "got his death" singing to her in the rain. She also thinks of Michael as she climbs the stairs to their room, while Gabriel—having been full of palaver all night—is thinking of what he can get out of her.

When Gabriel steps out on the dance floor with Molly Ivors, he steps into the political arena. She reproves him for writing for *The Daily Express*, a conservative paper that opposed Irish independence. She also reproves him for spending his summers in Europe, "to keep in touch with the languages," rather than on the west coast, where Gretta was born, and which was the seat of Irish nationalism: "And haven't you your own language to keep in touch with—Irish" (189). The mother tongue is suppressed in the country colonized by England. Gabriel, a writer as well as a speaker, chooses a language that keeps him out of touch with his country as well as with his native feelings: he thinks Molly Ivors is trying to make him look ridiculous and ignores the friendliness of her tone and the warmth of her grasp (205). Indeed, the language he chooses not only keeps him out of touch with Molly Ivors, Lily, his aunts, and his wife; it denies them voices and stories of their own.

In *Dubliners* Joyce was discovering the aesthetic and political power of absence. All the stories depend on what is left unsaid, sometimes on ellipses where we can fill in the meaning, or try to, through active reading and historical scholarship—that is, by asserting ourselves as conarrators and assuming our privilege as a member of the presupposed narrative community. But sometimes the narrator leaves us isolated, and the holes in the story cannot be filled in. For they are marks of absence in the language of power— which denies us access to the stories, as it denies selfhood even to those among the colonized and disenfranchised who use it.

Eveline is the clearest example. But if she cannot finish her story, Joyce can establish her as one of the most fully developed characters in *Dubliners*. We know what she does at the Stores, how she is harassed by the "edgy" Miss Gavin, and how much she earns. Indeed, Don Gifford uses her weekly wages of seven shillings as the basis for his discussion of monetary values (13–15). We know how she "keeps the house together," takes care of the two young children, and gives her entire wages to her father. We know that her father was a drunkard and threatened to beat her. We know that her mother lived a "life of commonplace sacrifices closing in final craziness" (40). We know that on her wall hangs a picture of the saint who paralyzed herself and was cured when she vowed to dedicate her life to God. We know that Eveline's imagination is aroused by the story of a noble girl kidnapped by gypsies. We know what kind of man attracts her, and that her vision of their life together is at best a fantasy and at worst a reality she cannot face.

In four-and-a-half pages Joyce depicts the social forces that shaped Eveline's consciousness. But, more important, he shows how they form the limit of her consciousness—indeed, the substance of each story establishes the limits of a character's consciousness. And the consciousness is embodied in the hole that makes each story (w)hole.

I should confront a problem of dealing with the discontinuities, absences, or holes in *Dubliners*—for I have been describing encounters with holes in the reading experience even though they have not been generally recognized. Early readers may not have gotten beyond the disruptions of propriety to be aware that they were reinforced if not shaped by what Joyce was doing with the form of the short story. Later readers may have become accustomed to what—with the influence of film and television—was becoming fairly conventional. But most of Joyce's contemporaries read *Dubliners* after *A Portrait*, where the gaps and leaps provoked strong positive and negative reactions. And one of my goals is to recover the power they generated.

2

A Portrait of the Artist as a Young Man: Stephen's Struggle with Author-ity

Edward Garnett, reader for Duckworth and Company, considered *A Portrait* "ably written," except for the end, where "there is a complete falling to bits." The reviewer for the *Glasgow Herald* judges this positively, saying that the novel "leaps confidently from one peak to another in the clear radiance emanating from the summits themselves." The reviewer for the *Liverpool Daily Post* was disturbed by a book "which flashes its truths upon one like a searchlight and a moment later leaves the dazzled reader in the darkness." H. G. Wells reacted positively to the "mosaic of jagged fragments that does altogether render with extreme completeness the growth of a rather secretive, imaginative boy in Dublin. . . . He breaks away from scene to scene without a hint of the change of time and place; at the end he passes suddenly from the third person to the first." But Joyce's rejection of the inverted comma and free use of dashes were too much for the persona Wells was developing. Except in the splendid Christmas dinner scene, "most of the talk flickers blindly . . . one has the same wincing feeling at being flicked at that one used to have in the early cinema shows."

The breaking and flickering generated in the gaps of the opening pages are like the jump cuts in films of the sixties that disturbed us, until they became conventional and were even appropriated by TV advertising. They also have a mimetic function, separating events that took place when Stephen was too young to have developed a sense of time. There is the story of the "moocow" when he was "baby tuckoo," his singing about "the green wothe botheth," his wetting the bed, his dancing for Uncle Charles and Dante, his hiding under the table after saying he will marry the Protestant Eileen, his mother declaring he will apologize, and Dante warning, "O, if not, the eagles will come and pull out his eyes" (7–8).

It may seem easy enough now to accept the row of asterisks following this traumatic scene as a conventional ellipsis. We have learned how to bridge the gap in space and time between the night-marish chant and that evening some years later on the football field of Clongowes Wood. And I want to emphasize "learned." For I do not think many first readers associated the eagle that would "pull out his eyes" with the "greasy leather orb" that "flew like a heavy bird" while "his eyes were weak and watery" (8). Indeed, I wonder whether anyone saw this link before the New Criticism, which taught us to read without recognizing that we were creating and not discovering the links, that we were domesticating the novel's terror, and that we were suppressing the social and politi-cal implications.

For if we accept the ellipsis as conventional, as standing for the natural passage of time, we might fail to recognize the disruptions in Stephen's life before and after he leaves home. We might fail to realize the full impact on Stephen when his mother and Dante collaborate in the nightmarish threat. Moreover, we might fail to be disturbed by the fact that the chant—"Pull out his eyes, / Apologise"— is not attributed to any character and issues from some generalized author-ity.

When they were grown up he was going to marry Eileen. He hid under the table. His mother said:
—O, Stephen will apologise.
Dante said:
—O, if not, the eagles will come and pull out his eyes.

> *Pull out his eyes,*
> *Apologise,*
> *Apologise,*
> *Pull out his eyes.*
> *Apologise,*
> *Pull out his eyes,*
> *Pull out his eyes,*
> *Apologise.* (8)

The implications of this scene become clear when we compare it to the original manuscript epiphany, upon which it is based. In the original, Mr Vance comes in with a stick, threatening "he'll have to apologise. . . . Or else . . . the eagles'll come and pull out his eyes." Mrs Joyce assents, "O yes . . . I'm sure he will apologise." And Joyce, hiding under the table, chants to himself, "Pull out his eyes, / Apologise . . . "(Scholes and Kain, 11).[1] The change not only shows how the women who nurture Stephen are implicated in the very power that represses them, it shows them to be agents of repression.

And, in displacing the source of the terrifying chant, it shows the repressive author-ity to be ubiquitous and totalitarian.

In accepting the ellipses as conventional, we might also fail to question the role of the male initiation story, or we might accept it as logical and natural. The Jesuit school curriculum is carefully ritualized to initiate adolescent boys, mostly from the upper middle class, into the power structure of Ireland, and to brutally exclude those who do not fit in. "The wide playgrounds were swarming with boys. All were shouting and the prefects urged them on with strong cries." Stephen felt small and weak; "he kept on the fringe of his line, out of sight of his prefect, out of the reach of the rude feet." Nor could he identify himself in the language of Nasty Roche, who called the Friday pudding "dog-in-the-blanket" and asked him what kind of name is Stephen Dedalus and "What is your father. . . . Is he a magistrate?" (8–9).

The second row of asterisks may give us a different kind of trouble, even though we could continue with the train of associations. On one side of the ellipsis Stephen dreams of lying dead like Parnell while Dante walks by proudly in her maroon dress and green velvet mantle. On the other side is the image of a red fire in the grate under the "ivytwined branches" (27). The dinner will feature another bird, a turkey, which is also what they called the pandy bat at Clongowes. And Parnell will be a key figure in the traumatic experience of Stephen's first Christmas dinner with the grownups.

But are we simply leaping ahead to a time connected in Stephen's mind by the images of Dante and birds? Why isn't this a flashback? Couldn't Parnell's death and the Christmas dinner have occurred the year before Stephen entered Clongowes? Would Stephen have been so disturbed by Dante's reaction at the Christmas dinner if Parnell had died while he was living among the priests? Wouldn't his experience at Clongowes be more "tragic" if the martyr with whom he identified had been not only betrayed by the Irish Church but the source of division in his family, so that it was no longer possible for him to dream of home as a refuge? I can now confess that I read this scene as a flashback when I first taught the novel, and for twenty-five years I have been suppressing what I thought was either careless reading or overpreparation. Not that I insist on reading the scene as a flashback, only that the text does not necessitate its being a successive event. It is certainly a unique event in the narrative, as David Hayman points out, for we leap from Stephen's limited consciousness, presented in free indirect style, to a dramatic scene ("The Joycean Inset"). It is a disruption of a narrative that secures itself through temporal succession and causal explanation.

John Paul Riquelme focuses on what he calls the "oscillating perspectives" to show that the novel is the autobiography Stephen has written once he found himself as an artist. The various shifts in styles and perspectives call attention to the process of narration and the narrative medium, as well as the kind of artist Stephen was to become. Riquelme analyzes these shifts carefully and systematically, but not to the end of realizing an experience of oscillation. Indeed, he points out the "striking fusion of inner and outer and character and teller" (56). I think his initial instinct was right, however. Joyce was discovering the possibilities of oscillation, not fusion. It is easy to recognize the role of the medium in *Ulysses* and *Finnegans Wake*. But it is important to recognize that Joyce was experimenting with the intrusion of the medium in his first novel. And—like the cubists who were leaping from perspective to perspective, the jazz musicians who were playing with the possibilities of syncopation, and the film makers who were experimenting with montage—he was discovering the potential of discontinuity.

If the novel is narrated by the artist Stephen would become, perhaps the best way to identify him is to look at what he wrote before he became the educated and self-conscious artist-*manqué* we see in the final chapter—or to look at a form that is not derivative. The dislocation from Bray to Dublin and his family's change in fortune embittered young Stephen, and he "chronicled with patience what he saw, detaching himself from it and testing its mortifying flavour in secret" (67). What he chronicled were three famous epiphanies: his aunt looking at a picture of "The beautiful Mabel Hunter," while a "ringletted girl" looks on and a boy mauls the picture with his reddened hands; old Ellen mistaking him for Josephine; and the children's party that ends with Stephen and E—C— waiting for the tram. Much has been written about what the protagonist of *Stephen Hero* defined as "a sudden manifestation, whether in the vulgarity of speech or of gesture or in a memorable phrase of the mind itself" (211).[2] I only want to call attention to the word "sudden," which is almost redundant, since how else could the spiritual manifest itself. And to the fact that what almost all forty of Joyce's original manuscript epiphanies have in common are ellipses—empty moments that punctuate the hollow speech.

Besides being a device of characterization, the three epiphanies young Stephen chronicles in *A Portrait* serve a narrative purpose; they illuminate moments during his early time in Dublin from the most subjective vantage in the novel. We might compare the short section chronicling three events, or epiphanies, with the opening passage, for in both Joyce was discovering what would be called the stream of consciousness. Even more than the opening, this section reveals that there is nothing like a stream connecting the moments of consciousness—each scene rises from a separate new source. In what Riquelme points out as "what must be the most unusual footnote" in *Interpretation of Dreams*, Freud insists that "there is at least one spot in every dream at which it is unplumbable—a navel, as it were, that is its point of contact with the unknown" (50). The epiphany is a sudden manifestation because it appears out of that navel.

The three epiphanies that Stephen chronicles include only one actual ellipsis, in Ellen's speech. But each is discontinuous with what comes before and each makes its impact because the narrator, young Stephen, has deliberately detached himself from it to test its mortifying flavor. The third epiphany, of the children's party, leads us to understand an important kind of discontinuity. It is the longest and the most detailed. We can picture the gay cocked hats, the sunbonnets, "the spoils of their crackers," and the gloomy boy in the corner hiding his "feverish agitation" as "her glance travelled to his corner, flattering, taunting, searching, exciting his heart" (68–69). We can picture almost everything at the party, that is, except for the subject of the pronoun "her." Her absence is notable when we think back to the other epiphanies. For we can clearly see the "ringletted girl" standing on tiptoe to peer at the picture of "The beautiful Mabel Hunter" (67), the boy who comes in from the street "stamping crookedly under his stone of coal" and mauling the picture with "his reddened and blackened hands" (67), and the "feeble creature," whose skull appears "suspended in the gloom of the doorway," and who in a whining voice mistakes Stephen for Josephine (68). But we cannot see the girl whose glance so excites Stephen's heart. We can clearly see the lank brown horses rubbing their noses together and shaking their bells, the conductor talking to the driver, and the empty tram seats with their scattered colored tickets. But all we see of the enchanting girl—as she goes up and down the steps, once or twice standing close beside him and forgetting to go down—is "her cowled head and her shoes [tapping] blithely on the glassy road" (69).

We see even less of her toward the end of the novel in the otherwise detailed picture when Stephen encounters her on the library steps with her companions:

The quick light shower had drawn off, tarrying in clusters of diamonds among the shrubs of the quadrangle where an exhalation was breathed forth by the blackened earth. Their trim boots prattled as they stood on the steps of the colonnade, talking quietly and gaily, glancing at the clouds, holding their umbrellas at cunning angles against the few last raindrops, closing them again, holding their skirts demurely. (216)

This passage is also based on one of Joyce's original epiphanies.[3] And, though not chronicled by Stephen, it was transformed from a conventional description to reflect the way the developing artist has come to see. It is something Stephen might have composed—in a form, unlike his villanelle, that is not derivative. Major connections in time and space are missing. After the literary opening, the formal elements of the medium are suddenly foregrounded, and the narrative eye leaps from a wide stylized view of the scene to a sharp picture of the girls' boots to a generalized view of the girls talking quietly and gaily, and then to a series of sharp images that focus on the purely formal elements of the scene—their glancing up at the clouds, holding umbrellas at cunning angles, closing them again, and holding their skirts demurely.[4]

The movement of the narrative eye and the formal elements of the medium are foregrounded—and so are the gaps. But the gaps may also be explained in terms of what Stephen is repressing: E—C—'s body. As in *Dubliners*, women are a threat throughout the novel. Or their physicality is a threat—their full and different presence. His childish thoughts of marrying Eileen (whose female otherness is compounded by her being Protestant) are associated with guilt and punishment: the eagle will pull out his eyes.

So there are two kinds of holes in *A Portrait of the Artist as a Young Man* as there were in *Dubliners*, with two different kinds of power and two different sets of political implications. There are the holes in the narrative, disruptions, shifts in perspective that embody Stephen's struggle with the language of author-ity and therefore lead to an inclusive sense of (w)holeness. And there are the holes in Stephen's vision, which deny the (w)holeness of self and society. How are they related? First, we should carry Riquelme's notion of Joyce's "oscillating voices" to the point where we hear at least two voices arguing about the best way to tell a story. Second, we need to understand the implications of this conflict, or dialogic.

In the beginning of *A Portrait* Stephen's father is telling him a story. He has a hairy face, and is looking down through what looks like a glass. The story begins traditionally, "Once upon a time and a very good time it was . . . " (7). That is, his father's story, like the story of the first father, begins at an ideal point in time, when a very good time it was. And it is designed to follow

the road, past where Betty Byrne sold lemon platt, to a logical
conclusion. Baby Stephen does not tell a story; he sings a song.
He even changes the words from "O, the wild rose blossoms / On
the little green place" to "O, the green wothe botheth." But the
song is obviously one that he heard his father sing. "Lilly Dale" is
about the love of a dead—safe—woman; the "green place" is
actually a "green grave." So Stephen's changing a "wild rose" to
a "green wothe" does not amount to much. Nor will he change
the romantic paradigm in the love lyrics he later conceives. Moreover, his father's way of telling a story prevails. The voice that
dominates the opening of the novel shapes it like a biblical chroni-
cle, which begins in an ideal time with an ideal father. Patricia
Tobin relates this form to that of the classical nineteenth-century
novel, where a commanding narrator traces the effects of an original cause, or "genealogical imperative." She is only one of the
many discerning scholars who have defined the father's way of
telling a story. Nancy Miller (who will become more pertinent in
my discussion of *Ulysses*) emphasizes one of its dimensions in the
Bildungsroman or *Künstlerroman*, which she calls an "ambitious
text," since its logic leads a male hero to success and power.

The logic of the story Mr. Dedalus begins to tell—the development of the artist—also leads to success and power. And, seeking
to achieve this goal, it overlooks, appropriates, or re-forms stories
that do not conveniently fit in. The little boy in this story may
require the services of Betty Byrne, or that he overcome her tempta-
tions, but he requires no knowledge of *her*. We follow the road
past where she sells lemon platt—just as we follow the road past
all the other female characters in the novel without hearing their
stories, or much if anything of their actual voices.

Let me quote every single line of direct female speech in the
novel. Well, every line except for those of Mrs. Riordan or Dante
(isn't it interesting that we don't even know her name?), for they
require special attention. Here is what Stephen's mother has to
say, and she is important enough to be his motivating force in
Ulysses—his last request of her in "Circe" being "Tell me the
word, mother" (474).

—O, Stephen will apologise. (8)

—Goodbye, Stephen, goodbye! (9)

—Sit over.
—For pity's sake and for pity sake let us have no political discussion on
this day of all days in the year.

—Mrs Riordan, I appeal to you . . . to let the matter drop now.
—Really, Simon . . . you should not speak that way before Stephen. It's not right.
—Mrs Riordan, don't excite yourself answering them. (29–38)

—Then I suppose . . . he will be able to arrange it. I mean about Belvedere.
—I never liked the idea of sending him to the christian brothers myself.
—I'm sure he'll work very hard now . . . especially when he has Maurice with him. (71)

—O, he didn't, Simon! (72)

—Some place that's not too dear. . . . Yes. Some quiet place. (97)

—An hour and twentyfive minutes. . . . The right time now is twenty past ten. The dear knows you might try to be in time for your lectures. (174)

Dante, as we'll see, has a bit more to say. I will come to her in less than a minute, which is enough time for us to take in all the other women's voices in this 250-page novel:

—The beautiful Mabel Hunter!
—What is she in, mud?
—In the Pantomime, love.
—The beautiful Mabel Hunter!
—Isn't she an exquisite creature? (67)

—Is that Josephine?
—No, Ellen. It's Stephen.
—O . . . O, Good evening, Stephen.
—Do you want anything, Ellen?
—I thought it was Josephine. I thought you were Josephine, Stephen. (68)

—Good night, Willie dear!
—Give me a kiss. (100–101)

—Hello, Bertie, any good in your mind?
—Is that you, pigeon?
—Number ten. Fresh Nelly is waiting on you.
—Goodnight, husband! Coming in to have a short time? (102)

—Goneboro toboro lookboro atboro aboro houseboro.
—Becauseboro theboro landboro lordboro willboro putboro usboro outboro. (163)

—Katey, fill out the place for Stephen to wash.
—Boody, fill out the place for Stephen to wash.
—I can't, I'm going for blue. Fill it out, you, Maggie.
—Well it's a poor case . . . when a university student is so dirty that his mother has to wash him. (174–175)

—Yes, father?
—Yes, father.
—Yes, father. (175)

—Ah, gentleman, your own girl, sir! The first handsel today, gentleman. Buy that lovely bunch. Will you gentleman?
—Do gentleman! Don't forget your own girl sir!
—Buy them lovely ones, will you sir? Only a penny.
—Well, sure, you will some day, sir, please God. (183–184)

That is every line of direct female speech in *A Portrait of the Artist as a Young Man*, with the exception of Dante's. In a frame of their own they make a group portrait of subservience and self-effacement. They also lead us to wonder about Stephen's prospects when he goes off to forge in the smithy of his soul the uncreated conscience of *his* race.

It is a cruel irony that the women who nurture Stephen invest the story's language with its most threatening potency, for it is his mother who says that Stephen will apologize for saying he will marry Eileen, and Dante who pictures the punishment. "O, if not, the eagles will come and pull out his eyes" (8).

Dante requires special attention, because of her power in this traumatic scene, because she has more lines of direct speech than all the other female characters in the novel, and because of the role she plays at the Christmas dinner. David Hayman singles out the Christmas dinner scene as an "inset" because it breaks from the dominant mode of free indirect discourse and achieves its effect through the direct presentation of its characters' voices. But the characters speak a language, which, despite their powerlessness, is the language of power.

The ineffectual men, Stephen's father and Mr. Casey, begin by talking of Christy, who manufactured "champagne for those fellows"—that is, bombs for the Fenians (28). They go on to vituperate against the priests for betraying Parnell and rending him "like rats in the sewer" (34). This leads into Mr. Casey's story, which concludes with his bending down to the "harridan" who was "bawling and screaming" about Kitty O'Shea and spitting a mouthful of tobacco juice, "*Phth* . . . right into her eye" (36–37).

Dante opposes the men, but it is important to realize that she collaborates in telling their story by goading them on. One response actually incites Mr. Casey to tell the story of the famous spit. "I will defend my church and my religion," she tells Mrs. Dedalus, "when it is insulted and spit on by renegade catholics" (34). And her reactions are voiced in the violent language of the

Church: "*It would be better for him that a millstone were tied about his neck and that he were cast into the depth of the sea rather than that he should scandalise one of these, my least little ones.* That is the language of the Holy Ghost" (32). Indeed, she slams out of the room shouting, "Devil out of hell! We won! We crushed him to death!"—which brings tears to the men's eyes (39).

Mr. Casey and Mrs. Riordan become caricatures as they caricature the very language that builds on violence and denies them individual self-realization. But Mr. Casey's characterization is positive in contrast to Dante's. He may be a blowhard but we empathize with his outrage, exult in his victory, and share in his laughter. Moreover, he gets the chance to tell his own story—and to picture himself as a kind of hero.

Mrs. Riordan, on the other hand, is identified with the harridan of Mr. Casey's story. She is not allowed a story of her own. In fact, she is characterized by Stephen's father, who was identified with the authorial voice. Mr. Dedalus had told Stephen that Dante "was a spoiled nun and that she had come out of the convent in the Alleghanies when her brother had got the money from the savages for the trinkets and the chainies" (35). But how did Dante get to America? Why did she enter the convent? Did she choose the convent as a positive alternative to the patriarchal family as so many women did in the nineteenth century? What did she do in the convent? Did she come out of the convent willingly? Could the America Stephen pictures be related to the "Wild West" that excited the young narrator's imagination in "An Encounter"—as similar adventure stories excited the imaginations of both the colonizers and the colonized? What are we do make of her being *rescued* by a brother who exploited "savages"?

It helps to know that Dante was modeled on a woman "embittered by a disastrous marriage," who had been on the verge of becoming a nun in America when her brother, having made a fortune in Africa, died and left her 30,000 pounds (Ellmann, 25). But it helps more to know that the Allegheny convents were not what was pictured by the male imagination, that they were not benighted retreats from the world but centers of care and learning, that they adapted to the customs and needs of the New World rather than perpetuating the traditions of the European closed convent, that they developed the first professionally trained nurses in the country, that they had the most advanced education for wealthy girls, that the tuitions helped pay for educating the poor, that some sisters managed businesses to support their charitable work, that many orders had their own constitutions, which meant they were under the jurisdiction of neither a European mother-house nor a bishop and were therefore freer than nuns, perhaps all women, anywhere else in the world.[5]

Knowing all this might lead us to imagine a story for Mrs. Riordan that neither Stephen's father nor the novel's primary narrator could tell. Dante was probably one of the poor girls, educated in sewing rather than Latin. But had she entered the order, her education would have changed. Indeed, we know she was exposed to books, had an appetite for knowledge, and an attraction for what was beyond. After all she taught Stephen "where the Mozambique Channel was and what was the longest river in America and what was the name of the highest mountain in the moon" (11). Had she not been "rescued" by a brother who made a fortune exploiting "savages," she might well not have become the narrow-minded harridan pictured in *A Portrait of the Artist as a Young Man*.

I do not mean to rewrite Dante's story, only to reflect on the nature and power of male author-ity and demonstrate how story-telling is a political act. Stephen feels the oppression of the Irish family, church, and state. And he rebels against them. But he does not escape the language of the fathers. Indeed, he transgresses in a way that keeps the eagles from pulling out his eyes. He rebels only against the conventions of ordinary people, thereby adding his voice to that of the fathers—for he embraces the conventions of the Church and High Art.

The language of the Church is epitomized in Father Arnall's violently charged sermon; it stimulates all the senses to perceive the individual as totally dependent. The language of High Art is not violent, but it violates the integrity of the *other* by appropriating the subject to its logic, especially when the subject is a woman. The limited nature of Stephen's rebellion is highlighted in the sequence on the strand, as he begins to identify with the original Dedalus and ignores his earthbound friends. He then looks but does not see a young woman wading in the strand; he transforms her into an angelic seabird. Robert Scholes was right in arguing for our acceptance of Stephen's villanelle as a true work of art ("Stephen Dedalus"), but his argument depends on our privileging religious and aesthetic conventions Stephen would have to reject to become an independent artist.[6]

Stephen's epiphanies, while more authentic forms of story-telling, do not enable him to escape from the language of the fathers. But at the end of the novel he chooses the form of the diary, which allows him to create himself anew each day. It also enables him to reflect, if still not actually picture, E—C—as an independent other. Feeling sorry and mean for the way he first responded to her, he "turned off that valve at once and opened the spiritual-heroic refrigerating apparatus, invented and patented in all countries by Dante Alighieri. Talked rapidly of myself and my plans. In the midst of it unluckily I made a sudden gesture of a revolutionary nature. I must have looked like a fellow throwing a handful of peas into the air" (252). If we still do not know her full name or hear her voice, we do see from her perspective.

The diary is not an official form of art. It has always been a private, and unofficial form of writing. It invites writers who are denied the continuous kind of time required to compose novels, and whose development would not be toward the achievement of success and power. And it invites a kind of thinking that is not directed toward a single end, but can emphasize multiplicity and relationship. It is predominantly a woman's form. If budding male novelists also kept diaries (which they might have called journals), they rarely used the diary form in their novels, unless it was to characterize a girl or woman. Two notable exceptions are Turgenev's *Diary of a Superfluous Man* (which influenced Joyce) and Gogol's *Diary of a Madman*—which go even further in showing this form as most congenial to the alienated and disenfranchised.

In choosing an alternative to the language of the father, Stephen may be discovering his way to independence, or creating himself anew. In discovering the values of discontinuity, he may be discovering a new way to tell the story of an artist as a young man. Two voices contend over the best way to tell a story in *A Portrait*, and demonstrate that storytelling is a political act. A traditional voice of author-ity, like that of Stephen's father in the opening lines, tells a linear story of development in the language of power. It seeks control and a final goal—the young man becoming an artist. And it denies the presence of what threatens it. The holes in its story are absences, denials of the (w)holeness of individual selves and society. A rebellious voice disrupts the traditional storyline in ways that excited and disturbed Joyce's contemporaries, though they have become conventional to us. It manifests itself in the epiphanies, but more successfully in the form of the diary. Of course, the authorial voice wins. For the virtues of the diary are its inclusiveness, its openness, its preference for association over logic, discontinuity over completeness, experimentation over mastery, relationship over goals, individual empowerment over the drive for power. And these are liabilities in the struggle for author-ity.

Moreover, the diary ends with Stephen speaking unconsciously in the language of power and enthusiastically in the language of High Art. His mother is putting his clothes in order and praying for him. He is going forth for the millionth time to encounter the reality of experience and to forge in the smithy of his soul the uncreated conscience of his race. "Old father, old artificer, stand me now and ever in good stead" (253).

Joyce had to tire of Stephen and discover Poldy before he could find the form that could not only contend with but reduce the father's to one among many independent voices and ways of telling a story—though this would generate a new set of complications.

3

Defining Terms: Author-ity, Voice, and the Body-Text

In distinguishing the two voices in *A Portrait*, I am borrowing from Mikhail Bakhtin, whose theory has special pertinence to Joyce and the modern novel, even though he was dealing with works that now seem very conventional. As I pointed out in my introduction, Bakhtin distinguishes between the monologic novel—where the voice of the author dominates—and the dialogic or polyphonic novel—which is like a carnival, where the voice of the author is only one among many voices that speak, argue, harangue, cajole, mock, imply, and take joy in their contradictoriness. The monologic novel reflects a unified sense of character; it relates to the self as an object, which is at least developing toward some final form. The polyphonic novel recognizes the self as other, independent, multiple, and indeterminate; it relates to the self as a subject, through various forms of dialogue.

I am using the term "voice" in a way that is both narrower and broader than Bakhtin's use of it. I am narrower in focusing only on voices that tell stories. But I am broader in trying to show how Joyce generated a subversive voice not from his characters but from the physical text itself, the printed page. I realize that my use of the term "voice" may seem metaphoric or abstract, especially when it is harder to hear than to feel as shaping force. Moreover, I am no longer acknowledging what David Hayman calls "the arranger," or narrative "counterforce" (*Mechanics*), and what other critics (including myself) have described as a self-generating medium. Shari and Bernard Benstock focus the problem by asserting that we should use the term "narrator" only when he or she is present in person, and that the term "narrative voice" is most often a misleading metaphor. It should be used only when there is "a speaker telling a story, a speaker present and identifiable through the story, who cannot be separated from that story, in whom and through whom that story exists and without whom there would be no story" (17). Various forms of textual representation "produce the illusion that speech acts occur in written narrative; they do not" (17).

Stephen Ross helps us solve the problem. He reminds us that language is abstract (*langue*) until it is embodied (and becomes *parole*). In speech it is embodied in sound; in a literary text it is embodied in print. And the medium of embodiment augments, modifies, contradicts—or adds meaning that goes beyond the meaning of the words. "Voice," according to Ross, names that part of the meaning generated by the medium that embodies language.

In the speech act we hear an actual voice, which adds meanings through tone, volume, and rhythm. In a novel, of course, we do not hear sounds (though many of us subvocal readers think we do). But we respond to what Ross calls a "mimetic voice": a collection of features that leads us to think of a particular passage "as the utterance of an imagined person (character, narrator, 'author'). . . . These features include the mechanics of written dialogue (punctuation, speech identification, etc.); the conventions of imitating speech (phonetic spelling, colloquial phrasing, etc.); and grammatical forms (such as 'shifters') that call attention to the source, time, and place of utterance. We could also include any feature of the discourse governed by 'expressive identity' . . . the word choice in dialogue, for example, in *style indirect libre*" ("Voice," 305).

The value of the term "mimetic voice," besides justifying the use of "voice" for a medium that does not speak, is that it leads us to understand what Ross calls the "textual voice." Textual voice functions like voice in speech. It arises from those elements that "prompt or allow the reader to regard the printed text as a source of signification" ("Voice," 306).

In modern fiction, when the physicality of the text enters the reader's field, this term becomes very useful. But "textual voice" may be too abstract, or disembodied, for a voice that liberates the wild heterogeneity suppressed by the language and stories of the fathers—the energy of the other that Conrad identified with the "savage" body of Kurtz's mistress, that Dinesen embodied in texts composed of women's blood, and that Julia Kristeva identifies with the *jouissance* of the "semiotic." So I will call it the voice of the body-text, when this expression is not too awkward. This is the voice that, in *A Portrait of the Artist*, disrupts the traditional narrative with blank space or asterisks, that prints the items as they would look on a pawn ticket, that arranges print and syntax to have the look of a diary, and that intrudes in the form of newspaper headlines to initiate a hijinks of visual intrusions in

Ulysses. And these disruptions augment, modify, or contradict meanings conveyed by the words and governed by the (mimetic) voices of characters, narrators, and implied author.

But voice of the body-text need not be so assertive or obvious. At a minimal level, the very transformation of voice into print—as in the opening paragraphs of *A Portrait*—adds a tone and a meaning to that of an ostensible speaker, and it may serve the interests of the authorial voice.

Once upon a time and a very good time it was there was a moocow coming down along the road and this moocow that was coming down along the road met a nicens little boy named baby tuckoo. . . .

His father told him that story: his father looked at him through a glass: he had a hairy face. (7)

Mr. Dedalus's story is filtered through the consciousness of baby Stephen, though the thoughts of baby Stephen are silently augmented free indirect speech. We know that Stephen did not think in these words, but we easily accept them as embodiments of what he heard. Nonetheless, a tone of amused superiority arises that goes beyond the enjoyment the father obviously takes in telling his story, and is certainly different from what "baby tuckoo" felt while listening to it. There is a note of mimicry, a concealed parody, achieved by putting what baby Stephen heard into print. The very simplicity of the first run-on sentence leads us to see it as printed language standing for an oral language, or a voice, mimicking the simplicity of Stephen's mind. Simon Dedalus, who took such pride in oral performance, certainly told this story with pauses and emphases suppressed by the textual voice. But in the second paragraph—where two strong, unconventional colons emphasize the repetition—the textual voice conveys the power of the father.

"Voice" must refer to a speaker, and the Benstocks are right when they argue that the speaker must be present in the story and cannot be separated from the story. But the speaker need not be identifiable. What is significantly present is the "implied author"—which Wayne Booth defines as a persona of the author who governs the text but exists totally within it. And, I would add, whose presence is reflected in the mimetic voice and the voice of the body-text.

The term "implied author" seems so self-explanatory, or has been part of our critical vocabulary for so long now, that we need to recall its original meaning. According to Booth, as an author writes, he creates "not simply an ideal, impersonal 'man in general' but an implied version of 'himself' that is different from the implied author we meet in other men's works" (70f.). Two points are important to note. First, in contrast to the actual author, the implied author is a product of the text, even though his role is to control it. Second, the implied author is neither preconceived nor fixed, but evolves in the process of writing—and reading—the novel.

The implied author governs the text through the use of narrative conventions and what Bakhtin calls the "common language": "the average norm of spoken and written language for a given social group," which embodies the *going point of view* and the going *value*" (301). The implied author may accept the common language, use it for his own purposes, distance himself from it, or expose it—and he may do all of these in the same novel. The term "voice," then, makes us conscious of an implied author speaking in some form of the common language, with one inflection or another, and sometimes with an inflection that generates a concealed voice.

Hugh Kenner shows how Joyce concealed voices within his narrative as early as *Dubliners*. And he illuminates the "concealed" dimension of free indirect speech by renaming it "the Uncle Charles Principle" from a passage in *A Portrait*: "Every morning, therefore, uncle Charles repaired to his outhouse but not before he had creased and brushed scrupulously his back hair and brushed and put on his tall hat" (60). According to Kenner, Wyndam Lewis was wrong in attributing "repaired"—a literary word used by second-rate writers—to Joyce, or even to his narrator. For the word "wears invisible quotation marks"; it belongs to Uncle Charles, "who has notions of semantic elegance, akin to his ritual brushing of his hat." "The Uncle Charles Principle" is simply that: *the narrative idiom need not be the narrator's*" (*Joyce's Voices*, 17–18).

Actually, the word "repaired" belongs to the implied author, who, as the "invisible quotation marks" suggest, is mimicking Uncle Charles. I realize that I am conflating the arguments of Booth and Bakhtin at exactly the point where they conflict. Bakhtin might have consented to the notion of an implied author as a persona created within and by the text—but not to one where the positions ultimately cohere. For Bakhtin, the authorial voice "exaggerates, now strongly, now weakly, one or another aspect of the 'common language,' sometimes abruptly exposing its inadequacy to its object and sometimes, on the contrary, becoming one with it, maintaining an almost imperceptible distance, sometimes even directly forcing it to reverberate with his own 'truth,' which occurs when an author completely merges his own voice with the common view." But it is always "in a state of movement and oscillation that is more or less alive" (301f.).

I will use the term "voice," first, to identify the agency by which the implied author, relating now one way and now another to the common language, embodies meaning—either by imitating or mimicking sounds and gestures through unobtrusive conventions of print, or by manipulating the print on the page. And I will side with Bakhtin in saying that the implied author oscillates among different and sometimes conflicting voices.

Let me go one step further, though, and initiate an argument I will pursue throughout this study. There is a problem that Bakhtin recognizes but does not confront. The revolutionary impulse of the novel may derive from its variety of contending voices. But some voices have more power than others; their author-ity derives from tradition, or a canon, established by the class whose authority the authorial voice reflects.

Despite the variety, oscillation, and conflict of voices in a polyphonic novel, the authorial voice is the most powerful. It is enhanced by the reader's needs. As Booth points out, "the reader needs to know where, in the world of values, he stands—that is, to know where the author wants him to stand" (73). And the authorial voice meets our needs by selecting events, arranging the plot, creating a hierarchy of characters, but also by speaking through his narrator(s) and even his characters. Let me point out that I am using "authorial voice" in a way that differs from Bakhtin's, or in a way that comes closer to his notion of the "monologic." I do not mean the voice of the author, or even of the implied author. I mean the voice of author-ity that is inscribed in a language evolved and perpetuated by social institutions: the state, church, family, school system, great books, press, popular forms of entertainment, advertising. And whatever form or position the authorial voice takes, it cannot abdicate its author-ity, or the role of author. Nor can it divorce itself from the tradition of its power. Indeed, it often appropriates other voices for its own ends.

It is important to add, therefore, that authorial language is made up not only of words and syntax but of story forms implied authors have traditionally employed. And these stories are unified because they ignore, exclude, suppress, alter, or co-opt whatever threatens their coherence. I hope it is now clear why I use the masculine pronoun to represent the implied author. The authorial voice may distance itself from the common language, parody it, expose its hypocrisy, its narrow-mindedness, or its ignorance. But it cannot totally undermine the patriarchal power structure, of

which it is a part. Nor can it attack its own authorial and authoritative role in shaping a story to achieve a set of goals that are ultimately shared by those who control the "common" language.

This is not to say that the authorial voice cannot be attacked by
other voices within the novel, undermined by subversive use of the
body-text, or, as we will see, reduced to one among many independent voices and ways of telling a story. Only that we must understand its inherent power, see how it attracts and appropriates other
voices, identify the voices that attack it—and describe the power
relations. While it is important to recognize the range and variety
of voices and ideolects (which Joseph Valente captures so incisively
in "The Politics of Joyce's Polyphony" and R. B. Kershner delin-
eates so well in *Joyce, Bakhtin, and Popular Literature*), my aim
will be to show how these voices line up.

I am aware that by lining up the voices I will polarize the rich
field of voices in Joyce, Faulkner, and Woolf. But the authorial
voice turns the carnival into an agon, or reduces the number of
positions to two: those that enhance its power and those that
oppose it. As a result, it will often force me into undesirably dualistic and apparently essentializing positions, which I hope will be
deconstructed through an understanding of its power and of the
alternative positions I will try to illuminate.

But now let me be more precise in defining the conflict, or power
struggle, in Joyce's early work. Instead of "traditional" or "official," I can now use the term "authorial voice"—to emphasize its
source and power. The authorial voice in *A Portrait* maintains control by using a story form—the *Bildungs-* or *Künstlerroman*—that
is strongly linear and goal oriented. Moreover, it tells a story, the
coherence of which depends on the absence of certain kinds of
experience, characters, and language. And it is reinforced by canonical allusions, as well as by the languages of the Church and High
Art, which dominate Stephen's thought. The rebellious voice expresses itself in the body-text as opposed to mimetic voice. It disrupts the authorial story to reflect an "otherness" beyond its grasp
and to provide a base from which alternative values can be generated. Finally, it suggests the potential Stephen might achieve in the
alternative forms of discontinuous epiphanies and diary entries.
Our ambivalence about Stephen's prospects results from this narrative argument, or battle, where the authorial voice is not only more
powerful but has shaped the very ground upon which the struggle
takes place. In *Ulysses*, Joyce finds new ways to undermine the
authorial voice, and to change the shape of the battlefield.

4

Ulysses

In *A Portrait of the Artist* an authorial voice was struggling with a rebellious voice. But Joyce was not ready to give the rebellious voice full reign, let alone discover the possibilities of polyphony. Perhaps he could not discover these possibilities until he gave up on Stephen, or realized, as he admitted to Frank Budgen, that he was no longer as interested in him—for "he has a shape that can't be changed" (Budgen, 105). And perhaps Stephen's shape could not be changed because it was determined by the shape of his story.

Joyce chose Ulysses for his new model because he was the most "complete all-round character presented by any writer." But he also chose Ulysses because his story "did not come to an end when the Trojan war was over. It began just when the other Greek heroes went back to live the rest of their lives in peace" (Budgen, 15, 17). Ulysses achieved his identity, unlike the other Greek heroes, not by going out to war and fighting valorously—but by returning home after the war to live in peace. I will elaborate later on his return, where he kills Penelope's suitors and establishes his identity as a warrior, father, and king. But Joyce seemed to be motivated primarily by a hero's achieving identity in a time of peace rather than war, through a journey or process rather than an agon, and by returning home—to a sphere of relationships, and a set of values that were in direct conflict with those of the Homeric warrior. Moreover, in contrast to the other Homeric heroes, Ulysses was aware of himself as a physical being, and not only in *The Odyssey*, where he covered his naked flesh before Nausicaa, but in *The Iliad* when he argued with Achilles that glory was not enough: the army needed food for their bodies. That is, he was also motivated to realize a human dimension suppressed by a heroic tradition that kept physical nature under control. "In my book," said Joyce, "the body lives in and moves through space and is the home of a full human personality" (Budgen, 21).

In focusing on Ulysses, Joyce was reaching the point that divides *The Iliad* from *The Odyssey*, or where the traditional epic can be questioned. For Mikhail Bakhtin, to question the epic is a radical shift, which signals the passage from the epic to the novel. While his distinctions have been questioned, they illuminate the radical nature of Joyce's novel and a set of aesthetic and political values from which it was breaking away. The epic, for Bakhtin, is characterized by an "absolute past." The epic world is "a world of 'beginnings' and 'peak times' in the national history, a world of fathers and of founding of families, a world of 'firsts' and 'bests.' " It is also a world that is complete, or a past that is inaccessible to the author, whose point of view is that of a "reverent . . . descendent." The reverence is for an impersonal and sacrosanct tradition. "In the epic world view, 'beginning,' 'first,' 'founder,' 'ancestor,' 'that which occurred earlier' and so forth are not merely temporal categories but *valorized* temporal categories, and valorized to an extreme degree. . . . The epic absolute past is the single source and beginning of everything good for all later times as well" (13–15).

There is one point of Bakhtin's that is worth noting, partly because of the equivocation in a man who is usually so outspoken and unequivocal. This is the relation between class and gender values. "In a patriarchal social structure the ruling class does, in a certain sense, belong to the world of 'fathers' and is thus separated from other classes by a distance that is almost epic" (15). What Bakhtin seems not quite ready to recognize is that the values we usually associate with women—where relationship is more important than domination and where what comes first is only part of an ongoing process—are values of class. Jean Baker Miller helps us understand this by beginning *Toward a New Psychology of Women* with a chapter on "Domination-Subordination." She shows how the values of nurturing and relationship are delegated to those whose function it is to support the dominant group, or class. She also shows that, despite their importance in a world growing more mechanized and alienated, these values cannot be recognized. Caring for others cannot lead to power, or dominance; indeed, it is a sign of submissiveness. Moreover, for someone in the dominant group to recognize the need for care and relationship would be to signal his dependency. Values associated with women, therefore, cannot be recognized by the fathers, or the language of fathers; the relation of class and gender is more important than Bakhtin wanted to admit.

Epic distance, which places everything in the epic world beyond question, was overcome by laughter, or an ambivalent laughter that was at once cheerful and annihilating. Contemporary life was originally the object of such laughter—which generated a fundamentally new attitude toward language and the word. "Alongside direct representation—laughing at living reality—there flourish parody and travesty of all high genres and of all lofty models embodied in national myth. The 'absolute past' of gods, demigods and heroes is here, in parodies and even more so in travesties, 'contemporized': it is brought low, represented on a plane equal with contemporary life, in an everyday environment, in the low language of contemporaneity" (Bakhtin, 21). Through laughter, what was sacrosanct and beyond question could be brought in close, drawn into "a zone of crude contact," fingered familiarly on all sides, turned upside down, inside out, peered at from above and below, taken apart, dismembered, laid bare, and exposed (23).

This "elemental popular laughter" gave rise to a wide range of literature—mimes, bucolic poems, fables, pamphlets, the Socratic dialogues, Roman and Menippean satire, the Greek romance or novel, and ultimately the novel as we have come to know it. That the novel has this varied lineage is just the reason for its heterogeneous potential, its capacity for competing voices, its openness. However, Bakhtin points out, the absence of internal control creates a need for "an *external* and *formal* completedness and exhaustiveness, especially in regard to plotline" (31). The *line* of the plot in the traditional novel becomes part of the monologic, though Bakhtin does not seem to be aware of its power. It is a remnant of the epic that, in valuing what came first and a world of the fathers, continued to limit the range of human consciousness. It controls the heterogeneity—and the drives of the body-text that draw the sacrosanct into "a zone of crude contact." What Joyce contributed to the development of the novel, though this potential was anticipated by Sterne, is the comic disruption, dismantling, displacement of the plotline.

I should confront the problem, here, that many classical scholars criticize Bakhtin's view of the epic because they recognize elements in *The Iliad* as well as *The Odyssey* that are brought into the zone of laughter: heroes seen realistically, and deeds shown to be less valorous than willful. But if Homer actually ridiculed the heroes in his epic story, this is not the popular view reflected in Charles Lamb's version of *The Odyssey* that initially inspired Joyce.

In *Ulysses*, the authorial voice echoes Homer's popular patriarchal epic; it resonates with canonical allusions. Moreover, it wants to tell a story that masters Dublin—that is, a realistic story from which the city, if it were wiped off the face of the earth, could be rebuilt. But it must contend with a rebellious voice that is more wily and inventive than the rebellious voice in *A Portrait*. And, more important, it must contend with an alternative story form—which changes the field of contention.

One reason Joyce may have lost interest in Stephen, or why Stephen's shape could not change, is that character is dependent on the shape of the story. Stephen had reached a critical stage in a story dominated by an authorial storytelling voice, where the very notions of growth and change are restricted by the form of development—and the achievement of goals and power. Joyce could not begin to experiment with a new shape until he had a new character. Just compare the beginnings of the Stephen and Bloom stories in *Ulysses*.

In the first story, the stage is set by Buck Mulligan, who comes up from the stairhead onto the top of the Martello Tower "bearing a bowl of lather on which a mirror and a razor lay crossed." He holds the bowl aloft and intones the beginning of the Mass. Then he summons Stephen from the darkness. Stephen, "displeased and sleepy," looks "coldly at the shaking gurgling face that blessed him" (3).

With allowances for age, Stephen's story in *Ulysses* begins very much like his story in *A Portrait*, from a well-defined beginning point in time and space, and with a physical if not psychological tabula rasa. Onto an empty platform comes a character who will introduce the protagonist. Buck Mulligan is a father figure, and, though he may parody the Mass and the language of the Church, his mimicry enhances as well as undermines the authority of the Church, and his parody is contained within the traditional storyline. Buck Mulligan's voice is rebellious; it is appropriated, however, by an inobtrusive authorial voice that enjoys his blasphemy—and fits it into the traditional storyline. When Stephen appears, it is as a character firmly established on a geographical and historical base, with a beginning that implies linear development, even if he will meander physically. Stephen's voice—augmented by rebellious uses of punctuation and print—breaks the conventional storyline through the intrusion of his private associations and competes with the authorial voice more and more. When it finally destroys the storyline, in a chapter-long internal monologue on the strand, his story disappears into a large hole in the text. By the end of the novel we can see that Stephen's story contains more gaps than storyline. And these gaps are filled by the much more continuous story of Leopold Bloom.

Leopold Bloom appears out of nowhere. There is nothing to prepare us for him in Stephen's story, either in the past three chapters or in *A Portrait*. The white page simply gives way to "Mr Leopold Bloom ate with relish the inner organs of beasts and fowls"(45). His character is not dependent on an a priori setting or figure or storyline. He is solidly identified with his body, especially when compared to the intellectual Stephen, who is averse to eating and bathing. Of course, a setting and storyline develop; they are more firmly grounded and easy to follow than anything in the first three chapters. But Bloom begins a different kind of story. Many voices contribute to the telling of his story; indeed, each chapter brings in a new voice, which may augment, counterpoint, under-mine, or usurp the authorial storytelling voice. The authorial voice tries to draw the character into a line of development. It is en-hanced by allusions to *The Odyssey*, or echoes of an epic voice telling the story of heroic achievement.

Countering the authorial voice is the voice of the body-text, functioning like voice in speech as it modifies, contradicts, or adds meaning that goes beyond the meaning of the words. In so doing it leads us to regard the printed text itself as a source of signification. The voice of the body-text makes itself felt rather than heard by intruding the materiality, or physicality, of the print and in shaping "an epic of the human body."

Nancy Miller helps us understand this new kind of epic—or antiepic—in her distinction between the "ambitious" and "erotic" texts. The ambitious text embodies the story of conflict and strug-gle, where the narrative logic leads a hero to independence and power or tragic death. It is a male text, a paradigm of the patri-arch, reflecting the values of struggle, logic, and goal orientation. In the erotic text, a heroine is identified not with what she might achieve but with her sexual nature, that is, her body. And the structure, rather than being linear, is based on the dynamics of interrelationship. Psychologists Jean Baker Miller and Carol Gilli-gan show that normative development has been based on the ambi-tious text because men have been the primary objects of study. But the study of women provides a challenging alternative in affirming the values of relationship over ambition, engagement in the com-plex world over goals in an abstract future. To affirm the body is to live more intensely in this world.

It is important that Ulysses affirmed the body, that his story began after the Trojan War, that he seemed to prove himself not in that battle, but in the *process* of returning home. But in the end he still had to kill the suitors—and in doing so realized his identity as a warrior, husband, father, and king. The ending of *The Odyssey* turns the story into an ambitious text dominated by the language of power—which might explain why it was not only popular, especially when Joyce read it in the Lamb version, but a model for the adventure tale that, as Martin Green says, "England told itself as it went to sleep at night; and, in the form of its dreams . . . charged England's will with the energy to go out into the world and explore, conquer, and rule" (3).[1]

Joyce destroyed the epic distance between us and *The Odyssey*, brought *The Odyssey* into what Bakhtin calls the "zone of cheerful and annihilating laughter," first by leaving *The Odyssey* out. Even with the aid of Hanley's *Word Index* it is hard to find the four appearances of "Ulysses" in the text. And without Stuart Gilbert we might still be straining to relate the title to the story of a middle-aged man wandering through the streets of Dublin so that his wife could have an affair with a (Trojanless) stallion. Nor would it be easy to discern the pattern of that patriarch of Western epics, where a son goes out in search of a father and the father returns home to reclaim his domestic and political sovereignty.

I am exaggerating, of course, when I claim that Joyce left *The Odyssey* out of *Ulysses*—though in 1937 he told Nabokov that he employed Homer as "a whim," and that collaborating with Gilbert was "a terrible mistake . . . an advertisement for the book. I regret it very much" (Ellmann, 616n). But, more to the point, given the few actual references, there is a gigantic hole in our reading experience that—despite all the serious work of diligent and creative scholars—turns the allusions into a joke, or at least a form of parody. By bringing the Homeric epic into the "zone of cheerful and annihilating laughter," Joyce also opens a historical gap; he leads us to question the relation between the present and the past. Have we lost our heroic potency? Were there ever gods and heroes as they were depicted in the epics? Will we undergo some cataclysmic experience and return to the age of gods? Are the values of the past being transvalued? He also leads us to question the very nature of the traditional story, especially as it evolved into the quest and popular adventure story of the nineteenth century, or all the values associated with a shape and logic we have unquestioningly—and too reverently—accepted.

The second way Joyce undermined the epic was by creating a hero who not only recognized his bodily functions but could be identified with his sexuality. The schema he sent to Carlo Linati, which predates the one he authorized Gilbert to develop, emphasizes the body over the Homeric correspondences. And Richard Brown leads us to understand the extent of Joyce's "sexual politics." If Bloom's sexuality is ambiguous, it is because the caricature of male sexuality generated by the Citizen in Barney Kiernan's tavern has in fact dominated our thinking. Bloom is a man of love, and is aware that love does not mean domination. He does not seek power but relationship. The equanimity with which he does not slay but accepts Molly's suitors is based on an awareness of the complexities in 7 Eccles Street on June 16 and 17, 1904.

Bloom does not move, let alone think, in a straight line; he meanders, drawn from here to there by pressing realities of the present and the past. And just as relationship governs Bloom's action, it governs the form of his story. For set against the tenuous line of events is the stronger pattern of psychological and literary associations, or relationships. The major literary association, of course, is Homer's story of a son in search of his father and the father's resumption of patriarchal power. But the erotic text in *Ulysses*—the epic of the human body—has appropriated the ambitious text. Or domesticated it. Indeed, Joyce has given "domesticity" new meaning and power.

I do not mean to underestimate Homer's power over us in my reading of *Ulysses*. I want to insist that we recognize the author-ity of the Homeric voice, even as it is parodied, undermined, and transvalued. Nor am I forgetting that there are many other voices in this polyphonic novel—which amplify the narrative conflict, or dialectic, I have been describing. But opposed to the patriarchal paradigm is an alternative story form that values relationship and inclusion over development, mastery, exclusion, and achievement. And Joyce includes so much—overloads the storyline with such a multiplicity of allusions, includes such a variety of discourses, makes so many connections, refuses to make so many connections, breaks the storyline and shifts perspectives so often, interposes so many different stylistic lenses, intrudes so much of the material text, and engages us in so many events simultaneously—that he undermines the hegemony of the Homeric voice, the story of development, the ambitious male text. Or he changes the shape of the field so that the agon between the authorial and rebellious voices does not take a traditional form; there is no final goal but only a dialogue where the balance of power continually shifts. And he leads us to understand the strategies of appropriation through which the authorial voice maintains its power.

Let me demonstrate. In the "Sirens" chapter the authorial storytelling voice is displaced by what the wartime censors thought was a secret code. The rebellious voice of the body-text mocks the goals of a linear story and sets forth a story of relationship in its most outrageous form. It is hard to see the most poignant scene in the novel—as Bloom lives through the moment when Blazes Boylan knocks on Molly's door. But we can see it. In "Sirens" there is not so much a hole in the story as too much going on at the same time for us to distinguish separate, sequential events. Moreover, the physicality of the text is foregrounded. What we experience are multiple relations without any hierarchic ordering. We are engaged by the sounds, shapes, multiple references of words on the page, and by events happening on the streets and in the Ormond— by the "hoofirons, steelyringing imperthnthn," "Blew. Blue bloom is on the," "Jingle jingle jaunted jingling," "Prrprr. . . . Fff! Oo," by Miss Douce and Miss Kennedy flirting with the men at the bar, by Blazes "Boylan with impatience" for Molly, by Bloom passing Boylan on the street, following him into the Ormond, eating dinner with Richie Goulding, writing to Martha, thinking of Molly, while Father Cowley sings to Martha at the bar and Simon Dedalus touches "obedient keys," and Boylan jogs the mare, and deaf Pat waits, and the blind piano tuner makes his way back for his tuning fork.

The linear story is important, but shown as only one story in the carnival of stories that often echo and undermine each other at the same time. At the end of the chapter, the storyline is simultaneously recapitulated and negated by the rebellious voice of the body-text: "An unseeing stripling stood in the door. He saw not bronze. He saw not gold. Nor Ben nor Bob nor Tom nor Si nor George nor tanks nor Richie nor Pat. Hee hee hee hee. He did not see" (238). "Hee hee hee hee" are *words* laughing at Bloom, who chooses not to see what is happening between Blazes and Molly, or who is denying his "manhood." But they are also laughing at the ambitious male text, which is mocked again and canceled in the final lines. We hear the heroic last words of the martyred Robert Emmet, who wants his epitaph to be written only "when my country takes her place among the nations of the earth." At the same time the voice of the body-text intrudes, causing us not only to see but hear: "Prrprr. . . . Fff! Oo. Rrpr. . . . I'm sure it's the burgund. Yes. One, two. *Let my epitaph be. . . . Written. I have.* Pprrpffrrppffff. *Done*" (239).

In "Cyclops" the story of Bloom's development is foregrounded. It is also appropriated by the demotic voice of the nameless and belligerent but nonetheless powerless storyteller. The powerless storyteller gains power by picturing Bloom as a fool and a scapegoat. Of course, he gains power only among his cronies, or the male society that shares his powerlessness as well as his values. Indeed, the sharing of values and views—that is, being part of the narrative community—is a prerequisite to good storytelling, which, as Shari

Benstock points out, is why Bloom could not tell the story of Ruben J. Dodd to the men in the funeral carriage.

The more eloquently the nameless narrator of "Cyclops" fumes, the more he becomes a caricature of the traditional teller of ambitious stories. On the other hand, he lends his rhetorical power to the author-ity and power such storytelling reflects—the power that is, ironically, the very source of his own material and political powerlessness. But he also leads us to understand the inherent or willful blindness of the traditional narrator.

For, besides turning Bloom into an object for his own self-aggrandizement, the nameless narrator makes an important mistake—an omission, a hole in Bloom's actual story—that reveals a side of Bloom's character to which the narrator is blind. Bloom does not leave the tavern to collect on his bet; he searches for Martin Cunningham, with whom he will visit Paddy Dignam's widow. Of course, the nameless narrator could not have known what he was omitting, or that Bantam Lyons made a mistake in thinking Bloom gave him a tip on Throwaway. But the omission determines the shape of his story and, therefore, his characterization of Bloom. It also results in a story of violence—as the men in the bar, angry that Bloom will not spend his winnings on a drink, challenge his identity as a man, and as the citizen hurls a biscuit tin at him.

The rebellious voice of the body-text issues in the engorged mock-heroic style Joyce called "gigantism," continually interrupts the nameless narrator's story, leads us to lose all sense of connection, and changes the proportions. It is characterized by a verbal escalation feeding on itself until it goes out of control. And it magnifies the threat of violence seething beneath the surface of Dublin life. Moreover, it generates a powerful agon by raising the magnitude of all the characters and events. The final scene, narrated by the demotic voice, is comic: "all the ragamuffins and sluts of the nation" gather round the carriage, and Martin Cunningham tells the jarvey to drive on, and a loafer with a patch over his eye sings *"if the man in the moon was a jew, jew, jew* and a slut shouts out of her: —Eh, mister! Your fly is open," and Bloom shouts back that "Mendelssohn was a jew and Karl Marx and Mercadante and Spinoza. And the Saviour was a jew and his father was a jew," and Martin Cunningham tells him he had no father, and the citizen shouts "By Jesus . . . I'll brain that bloody jewman. . . . I'll crucify him so I will" (280). But as the citizen hurls the biscuitbox, the comic narrative gives way to a page-long epic description of an earthquake, a "catastrophe . . . terrific and instantaneous in its effect"(281), and we feel the impact of a violence that has been accumulating. Earlier, Bloom stood up to the chauvinistic men in the bar as a man of love; after the earthquake, when he ascends like Elijah, his confrontation takes on heroic proportions—until his ascent is described, "at an angle of fortyfive degrees over Donohoe's in Little Green street like a shot off a shovel" (283).

The demotic and mock-epic voices usurp the voices that have been shaping Bloom's story—in ways that lead us to understand their potential. The demotic voice of the nameless storyteller is especially welcome after the "Sirens" chapter where the music-making voices all but obscured the storyline. But—just because his literal and symbolic limitations are so clear, because he sees Bloom as an object in his linear, ambitious story, and because the hole, or what he leaves out of Bloom's story, is so important—we can see how the traditional storyline appropriates or shapes its characters to realize its own end. The nameless narrator may usurp the authorial voice, but, like so many powerless and frustrated among the colonized, he carries out its task.

Moreover, the narrative community of men in Barney Kiernan's tavern is a caricature of the narrative community aboard the deck of the *Nellie*, or the homosocial network that Eve Kosofsky Sedgwick argues grounded male power in nineteenth-century English society and literature. This narrative community will be caricatured again in "Oxen of the Sun," on a higher level of colonized Ireland's social scale—where Bloom joins Stephen and his (male) friends in the maternity hospital, and the narrative voice traces the gestation of English literature by mimicking the style of one great (male) author after another, and the (male) characters get drunk, while Mrs. Purefoy gives birth offstage. But just as the powerless narrator of "Cyclops" carries out the task of the authorial voice, the male narrative hegemony of "Oxen of the Sun" is recuperated. For we are required to identify the style of each great author in the tradition of English narrative and thereby perpetuate the reverence as well as the very canon that is being drawn into the "zone of crude contact."

Nonetheless, as a character in the rebellious story of relationship, the nameless narrator of "Cyclops" reveals the traditional authorial blindness. And the rebellious, mock-heroic voice disrupts, or creates holes in, the nameless narrator's ambitious text. It magnifies everything out of proportion. It creates a new set of proportions and illuminates dimensions of heroism and love to which the authorial voice is necessarily or willfully blind, and which cannot be told in the traditional ambitious story.

The story of Bloom's development is undermined by the rebellious voice throughout the novel, but nowhere so radically as at the end, where Bloom is reunited with Molly. For he is not actually reunited with her. Indeed, his story comes to an end, and hers begins just at their point of physical contact. And this introduces the greatest gap in the text.

Molly has been out of sight for almost the entire novel. She was introduced as part of Bloom's story, as it was shaped by both voices. She is identified with the negative "Mn" (46). She sends Bloom off to "get another of Paul de Kock's" (53). And until the last chapter she is no more than a presence (however powerful) in Bloom's mind and in the minds of male Dubliners. She is a wink in the eyes of the barflies, a "plump bare generous arm" flinging a coin to a one-legged sailor (185), a fantasy come to life in the male fantasies of nighttown, a creased photo shown to Stephen in the cabman's shelter, and finally an invisible person whose mystery is "denoted by a visible splendid sign, a lamp," in the penumbra of which Stephen and Bloom urinate and comically affirm their manly relationship (576f.). In the final chapter she becomes a physical presence and tells her own story, which begins and ends with the affirmation "Yes." How does Molly's story relate to Bloom's, to Stephen's, or to the novel as a whole?

We have watched Bloom urinating with Stephen in the penumbra of Molly's lamp. We have heard the double vibration of the jew's harp, which Stephen plays as he leaves 7 Eccles Street. We see Bloom alone, bumping his head against a walnut sideboard that has been moved across the room, burning incense, contemplating his solitary image in a giltbordered pierglass, cataloging the books on his shelves, removing his collar (size 17), compiling his budget for the day, considering four pages of objects in his drawers, discovering the imprint of Blazes Boylan in his bed, removing some flakes of Plumtree's Potted Meat, listing twenty-four men who might have been Molly's lovers, kissing "the plump mellow yellow smellow melons of her rump," telling her (with some qualifications, or gaps) what happened to him during the day, recalling that they hadn't had sexual intercourse for what we discover is a period of ten years, five months, and eighteen days, lying down next to Molly in a fetal position, and falling asleep while musing on Sinbad the Sailor.

But in the Ithaca chapter of Joyce's *Ulysses*—so overloaded with details from Leopold Bloom's last waking hour on that long day— we never hear him ask Molly to bring him breakfast in bed. And it is just this request that stimulates Molly's final monologue. It is just this request that leads us to think that Bloom has achieved his ("manly") identity. It is just this request that leads Molly to her affirmation of Bloom—and to an ultimate expression of universal harmony. "Yes because he never did a thing like that before as ask to get his breakfast in bed with a couple of eggs"(608). Molly introduces herself, then, not only with an affirmation but with a gap, the ultimate hole in the novel. Fritz Senn and Hugh Kenner cogently argue that she misunderstood Bloom's rambling about the "roc's auk's egg"(607), but in doing so they naturalize Joyce's daring omission—and the power of the rebellious voice.[2] Molly begins a new story, which liberates her from the male storyline that has embodied her, and turns Bloom and Stephen into characters of her story.

It should be noted that, by turning Bloom into a patriarch, she speaks with a voice that tells the kinds of stories men wrote for women or women wrote or fantasized in men's voices—like Gerty MacDowell. Certainly, her final yesses are expressions of acquiescence as well as independent affirmation. The dialogic novel is composed of at least two voices. Molly's monologue, composed of so many discourses, contains the authorial as well as a rebellious voice. And the authorial voice maintains a resonance of authority no matter how it is toyed with and subverted. But Molly contends with the authorial voice with far more independence than Gerty. And Gerty is far more assertive than readers have thought, for by comparing her to her prototype in *The Lamplighter*, Kimberly Devlin shows how she asserts herself in unladylike ways and escapes the stereotype imposed on her by the authorial voice. Moreover, Molly decenters the patriarch she creates by conflating Bloom and Mulvey in her final affirmation.

Molly's story is characterized by what Frances Restuccia describes as playful "leapfrogging," that is, grammatical subversions, puns, and other ways of toying with the phallic pen that undermine the kind of language designed to create a complete picture of Dublin or to tell stories of development.[3] It is also characterized by long run-on sentences, the kind of language that Joyce, in referring to Nora and his Aunt Josephine, generalized to all women (Scott, 70). Joyce was not denigrating women, for it is just this fluidity that characterizes the stream of consciousness, the movement by association or relationship rather than logic. That is, it characterizes the rebellious voice that began to assert itself in telling the story of Stephen, which succeeded in telling the story of Bloom, and which finally becomes em-bodied in the person of Molly as she tells *her* own story in the first person.

The long run-on sentences seem to be imitating the way Molly speaks. Anyone who has heard Siobhan McKenna's splendid rendition of the monologue knows that it derives its power from the pauses and shifts in tone that the actress supplies. But this is only one of any number of ways the written text might sound. The monologue's ambivalence, polyvalence, play is generated by words that are not pinned down by punctuated syntax. Susan Bazargan convincingly argues that "Penelope" is not a monologue but a dialogue—"Yes because . . ." being Molly's explanation to an ideal listener, thereby situating Molly in a " 'public' domain of language" rather than the private domain of her thoughts. But Molly goes beyond causal explanation and beyond the constraints of language. It is not only dialogue but dialogic. As Bazargan says, the rhythm of her unpunctuated sentences is "what Julia Kristeva calls the 'semiotic rhythm,' the 'air or song beneath the text,' that enigmatic and feminine space 'underlying the written' " (66). Her unpunctuated sentences subvert the monologic of the authorial voice, though the monologic asserts itself in the syntax of our silent punctuation. Molly's monologue or dialogue or "polylogue" (to use Kristeva's expression) does not characterize but em-body Molly—in all her plurality.

Moreover, as Restuccia shows, what we encounter is not an oral but a written text; most of the play comes from the way the words look on the page. The physicality of the text is not mimetic but actual, individualized, and rich. It reinforces the theme and other formal, or physical, instances that value physical presence as opposed to future goals. Indeed, it literally em-bodies them as it literally em-bodies Molly.

But what does it mean to em-body Molly, whose body Joyce foregrounds in such a revolutionary but nonetheless controversial way? While Poldy elucidates "the mystery of an invisible attractive person" (576–577), Molly is sitting on the chamberpot, having her period: "O Jesus wait yes that thing has come on me yes . . . O patience above its pouring out of me like the sea anyhow he didnt make me pregnant" (632, 633). Molly's menstruation has been used to argue that she is not the fertile *gea tullus* she appears to be in the closing pages. But Mary O'Brien—nurse and midwife for twenty-five years before becoming a political theorist and author of *The Politics of Reproduction*—helps us counter this argument and extend our understanding of Penelope. O'Brien would argue that this negative view of menstruation (as well as of the female archetype) is a mark of "male-stream thinking."

Menstruation, O'Brien shows, is not a sign of infertility. Menstruation and pregnancy are opposite, visible signs of the reproductive process, "communally understood signs of female potency, of the unity of the potential and the actual"(50). The language, or semiosis, of this potency is what Dinesen's old storyteller pictures as the women stand in the convent gallery looking at the body-texts of their communal experience; it is what em-bodies Molly in *Ulysses*. By menstruating, Molly liberates herself from the "symbolic" language of the fathers and asserts her humanity in a way that has been ignored or suppressed by the humanist tradition. Indeed, Joyce brings Dante's beatific vision into the "zone of crude contact"—imagine Beatrice sitting on the pot, having her period!

It is neither anomalous nor paradoxical that Dinesen's community is formed within a convent. For the convent was historically the only space that women could call their own. And knowledge of the reproductive process is not limited to women who bear children. As O'Brien points out, "the historical isolation of women from each other, the whole language of female internality and privacy, the exclusion of women from the creation of a political community: all of these have obscured the cultural cohesiveness of femininity and the universality of maternal consciousness. . . . It is a tribute to the indelibility of male-stream thought that we should have to make this point" (50).

And now Susan Bazargan's argument about Molly's dialogue with an ideal listener takes on added significance. Molly is the most isolated character in the world of *Ulysses*. Like many middle-class women of the time, she had no close friends. She may have had a physical relation with Boylan, but significantly this important scene is missing—a hole in the text. She is not very visible, audible, or successful in communicating with Bloom in their opening scene. She is in bed with Bloom in the end, but isolated by his being asleep and, even more, by a point of view limited to her mind. Perhaps all internal monologues are dialogues with imaginary listeners; Bonnie Scott argues that Gerty MacDowell's thoughts "contain an implicit dialogue with other female voices" (*James Joyce*, 65). They certainly are dialogues with many voices, or discourses, of the culture.[4] But it is important that we see Molly's ideal listener as a woman, who can share the "language of female internality" and the maternal consciousness—a visible sign of which is Molly's menstruation. Once I take this view, as a male reader I feel as limited as I do imagining the community of women standing before the blank page, sunk in deep thought. I understand how I am limited by the language of the fathers. But I also feel this constraint being mitigated by such a positive image of female otherness.

The distinction between the mimetic voice and the voice of the body-text is important in Penelope. In telling her story in the feminine first person, especially if it is to an ideal female listener, Molly liberates herself not only from the other stories in *Ulysses*, but from the language of the fathers as it shaped the story of her prototype, and the language of the male Dubliners which, until now, has shaped hers. Her liberation is not complete, especially given the residual power of the authorial voice. Indeed, Frances Restuccia cogently argues that Molly is used by Joyce to exorcise the fathers. And in a fascinating and persuasive essay entitled " 'Penelope' as Period Piece," Cheryl Herr argues that Bloom rather than Molly experiences menstruation, and that Molly is not a liberated character. She is not a character at all but a role to be enacted by any one of the major artistes of the day. Herr points to Molly's "monologue-ing, her sartoriocentrism, her stylized gestures, her great sentences sustained as an operatic tour de force," as well as the fact that "Molly's life is recalled on what appear to be stage sets—Molly by the Moorish wall, Molly on the promenade with an officer in Gibraltar, Molly on Howth. And it is not entirely off the mark to suggest that the performer who gives us this star turn is not necessarily a woman at all. Why not, in that era of relentless comic cross-dressing, a male performer? Why not a male performer doing a good imitation of La Duse doing a good imitation of a Dublin Hausfrau with trendily late Victorian 'excess libido'?" (135).

Herr illuminates an important point about Joyce's characterization. For just as Joyce destroys the hegemony of the monologic authorial voice and disrupts the plotline of the ambitious text, he also destroys, or deconstructs, the notion of a unified character. Just as there are several voices arguing with one another in the carnival of his novel, and several stories being told at the same time, there are several characters (personae, masks) vying with one another for the stage of the reader's imagination. I have been trying to argue that one of these Mollys, em-bodied in the voice of the body-text, liberates herself for a time from the authorial voice. And if her liberation is not complete, it allows her to stand out against them.

Penelope was strong and admirable in maintaining her independence from the suitors for nineteen years, but she could not tell her own story. She could weave and unweave her shroud to prevent the suitors from changing her role, but she could only define herself in the story of Ulysses. Indeed, she is contrasted with her serving women and Clytemnestra, who initiated, or acted out, their own stories—the serving women by dallying with the suitors and failing "to make the best of slavery" (338), and Clytemnestra through the "unwomanly" act of revenge. Penelope may try to take charge of her story when she tests Ulysses—by making him describe their marriage bed. But Ulysses preempts her. When he describes the bed he cut from a living tree, he asserts his mastery over nature and women—and over his story, the logic of which leads to his meeting with the other Homeric heroes in Hades and swooping down on his enemies with "a terrible war cry" before he can rule his family and country in peace (365).

. Following the Pythagoreans, the Greeks divided the world into two categories. One included reason, light, straight lines, order, the city, men, and good. The other included the irrational, darkness, curves, disorder, nature, women, and bad. Homer's *Odyssey* is the story of a reasonable man who meanders for nineteen years but the logic of whose journey leads him back to the city, where he reestablishes order—or where he reestablishes his mastery over the irrational, darkness, curves, disorder, nature, and women. Joyce's *Ulysses* tells not one but three main stories, where the irrational, darkness, circularity, disorder, or diversity, nature, and women are not mastered but asserted and affirmed as good. The rebellious voice delves into the darkness of the wild, the contradictory, and the unconscious. Each story is contained in its own circle. If the city could be rebuilt from the pages of *Ulysses*, the bodies of men and women are affirmed in all their functions and the novel ends on a paean to nature. The body is also affirmed by including the physicality of the text within the experience of the story—the typography, the visual and aural puns, the white spaces, the stimuli to turn the pages back and forth. And the rebellious voice not only affirms values of relationship that have been associated with women, it finally embodies itself in a woman speaking in the feminine first person.

If the three stories are contained within their separate circles, this is because the structure of the novel acknowledges gaps, or holes, as part of the (w)hole. There are two kinds of holes in *Ulysses*, as there were in Joyce's earlier work, but here Joyce has found a way to realize their potential. The holes in the stories shaped by the authorial voice result from a blindness to what does not fit its preconceptions and the storyline, or a suppression of what threatens them. By not recognizing the holes in its story, the authorial voice appropriates or reshapes its subject, turning it into an object. The holes in the stories shaped by the rebellious voice of the body-text result from what cannot be known or mastered, and what is affirmed in its otherness. We will never know why Bloom and Molly have not had complete carnal intercourse for ten years, five months, and eighteen days, or why Stephen left Bloom singing an anti-Semitic song, or whether Bloom asked for breakfast in bed, or the answers to any number of questions that keep us from rebuilding Dublin on 16 June 1904 from the pages of Joyce's novel. By not only recognizing but valuing the holes in the story—or the discontinuities between three independent but related stories—the rebellious voice asserts the independence of characters from one another's stories, as well as from a controlling author-ity. And it asserts the readers' independence from the authorial voice that tries to draw us into a storytelling community, or fool us into imaginatively collaborating with those who would deny us our own voices. Through its disruptions, the rebellious voice creates a story of relationship, which includes the authorial voice and the ambitious story within its range, and where all the voices can relate to each other as subjects in dialogue.

Still, we need to recognize the residual power of the authorial voice as it requires us to master and hence valorize the classical sources Joyce undermines, as it seduces us into calling the chapters by the Homeric names that Joyce declined to use, and as it necessitates our filling in some holes and setting up authoritarian structures to teach the novel. Moreover, while Molly may liberate herself from the men's stories in a chapter not required by their plot, she cannot escape the power of their frame. For, with a shift in perspective, we can see her independent frame securing her as a permanent outsider, more alienated than Bloom, who participates in the male story. Indeed, we can see her being framed for us by the authorial voice, on display as an independent woman; that is, as an exception. We can see also her as an object of the male gaze, eroticized by her desires. We can see her as an hysteric, who—after what Breuer and Freud called a talking cure where she lets it all out—will be recuperated and return to being a good wife. And we can see her as an essentialized, idealized figure of feminine vitality, who can restore order and bring an ideal closure to the male plot. Moreover—even if we reject her essentialization and idealization, even if we see Molly as an individual with multiple desires of her own, even if we recognize that she decenters Bloom or conflates him and Mulvey in her final affirmation—our very desire for a happy ending implicates us in restoring the male plotline.

I want to end my discussion of Joyce on this ambivalent note to emphasize the instability of the dialogic, or the continual struggle for author-ity, and the need to identify and understand the power of traditional narrative forces. The extent of this power will become clearer in my discussion of Faulkner, who was more ambivalent than Joyce, and Woolf, who had more to contend with and could bring it into historical and political focus.

William Faulkner

5

Can a Woman Tell Her Story in Yoknapatawpha County—Even with All Those Yarns?

Bakhtin points out that, despite the competition among voices in the carnival of a novel, there is an "internal politics of style" (284). What he calls the "unitary language," shaped by historical, linguistic, and ideological "destinies" becomes a force that may dominate the varied field of voices, or the "heteroglossia" (270). But he does not devote his attention to analyzing or measuring the power relations partly, I suspect, because he was trying to illuminate the revolutionary potential of the novel, partly because the power relations are clearer in the novels with which he was working, and which we now see as traditional, and partly because the fecund model of the carnival led him to such a prolific poetic schema. I have tried to show that what makes the "unitary language" unitary is the power of the authorial voice in imposing its kind of story and avoiding, suppressing, or appropriating other kinds of stories, voices, and languages—thus the holes I have designated as absences. Joyce found ways to undermine the authorial voice by creating holes in the unitary fabric, expanding the range of fictional voices, generating dialogues among them, and foregrounding the struggle for authority to give us a greater sense of the whole.

Faulkner also undermined the "unitary language," as anyone recalling her or his first encounter with *The Sound and the Fury* will attest. But his relationship to the language governing the American South was ambivalent. He both idealized and satirized Southern heroism; he depicted racial injustice, but perpetuated the values of the Southern "community" and argued against national desegregation.[1] And his ambivalence is reflected in his use of Southern oratory and the tall-tale—American extensions of the high style that colonized Irishmen imitated so well and the adventure story that rationalized and energized British imperialism.

His ambivalence is also reflected in the complex politics of narration that evolve in his major novels. A variety of storytelling characters represents a wide range of classes. Faulkner's authorial voice, in contrast to Joyce's, is a hovering presence. It is ambivalent, troubled, searching, sometimes echoing, sometimes holding back, but never quite giving way to the storytelling voices of his characters.

Regardless of Faulkner's vacillation, though, his authorial voice is a source of narrative patterning—and of a wide range of authorial strategies. It establishes the order of events, even when they seem arbitrary. It chooses who will narrate or explain what event. It denies some of his major characters the chance to tell their stories. And it gives different storytellers different degrees of credibility, or power. Let me give an example of the kind of a authorial power against which some of Faulkner's heroes, but mainly his heroines, must contend, by turning to a story in the frontier tradition of tall tales that Faulkner so brilliantly exploited.

In *The Land Before Her* Annette Kolodny describes the story of a singular frontier heroine. A fifteen-year-old girl runs off with a young clerk. They are pursued by her father's henchmen, escape into the forest, and then are captured by Indians. The girl watches her lover being tortured and killed, but manages to escape before she is ravaged. After living off the land for fourteen days, she is captured and carried off to a cave by "a man of gigantic figure." When she refuses to lie with him, he ties her up, lays out his sword and hatchet, and warns her to reconsider his proposal before morning. While he sleeps, she chews through her bindings, seizes the hatchet, and with three blows puts "an end to his existence." But that's not all: she chops off his head, cuts his body into quarters, carries him piece by piece a half-mile into the woods, and covers him with brush. In the back of the cave she finds some corn, which she plants, and lives contentedly alone for nine years.

Until she is "rescued" by two hunters.

Actually, the story of the hunters frames the story of the woman. They are shooting game in the wilderness and hear a voice. "Uncertain whether the voice was . . . human . . . or that of some bird," they make their way up a hill, through the brush, and into a large opening where they behold a beautiful young lady sitting by the mouth of a cave. At the sight of the hunters the lady screams and swoons, but they quiet her apprehensions and prevail upon her to tell her story. Then—and this is the conclusion of a tale so popular that it was reprinted at least twenty-five times between 1788 and 1814—the hunters take her home, where she is reconciled with her father just before he dies and leaves her a fortune (57–61).

I should emphasize that the original "Panther Captivity" is quite different from my retelling, since I start with the woman's story—thereby giving the heroine's voice an authority it was denied. The original story starts with the frame, in which an authorial voice is embodied in the pseudonymous Abraham Panther. He is answering a letter requesting the account of a journey into the wilderness. Panther—a hunter and a writer, an *authority* on the wilderness as well as a professional *author*—not only frames but appropriates the young woman's story for his own ends, or the ends of the established male community, which the reader comes to accept as his or her own. Moreover, he subverts its meaning and power, even though he allows her to speak in the first person. In the opening of the frame, Panther pictures the woman as a nature goddess, who by screaming and swooning is turned into the helpless heroine of romance. In the closing of the frame, he adds an ending to her story by taking her back to civilization—the world of fathers and hunters—where she is rewarded with a fortune made in the fur trade. The woman—who cannot only kill but decapitate and quarter a giant, who can live in the wilderness alone and content, who chooses not to hunt with the weapons she can handle so well but to plant seeds, and who has even discovered a voice the hunters cannot categorize—is domesticated, made safe, and then rewarded for returning unblemished to the world of her author.

Of course her story was heard, and, as Kolodny points out, she became a heroic model for women of the period. To use Bakhtin's terms, "The Panther Captivity" is a dialogic narrative where two voices contend. But even though each voice is strong in its turn, the authorial voice comes to dominate—thereby inscribing the reader in the text as a member of his community. Was the commercial success of this anomalous frontier story due to the narrative strategy—to the power of the authorial voice, or the politics of storytelling? If so, then what did the women of the period actually hear? Was it the heroine's own voice, somehow making its way through her author's language and shaping force? Or was it a safe—*author-ized*—voice?

THE SOUND AND THE FURY

Four storytellers compete in *The Sound and the Fury* and fifteen compete in *As I Lay Dying*. Both novels are designed to undermine, disrupt, escape, even ignore the unitary voice. But how multiple is their multiple perspective? How would a captive daughter contend in this new narrative field? Could a woman tell her story in Yoknapatawpha County—even with all those yarns?

Certainly not Caddy.

Faulkner claims that in *The Sound and the Fury* he simply wanted to tell the story of a little girl, or, as he says in his more revealing syntax, "of the muddy seat of a little girl's drawers in a pear tree, where she could see through a window where her grandmother's funeral was taking place" (Stein, 73). He certainly cared about Caddy. He created a character doomed by her natural, selfless, and spontaneous love. And he designed a novel to question the social order that destroyed her. But from the original conception, Caddy is identified with her body, sexuality, and death. Her image is so difficult to grasp or so threatening that her story must be told through four voices—though not one of them is hers, and all of them, as I will show, are male.

This is not to say that we do not get to know Caddy, or that we do not hear her speak. Minrose Gwin focuses Caddy's presence and tunes in her voices in a sensitive, eloquent, and important new reading—or as she describes it, "listening" through the hegemony of male discourse. Gwin builds on Linda Wagner's point that Caddy brings Benjy "to speech" through the language of love and interconnection—thereby deconstructing the male messages of a world full of sound and fury signifying nothing. Gwin also shows how, as Caddy's space constricts and her text becomes bounded, she becomes what Luce Irigary calls the "*disruptive excess.*" When Quentin recalls his fear of the dark house he calls a dungeon, Caddy bursts into his thoughts, declaring she would become "*King*" and "*break that place open and drag them out.*" And she rises in his mind to speak of her "unending pleasure in her own sexuality," her transgressive and excessive desire for Dalton Ames. Unlike her brothers, especially Jason, Caddy gives without taking away. She even breaks through Jason's story, though he reduces her to "an ideal victim because of her willingness to give excessively." For when she is completely helpless, after managing only a glimpse of her daughter, she takes on the role of the hysteric, who Cixous argues "is the nuclear example of women's power to protest" (Gwin, 34–62).

Indeed, we get to know Caddy and to hear her multiple voices, and she becomes the main source of alternative values in *The Sound and the Fury*. But we do not hear her story. For Caddy is both expelled from the family and excluded from the family of storytellers. And the *family* of storytellers includes the authorial voice that restores the social, psychological, and aesthetic order in the last section of the novel. Moreover, it gives us the most author- itative view of Caddy. In an appendix written fifteen years later, we see her as the woman in a picture—"hatless . . . ageless and beauti- ful, cold serene and damned," and, most important, standing be- side a Nazi general (415). The authorial voice may value Caddy as a singular character capable of selfless love, but it associates her sexuality and independence not only with the destruction of the family but with what (especially in 1946) could be understood as pure evil. Nor is her identification with nazism merely one of association. As the appendix restores the novel's chronology, it also establishes its logic: Caddy's story has large gaps, but it begins with sex and ends with Hitler.

That Faulkner wrote the appendix fifteen years later only adds to our sense of its objectivity and authority. Indeed, he told Robert N. Linscott that he should have written it when he wrote the book itself. "You will see how it is the key to the whole book . . . the 4 sections as they stand now fall into clarity and place" (*Letters*, 220–221).[2]

The appendix of *The Sound and the Fury* is like the climactic shot in *Citizen Kane*. The film claims to be telling Charles Foster Kane's story from four different, subjective points of view, and the objective investigating journalist concludes by saying that we will never be able to understand the meaning of "Rosebud," Kane's last word and the apparent motivation—or cause—of his behav- ior. Then in a spectacular crane shot beginning high in the air, the camera surveys Kane's universe of objects, travels directly toward what turns out to be the furnace, and finally into the flames, where in a tight close-up it shows us the sled with its Rosebud emblem. By causing us to recall the opening scene—where young Kane holds tight to his sled as his mother sends him off to become the richest man in the world—the authorial camera establishes the sequence and logic and leaves us with a privileged, authoritative version of Kane's story.

The authorial voice in *The Sound and the Fury* seems to efface itself by scrambling the chronology, disrupting the storyline, and giving in to the voices of its characters. But it emerges in the Dilsey section and asserts its author-ity in an appendix—the last words in the novel, which issue from an omniscient point of view, set the chronology straight, establish the ultimate pattern of cause and effect, and pronounce the final judgments.

Moreover, while scrambling the chronology may be disruptive, it does not really undermine the novel's logic—or the power of the authorial voice. Quite the contrary. It compels *us* to set the dates—first of Benjy's story, then of the four sections—in proper chronological order. So, while it succeeds in making us active readers, it also draws us into the presupposed narrative community— or turns us into accomplices in putting Caddy in her place. *We* impose a chronological order on the novel—using the facts its storytellers tell us are important—to discover a pattern of cause and effect, or to find the ultimate cause of lost values and the dissolution of an aristocratic Southern family. And, as we impose a linear pattern of cause and effect, we also impose the language of author-ity or the values of a society that expels Caddy and will not allow her to tell her story.

The novel opens on April 7, 1928, with Benjy's unmediated and "innocent" perceptions. Because they are organized by association rather than chronology, they seem disordered—the ramblings of an "idiot" that establish the meaning of the title. Benjy's story also establishes the selflessness of Caddy's love, and the effect of her falling in love with Dalton Ames. When she fell in love, Caddy was becoming independent, or was trying to begin a story of her own, but Benjy keeps her as a character in his story by making her wash off the perfume she wore on her first date. Of course we do not really "understand" Benjy's story until we finish Quentin's and reestablish the chronology. When we do, we discover that the first event was Damuddy's death, or the scene where Caddy climbed the pear tree to look in the window, revealing her muddy drawers. In this first scene Caddy is identified with death and sexuality, but even more threatening, with the kind of independence usually associated with boys. If the scene with Dalton Ames is the causal scene of Benjy's innocent story, the scene in the pear tree, being prior as well as symbolically predictive, functions exactly like the scene in the garden that established Eve's guilt—for her curiosity and sexuality—and the inescapability of original sin.

When we reestablish the chronology of the novel as a whole, we discover that Quentin's story comes first, for it is dated June 2, 1910. Putting Quentin first gives him a kind of priority, which is reinforced by his being first in the patrilineal succession; despite his obsession, he has the intelligence, sensitivity, and sense of language to be identified as a reliable narrator. We look to his story for the best answers. But to privilege Quentin is also to privilege the values of the old South and the language of the fathers, with whom he is the most closely related.

If Quentin's father was not one of the founders of the South, he was the son of Jason Lycurgus:

Who, driven perhaps by the compulsion of the flamboyant name given him by the sardonic embittered woodenlegged indomitable father who perhaps still believed with his heart that what he wanted to be was a classicist schoolteacher, rode up the Natchez Trace one day in 1811 with a fine pair of pistols and one meagre saddlebag on a small lightwaisted but stronghocked mare which could do the first two furlongs in definitely under the halfminute and the next two in not appreciably more. . . . Who within six months was the Agent's clerk and within twelve his partner, officially still the clerk though actually halfowner of what was now a considerable store stocked with the mare's winnings in races against the horses of Ikkemotubbe's young men . . . and in the next year it was Ikkemotubbe who owned the little mare and Compson owned the solid square mile of land which someday would be almost in the center of the town of Jefferson. (406–407)

Quentin's grandfather is one of the original fathers of the aristo-cratic, slave-owning South; he is also identified with the classical fathers of Western civilization.[3] Therefore, he combines violence (his pair of fine pistols) with cunning (his ability to exploit meager resources), with almost superhuman powers (his miraculously fast rise from a propertyless frontiersman to a businessman to a planta-tion aristocrat). His (tall) story—almost a parody of the ambitious text—is powerfully chronological and logical: it establishes his identity through a long series of clauses that link his qualities as a man of violence and cunning into a line leading from zero to patriarchy.

Quentin's father, Jason III, is not given a story of his own in the appendix but emerges midparagraph in his father's story (409). In fact, there is nothing to his story in the appendix except that he was "bred for a lawyer" and "sat all day long with a decanter of whiskey and a litter of dogeared Horaces and Livys and Catul-luses" (409–410). He protests that time is "the mausoleum of all hope and desire" or that "Christ was not crucified: he was worn away by a minute clicking of little wheels" (93f.). But he still affirms the value of time, or that everything can be traced back to the original father and the first cause.

Despite Quentin's attempt to stop the clock by committing sui-cide, he too affirms the value of linear clock-time in the telling and acting out of his story. Quentin may smash his watch, but he orders every moment of his day—and story—from the moment he wakes up until the moment before the clock strikes his last hour. Quentin continually breaks the storyline and drifts back to moments from the past. But his pattern of associations is as mechanical as Benjy's, with every moment leading back to a first cause. The temporal pattern of Quentin's story reinforces the pattern of cause and effect, or its explanatory logic. And it identifies him with the authorial voice—who has designed the novel to implicate his readers. Whenever Quentin breaks the storyline and leaps back in time, we become his accomplices and fit the disordered moment back into its chronological and logical pattern.

The immediate cause of Quentin's story, we affirm, is the announcement of Caddy's wedding. But the initial cause is Caddy's affair with Dalton Ames, and the original scene is associated with her muddy drawers. If Benjy stops Caddy's story, Quentin continually tries to rescue it from the stories of other characters and appropriate it into his own. Innocent in her choice of Dalton Ames, she becomes the seduced young woman in the story of her seducer. Quentin tries unsuccessfully to change this story, first taking on the role of an outraged brother-lover-hero, then by turning it into a story of incest. Then Caddy becomes the pregnant daughter in the story of a Southern mother. On the day Quentin begins his story, Mrs. Compson has found Caddy a husband. He appropriates both his mother's story and Caddy's by committing suicide. And in his recollections on June 2, 1910, he selects and organizes the events of Caddy's life to fit into the romantic story of a bright, sensitive, young man who dies for pure love.

Jason is an almost totally unsympathetic character. But, while our judgment of Jason reflects an ideal embodied in the absent Caddy, it is important to realize that it also reflects the values of the implied author—whose moral scale cannot be separated from his sociopolitical hierarchy. For Jason is antithetical in every way to the ideal of the Southern gentleman. But if Jason is not identified with the values of the old South, he is at least validated as a narrator by being situated so squarely in the comic-realistic tradition. His story is perfectly linear. It explains everything within its compass. And the very fact that he depicts himself as a comic character affirms his detachment and trustworthiness as a storyteller. He does not pretend omniscience, and certainly not broad-mindedness; indeed, his continual victimization results from his limited view of the world. But what he tells us is factual, however prejudiced his language, and this lends credence to his judgments—which are always explicit and rational.

"Once a bitch always a bitch," says Jason in the opening line of his story. "I says you're lucky if her playing out of school is all that worries you. I says she ought to be down there in that kitchen right now, instead of up there in her room, gobbing paint on her face and waiting for six niggers that cant even stand up out of a chair unless they've got a pan full of bread and meat to balance them, to fix breakfast for her" (223). We may not like Jason's sexist and racist language, but we laugh at his lines because they caricature what we are convinced is true. There may be more delicate ways to picture Quentin making up her face, but "gobbing paint" on it is sharp and accurate. He may perpetuate the stereotype of lazy blacks, but, except for Dilsey, they do live off his hard-earned money, and what work they do does not pay for all they eat. We may hate him for the way he restricts Quentin, but her actions are designed to provoke Jason as much as to assert her independence.

No matter how nasty or vindictive, Jason's aphorisms continue to be sharp and accurate on many levels at once. His reliability, that is, allies him with the authorial voice. It is true that he "never had time to go to Harvard like Quentin or drink myself into the ground like Father" (224)—the word "time" having a resonance that Jason does not supply. Moreover, he gives us our first realistic picture of Benjy when, frankly trying to maintain the family name for business reasons, he complains that "it dont take much pride to not like to see a thirty year old man playing around the yard with a nigger boy, running up and down the fence and lowing like a cow whenever they play golf over there" (276). And Jason is frankly realistic in telling his own story. He spares no sympathy on himself when he tells us how he is outwitted by Quentin, chasing her all over the countryside and ending up cornered by a hunting dog against a bush with "beggar lice and twigs and stuff all over me, inside my clothes and shoes and all, and then I happened to look around and I had my hand right on a bunch of poison oak" (300).

Jason's story takes the form of a comic chase, the breathless pacing of which heightens its linearity. His failures only emphasize the shape of the American success story into which he is so desperately trying to fit. Unlike Benjy, he tells it completely in the present tense, but it continually emphasizes what he feels is the first cause of his failure: if Caddy hadn't gotten pregnant by Dalton Ames, he would have had a position in Herbert Head's bank. Jason's rage at the daughter is fueled by his hatred for the mother who started him on the road to failure. His story leads to a conclusion that rationally justifies the judgment of its opening lines. Though it heightens our sympathy for Quentin and Caddy, it nonetheless leads us to feel that they threaten the order Jason works so desperately to maintain.

It is important that Jason's story does not end during his monologue but reaches its climax in the Dilsey section. It is also important that the Dilsey section is not narrated by Dilsey but by an omniscient narrator. For the omniscient narrator's view of Jason, being no different from his own, validates his judgments. Moreover, the omniscient narrator speaks with an author-ial, male voice.

Dilsey's story is the story of a heroic woman who provides a perspective on the Compson family. But it is also the story of a Southern stereotype and fantasy: the ideal, timeless mammy—which, as Gloria Naylor points out, was a fiction created out of "the need to view slavery as benign" (65). Dilsey is a figure of strength, selfless love, and piety. She is also safe as a woman without sexuality, a mother without blood ties, a servant who can hold the family together and maintain its tie with the past. And we are assured by the final lines on the final page of the appendix:

DILSEY.
They endured.

But what are we assured of? Does "they" imply that there is more than one Dilsey in the world? Does "they" unite Dilsey with Faulkner's own "mammy" Caroline Barr (who served as Dilsey's model) and all the black "mammies" who maintained (or were constructed to maintain) the very order that originally enslaved them? And aren't the words "They endured" placed at the very end of the novel by the authorial voice that seemed to efface itself in the disorder and irrationality of the sections ostensibly narrated by the three males of the family?

We do catch a glimpse of Dilsey that is independent of the story shaped by the authorial voice—in the picture that introduces her section. What dominates this singular image is Dilsey's awesome body. And the language is not one of power and control as the authorial voice pictures her standing in the bleak chill dawn. In fact, the authorial voice loses control; it does not create anything we can coherently picture.[4] And, since the language evoking Dilsey breaks the laws of logic and syntax, it is not a language at all but what Kristeva calls "semiosis." "She had been a big woman once but now her skeleton rose, draped loosely in unpadded skin that tightened again upon a paunch almost dropsical, as though muscle and tissue had been courage or fortitude which the days or the years had consumed until only the indomitable skeleton was left rising like a ruin or a landmark above the somnolent and impervious guts, and above that the collapsed face that gave the impression of the bones themselves being outside the flesh" (331). The authorial voice cannot capture Dilsey. However, in the disruptions of its discourse it evokes the excess of Dilsey's spirit and the plentitude of her body, which has comforted all her children—but which also "seed" the beginning.

The Dilsey section subordinates the figure of Dilsey to the story of the Compson family. Actually, this section contains two alternating, parallel stories: the climax of Jason's story and a story focusing on Dilsey. The line of Jason's story leads him in pursuit of his niece, his lost money, and his lost opportunity. Its breathless pace contrasts with the stately pace of Dilsey's story as she walks from home to church. The line from home to church leads to a stability that, for many readers, replaces or at least balances the novel's despair with hope. But we should examine the logic of this storyline, as it leads from the disintegrated Compson family to the climactic sermon and to the speech that establishes Dilsey's role in the novel.

The congregation waits in suspense for the preacher from St. Louis. They look in disbelief at the "undersized" visitor "in a shabby alpaca coat" with "a wizened black face like a small, aged monkey." But when the visitor rises to speak, they forget his appearance and sigh "as if . . . waked from a collective dream." What wakes them is a voice that "sounded like a white man . . . level and cold . . . too big to have come from him." The preacher tells the story of Christ from his birth to his crucifixion to his resurrection. His story gains in immediacy, power, and authority—indeed, it identifies him with God the Father—because he sees it all at once from beginning to end: "I sees de light en I sees de word," and he "sees de day" when "Ma'y settin in de do' wid Jesus on her lap" and "de angels singin de peaceful songs" and "Mary jump up, sees de sojer face" and the soldier tells her "We gwine to kill yo little Jesus!" And he "sees de blastin, blindin sight . . . sees Calvary" and "sees de resurrection en de light"—and Jesus saying, "I died dat dem whut sees en believes shall never die" (365–370).

Thadious Davis points out that the Rev. Shegog "sheds his cold level 'white man's' voice," slipping unnoticeably into negroid intonation and pronunciation. He identifies with his black congregation and reaches them at a level beyond language. She goes on to show how sensitive Faulkner was to the power of black oratory and the black church in maintaining a sense of community and self-worth (116ff.). Still, it was a white man's voice that described Shegog as "undersized" and compared him to a monkey. And it was the white man's voice that woke the congregation, that gave Shegog his initial power and authority, the congregation failing to notice his shift into their language. As André Bleikasten concludes, "Shegog has become the docile servant of the Word" (*Most Splendid Failure*, 196). But Bleikasten is developing an eloquent argument for a collective, mythic, and hence universally hopeful moment in the novel. And he does not seem to fully realize its implications. For what holds the black community together is a religion that fosters submission to the society that continually undermines their community, or collectivity, and sense of self-worth.

I do not mean to underestimate the cohesive and subversive power of an institution that has played such an important role in African-American history, and that Davis describes so well, or the unusual achievement of a Southern white writer in evoking it. But I do want to point out that the black voice—taking on "a sad, timbrous quality like an alto horn, sinking into their hearts and speaking there" (367)—is competing with a voice of greater narrative power and author-ity. And the relation between the two voices reflects the power relations in Jefferson society.

In the Dilsey section, then, an omniscient narrator tells two parallel, linear stories, one of which leads to a story of the Son of God told by a black man in the voice of a white man and with the omniscience of God the Father. But this is only part of the climax. For the storyline leads out of the church, where on her way home Dilsey declares: "I've seed de first en de last" (371). Dilsey not only identifies with God the Father, she takes responsibility as a mother. For "seed" is a pun by which the authorial voice, overlaying her innocence with his irony, implicates her in the original mother's sin.

When Dilsey arrives home, Jason is twenty miles away searching for a circus man in a bright red tie. His story leads to his ultimate defeat: he learns that Quentin got away, he is nearly killed when he insults a mad old man, and he is overcharged by a Negro for a ride home. But it also leads to the final scene where the two storylines are drawn together. Young Luster is driving Benjy to the cemetery to visit the graves of Quentin and Mr. Compson. When Luster drives the wrong way around the Confederate monument, Benjy starts to howl, and Jason comes to the rescue, "jumping across the square and onto the step." In the end, after Jason turns the horse around, Benjy sees the objects flow by "smoothly once more from left to right; post and tree, window and doorway, and signboard, each in its ordered place" (400f.).

The chase scene was perfected in film by D. W. Griffith. It began with parallel editing, or the intercutting of two storylines, and concluded with a "last minute rescue" that drew the two storylines together. And it restored social as well as aesthetic equilibrium. It may have been a coincidence that the chase scene was perfected by a frank advocate of white patriarchy, but it epitomizes the language of the fathers in its linearity, causality, omniscient controlling force, violent action, and the achievement of a goal that combines power and order.

Though *The Sound and the Fury* begins in the mind of an idiot and the original timeline disintegrates, the authorial voice manipulates the disorder all along—which is why the associations are so mechanical. It privileges Quentin's story and validates Jason's. It appropriates Dilsey's voice and story. And it ends on a note of order, which is validated by the order in the chronological appendix. There are important arguments among the aristocratic Quentin, the middle-class Jason, the innocent Benjy, and the narrator of the Dilsey section. Moreover, their heterogeneity and independence, as well as their defiance of logic and chronology, undermine traditional narrative author-ity. But however socially diverse and independent, the narrating voices reflect a unity among the social classes, as well as the historical, rational, natural, and religious orders. They combine in telling a story that excludes the voice of the woman they define as responsible for its "tragic" conclusion. They fragment the storyline but not its implicit logic which leads from the scene of original sin (Caddy sitting in a pear tree with muddy drawers, looking in at her grandmother's funeral) to the causal event (her affair with Dalton Ames), to Quentin's death, to the dissolution of the family, and finally to a picture of Caddy standing beside a Nazi general.

As I Lay Dying

It may be no accident that the names of Caddy and Addie are so much alike; they are both identified with their sexuality, and they both hold together as well as threaten a family. But Addie is given a chance to tell her own story—even though she must contend with fifteen other storytellers. In *As I Lay Dying* Faulkner takes up the challenge of giving his heroine her own voice.

Each member of Addie's family, a choral group from the community, and two outsiders alternate in telling the story of Addie's death and burial. Addie's story is shaped into a ritual journey through fire and flood, and leads from a rural world to a developing city, from Addie's home to the home of the new Mrs. Bundren, from death to rebirth.

But the characters also tell of themselves as they tell the main story, and in so doing they subordinate Addie's story to theirs.[5] Darl opens the story of Addie's death by focusing on Jewel, with whom he is striving for his mother's complete love. Cora begins, "So I saved out the eggs and baked yesterday" (6)—and embeds Addie's story in a story in which she focuses on herself as a thrifty and godfearing but also energetic and enterprising housewife. Jewel, a violent man of action, speaks only once, revealing his jealousy and hatred of the others and wishing "it would just be me and her on a high hill and me rolling the rocks down the hill at their faces" (15). Dewey Dell must tell of her condition; her story is shaped by her loneliness and need for an abortion. Anse speaks only twice: first to emphasize his sacrifice in going to Jefferson to do the right thing by Addie, then to excuse his failure as the head of the family. Except for a moment when sympathizing with Darl, Cash can only speak of his calculations; he calculates in making the coffin and worries about its being off balance, and he calculates when he justifies sending Darl to the madhouse, or as he balances human values against property values—"I dont reckon nothing excuses setting fire to a man's barn" (223). Vardaman reflects a loss and a resulting series of events that are beyond his comprehension. Whitfield's story is designed to rationalize his arriving too late. Tull, Armstid, Samson, and Peabody are relatively disinterested outsiders, choric characters, but members of the community that excludes Addie. Moseley and MacGowan provide an outside perspective. But Moseley uses the pregnant Dewey Dell to reflect himself as a "respectable druggist, that's kept a store and raised a family and been a church-member"(192). And MacGowan uses her to show himself as a wily seducer who will give her something that smells like turpentine and then take her down to the cellar for the rest of the treatment.

Addie is dead and therefore absent from both the main story and the stories the characters tell of themselves—but it is she who unites them. Indeed, her absence defines the relationship that gives meaning to each character, the family, the community, and the journey itself. She is a hole in both sets of stories, which, ironically, gives shape to the (w)hole. And she tells a story of herself that, as we will see, builds on negation.

Besides the characters telling the stories, there is an authorial figure who hovers nearby, sometimes near, sometimes farther away from each character, adding his voice to theirs, or imposing his views, mainly through images and metaphors inconsistent with their sensibilities or education.[6] And there is a voice that disrupts the narrative and flaunts the logic of naturalistic explanation, or rebels against the authorial voice. Stephen Ross explains that the chapter headings and other purely textual signs function like voice in speech, for they "prompt or allow the reader to regard the printed text as a source of signification" ("Voice," 306). They are elements of a "textual voice," which I have been calling the voice of the body-text to emphasize its physicality and its relation to the body of the mother. Darl's clairvoyant passages and Addie's disturbing monologue arise from no source we can identify other than the chapter headings —"*Darl*," "*Addie*"—which are set off by themselves on a blank half page and ambiguously related to the narratives that follow. They issue, that is, not from the characters speaking or thinking, or from the hovering narrator, but from the rebellious voice of the body-text.

Darl is the chief storyteller of the main story, until he goes mad. As his language loses its coherence and logic, he begins to fail as a storyteller. But most of the narrative sections are his. He also narrates the most important events: Addie's death, rescuing her body from the fire, and saving it from the flood. He is an ideal storyteller, for he is articulate, observant, and even poetically sensitive.

He is able to describe the scene of Addie's death with extraordinary insight even though he is miles away when she dies. He pictures Dewey Dell in a way that reflects her loss of not only a mother but the only other woman in the family, the only person with whom she could possibly share her experience of being pregnant. "She flings herself across Addie Bundren's knees, clutching her, shaking her with the furious strength of the young before sprawling suddenly across the handful of rotten bones that Addie Bundren left, jarring the whole bed into a chattering sibilance of mattress shucks, her arms outflung and the fan in one hand still beating with expiring breath into the quilt" (47–48). Vardaman, too young to comprehend, peers in awe "from behind pa's leg . . . his mouth full open and all color draining from his face into his mouth, as though he has by some means fleshed his own teeth in himself, sucking" (48). Cash, who can only express his relationship to Addie by making a perfect coffin but develops into the one character capable of reflecting on Darl's madness, looks "down at her peaceful, rigid face fading into the dusk as though darkness were a precursor of the ultimate earth, until at last the face seems to float detached upon it, lightly as the reflection of a dead leaf" (49). But most insightful and sympathetic is his view of Anse, who couldn't work because he was afraid he'd sweat and "catch his

death from the sickness"(25), who believed that if the Lord wanted
us to be on the move he'd make us "longways, like a road or a
horse" (35), and whose first words after Addie's death are
" 'God's will be done. . . . Now I can get them teeth.' " For just
before that speech, Darl pictures Anse in a moment of awkward
tenderness: "He touches the quilt as he saw Dewey Dell do, trying
to smooth it up to the chin, but disarranging it instead" (51).

There is no naturalistic explanation for Darl's clairvoyance; indeed, his objectivity is inconsistent with his obsessive jealousy of
Jewel. But there is a formal rationale, which reflects Darl's potential as an artist. Even more, it identifies him with the traditional
omniscient narrator, or the hovering authorial voice. It also authen-
ticates the main story and firmly establishes it in the tradition of
heroic journey stories that affirm the social order. What we have in
Darl, then, is a double voice, or an agon between an authorial
voice and a rebellious voice, which is abetted by the textual voice
Stephen Ross describes so well. But the rebellious voice fails to
realize itself in Darl, because he takes on the role of the artist who
is destroyed by society.

A key event in the ritual journey that governs this novel is the
rescue of Addie from the flood—for it focuses the action of the
journey as well as the capacity of selfish characters for selfless
sacrifice. Darl pictures the family and friends pulling together to
save not only Addie but Cash and his tools. Detached and sympathetic, as he was in describing Addie's death, he takes on the
traditional role of artist and omniscient *author-ity*. Tull provides a
choric perspective, which is complemented by Vardaman's close-
up view connecting his mother with a fish. And Cash gives a
rational explanation for the catastrophe: "It wasn't on a balance"
(157). Neither Anse nor Jewel joins in the telling of this story, but
they are characterized by their reticence, Anse as a result of his
laziness, Jewel because he is a man of action. So, with them accounted for, we sense that the community as a whole shares in
telling the story of the community in action.

But only if we fail to think about the characters who do not
share in telling this story—Dewey Dell, Cora, and Addie. Which
means that this community of storytellers—author-ized by Darl's
omniscience—is all male. Cora's absence is logical, or explained
by her being a woman whose role it is to tend the farm, but this
explanation is sufficient only if we fail to question why her husband, Tull, is more expendable at the height of the harvest season.
It highlights the hegemony and author-ity of male narrators—as it
highlights the exclusion of women from the community of those

who can tell the important parts of the main story. And this exclusion is most noteworthy in the case of Dewey Dell, who is given only two sections in the narrative, the first to tell us how she became pregnant picking down the row with Lafe, and the second reflecting on her aloneness and Vardaman's reaction to Addie's death.

Addie's absence from those who tell the story of the flood is also logical, for she is dead. However, this logic becomes questionable when she takes her place among the novel's narrators. Addie's story is untraditional, indeed, unnatural as well as illogical—the dead woman disrupting the story of her funeral journey after the community of storytellers saves her from the flood. But she begins her story in a traditional and apparently natural and logical way: with her meeting of Anse. For Anse would give her the identity of wife and mother, or, more specifically, of a woman whose life consisted of laying and dying. She also grounds her identity by remembering her father, who used to say that "the reason for living was to get ready to stay dead a long time" (161).

Nonetheless, Addie's story is hard to follow and understand, because it is untraditional, "unnatural," and illogical—that is because it defies the authorial voice— but also because her illogical story is linked by series of logical transitions. "When the switch fell I could feel it upon my flesh . . . and I would think with each blow of the switch. . . . Now I am something in your secret and selfish life, who have marked your blood with my own for ever and ever. *And so* I took Anse" (162, my emphasis).

"And so," "and so," "then," "and so," "and then," "then." Addie leads us through her illogical story with logical connectives that ultimately come to link the births of each child: from Cash (who taught her that "motherhood was invented by someone who had to have a word for it") to Darl (whom she was tricked into by Anse's words of love) to Jewel (whom she was tricked into by Rev. Whitfield talking of God's love). And they lead to what is shaped like a logical conclusion: "I gave Anse Dewey Dell to negative Jewel. Then I gave him Vardaman to replace the child I had robbed him of. . . . And then I could get ready to die" (163–168).

Descending from Puritan Calvinism and secularized into the language of business calculation, the language and logic of the fathers is deceptive, manipulative, coercive, and life denying. It not only excludes the weak and disenfranchised but co-opts them into believing in the interrelated values of submission and balancing one's books.

Only one other character in the novel combines the language of business calculation with logic, and indeed with righteousness. Like Addie, Cora is excluded from the power such language implies, but she has accepted and internalized the ideology and therefore provides a contrasting perspective. "So I saved out the eggs and baked yesterday." While Addie lies dying, Cora brags to Kate and Eula about not only the cakes, which "turned out right well," but about how she increased the net value of the flock, saved the eggs out one at a time so that they "wouldn't be costing anything," and (since the hens laid so well) so that the "flour and the sugar and the stove wood would not be costing anything" either. As it turns out, the lady who ordered the cakes changed her mind, but Cora is not disturbed. "Riches is nothing in the face of the Lord." Besides, "it isn't like they cost me anything. . . . Mr Tull himself realises that the eggs I saved were over and beyond what we had engaged to sell, so it was like we had found the eggs or they had been given to us" (6–8).

Cora seems to be a self-centered, self-righteous, narrow-minded woman. She puts herself, rather than Addie, in the center of her narrative. And her narrow obsessions make her unreliable in almost every observation about Darl, Jewel, Anse, and Addie. Obsessed with swapping and selling and saving, she has completely internalized the ideology that associates good works with business success. But are we being fair to Cora? In their study of rural women in preindustrial society, Louise Tilly and Joan Scott point out that farm wives who sold milk, chickens, and eggs "often brought in the only cash a family received" (45). Tull certainly received some cash for the crops he did not use for feed, but given the subsistence level of his farming, it probably went for seed or harnesses or new stock or even toward the mule that Snopes would cheat him out of. Didn't Cora have the right to be proud of her business skills? Though limited by necessity, she not only managed within the limits of her narrow world, but exceeded them with her ingenuity and energy. She had the power to create the cakes out of nothing.

Nonetheless, in her storytelling she accepts, indeed affirms, the system of power from which she is excluded by both class and gender. Her "so . . . so . . . because . . . so" are logical links in the caricature of a success story. She cannot become angry at the rich lady who changed her mind about the cakes, for this would be an admission of failure. So to authorize her achievement, she invokes the Lord (to whom "riches is nothing") and her husband "Mr Tull" (who "himself realises that the eggs I saved were over and beyond what we had engaged to sell"). Since she accepts the ideology that limits her identity, Cora's ingenuity and energy turn her into a caricature.

Addie is not a caricature but a memorable and disturbing character. Her story is not of acceptance but of rebellion—of saying no to every demand imposed on her by society. She refuses to use the language of the fathers, and the scene Cora narrates reflects her isolation from the community of women who have internalized it. Moreover, her monologue is disruptive. Breaking into the middle of a much more linear story, breaking the rules of verisimilitude as well as logic and decorum, Addie turns a multivoiced but predominantly monologic novel into a carnival. She is not only unconventional and indecorous but subversive, indeed blasphemous. She gives voice to what Cora suppressed: a woman's outrage at her social restrictions and her social construction. Moreover, she breaks through the language that has constructed her. And she also gives voice to what breaks through in the disordered opening description of Dilsey. That is, to what Julia Kristeva calls the semiotic chora—the totality of creative but also destructive drives that precede the language of the father and relate to the mother's body, the disruption that in a patriarchal society is a mark of difference, otherness, shifting identity.

The chora, though characterized by rupture, is also mediated and constrained by social organization and the language of the father. Addie cannot break from society, or even escape her social construction. But she does not give in to it. The form of Addie's story reflects her struggle—as she tries to fit the "logic" of her life into the only language—and logic—she knows. She can only articulate her self through acts of negation: by hating the fathers, by rejecting the demands of her children, and by dying. Still, she achieves an identity by violating the "laws of logic" and language of authority, and, thereby, powerfully conveying the intrusions and violations in a woman's life.

Moreover, her story is a major disruption in the main—and traditional—storyline. The improbable voice of a dead woman disrupts the story and the ritual journey to tell a story that no one in the community would want to hear. Ironically, Addie's story is the impetus to the main story. After Darl was born, she made Anse promise to take her back to Jefferson when she died. Her comic revenge on Anse motivates the journey, the ritual, and the novel itself.

So in answer to the question of my title—can a woman tell her story in Yoknapatawpha County, even with all those yarns?—we could say yes, as long as she is dead. But that would underestimate the distance Faulkner traveled since his first experiment in narrative form. The narrative politics of both novels reflects the power structure of Faulkner's society—as the authorial voice attracts, subverts, appropriates, and finally dominates the field of independent, contending storytellers. But in *As I Lay Dying* we hear more than the voices of a community that co-opts, excludes, and suppresses the voices of its women. We also hear a woman's voice, saying no—struggling to tell her poignant and dangerous story in the only language available to her, and making it not only heard but central.

6

Widening the Gyre: *Light in August*

It may be argued that in emphasizing power of narrative authori-ty, despite Dilsey's disruption, I am applying a differ-ent standard to Faulkner, for in my discussion of Joyce I gave far more weight to the power of rebellious voices. And I want to confront this issue before looking at the novel in which Faulkner deals most completely with the range of Southern society. As we develop from naive or common readers into teachers and critics, we lose sight of our initial responses. As common readers we were more disturbed and affected by the leaps, gaps, disruptions— though not by the absences, or the voices and stories left out, suppressed, appropriated. But we were also drawn and gave more weight to the most traditional sources of narrative author-ity. For Faulkner's authorial voice addresses (or inscribes) the reader as a member of his presupposed narrative community. Moreover, to develop Wayne Booth's point, implied author-ity is not created by the author alone but also by the needs that have been developed in the reader. It may be important to teach people different ways of reading (in the fifties I was taught to read the end of the novel first so that I would not be governed by the plotline). But we should recognize, first, that this is a political as well as a pedagogical decision, and, second, that it might not have a very widespread impact. Nor will the impact be long-lasting unless we also teach people to understand the power of traditional author-ity, and in-deed how "careful" reading is often a way of ignoring the context of its power. Interestingly enough, the New Criticism and Bakh-tin's dialogic both aim at decentering traditional sources of author-ity. But the New Criticism enhanced them all the more by cutting the text out of its social and political as well as its authorial con-text, thereby insulating its ideological assumptions from critical questioning, and even legitimate scrutiny. And the Bakhtinian ap-proach may run a similar risk if it does not recognize that some voices, stories, and narrative strategies have more power than oth-ers because of the conditioned needs and habits of the common reader.[1]

The question may arise, then, why this argument should not apply to Joyce as well as Faulkner. Actually it does, for I have been describing a narrative dialogic, an agon between authorial and rebellious voices, which, as I argued at the end of the *Ulysses* chapter, is by definition unstable. Moreover, Joyce was more rebellious than Faulkner. He was rebellious in his feelings about his country, his language, his religious heritage, and the dominant attitudes toward sexuality. Faulkner, on the other hand, was iconoclastic, independent, ornery, and a sharp critic of American society. But he was not as consistently rebellious—especially in his public statements about America, the South, God, and black people. His ambivalence about authority is reflected in his use of Southern oratory, the tall tale, and the very shaping of his novels. Therefore, he leads us to understand the great variety of ways in which the authorial voice maintains its power.

Light in August begins where *As I Lay Dying* left off, in Jefferson. Jefferson may be no more than a small town grown large, but, when the Bundrens arrive, we see that what remains of a community is the accumulation—indeed escalation—of selfish concern, narrow-mindedness, materialism, and violence. Lafe may take advantage of Dewey Dell's innocence as they pick cotton down the row, but MacGowan takes advantage of her helplessness as she tries to articulate her needs in the Jefferson drugstore. Dewey Dell may resent Darl's knowing looks at home, but in Jefferson she turns on him with a vengeance. Cash is concerned with the material of his craft while building the coffin outside Addie's bedroom, but in the city he can reckon a barn is worth more than his brother's life. Anse is lazy and ineffectual on the farm, but in town he is able to acquire a new set of teeth, a new wife, and even a phonograph.

What is partly hidden by the bucolic cartoon style of *As I Lay Dying* erupts in *Light in August*. Here the main story is of Joe Christmas, a rootless man, who lives thirty-three years denying his identity—now as a black man, now as a white man—whose final denial, or negation, is to kill Joanna Burden and define himself as a "nigger-murderer." He is chased by men and dogs, gives himself up, escapes from prison, and is finally castrated and killed by a mindless young fascist. His story is told by the timekeeper of a saw mill, an unemployed religious fanatic, an old woman, a chorus of townspeople, a lawyer, and a narrator who though rarely omniscient can focus on Christmas's consciousness as well as those of his storytelling characters, and who mixes his voice with theirs. So this novel not only brings to light what was implied in Faulkner's earlier novel, it expands its focus and source of explanation from the family to a more complex representation of Southern society.

Christmas's story does not begin with his beginning. It begins when mill hands in Jefferson look up to see a stranger with serge trousers and soiled white shirt and a straw hat "cocked at an angle arrogant and baleful above his still face" (33). Actually, it begins four times. It begins again the night before he kills Joanna Burden; and again the day of his earliest recollection, in the orphanage, getting sick in the dietitian's closet while she makes love to an intern; and finally it begins with his biological beginning, the day his mother ran off with a dark-skinned circus man and conceived him.

The indecisiveness and dislocations in Christmas's story reflect the disorder of his life—and, more important, the two main holes, dislocations, enigmas in his biological and existential identities. We can never know whether his father was black (whatever that might mean). For Milly told old Doc Hines that the father was Mexican, while Doc Hines insists that he "knowed better"— though he never saw the man (and even shot him in the dark). Nor can we know what Christmas was thinking at the moment he killed Joanna Burden. For the main narrator omits the moment— leaving a blank space in the text—after the hammer of Joanna's pistol flicks away and before Christmas finds himself in the middle of the road flagging down a car.

Many readers and even critics note the enigma of his birth but still think of him or continue to speak of him as being black, or mulatto. Fewer note that, though Christmas knew that "*something was going to happen*" and took his razor to Joanna's room, he waited—"watching the shadowed pistol on the wall" and that he was still "watching when the cocked shadow of the hammer flicked away" (310). He did not act but react; he was not a murderer—except in the eyes of Jefferson society.

By continuing to think of Christmas as black and as a murderer, readers are assenting to the view of Jefferson society. And, as John Duvall convincingly argues, the interpretive community—main-line critics since Cleanth Brooks—joins the Jefferson community in its racist complicity. But for good reason. They are not misreading. The novel is designed to make us forget, minimize, or at least feel ambivalent about these passages. For besides the various story-tellers, there is an authorial voice, and its role is much more intrusive than that in *As I Lay Dying* or even *The Sound and the Fury*. Nor is *Light in August* designed to provide the balance of multiple perspectives that Hugh Ruppersburg in his useful study of *Voice*

and Eye in Faulkner's Fiction says "combine in an evocation of the
nature of human experience, with Joe Christmas as the archetypal
individual" (56). No doubt Faulkner intended to universalize the
experience of his novel; certainly the authorial voice does as he
speaks through his main narrator. But we should realize by now
that "universal" is a loaded term, that the notion of "all human
experience" is limited by one's social position, that the perspectives, therefore, are not balanced because the authorial voice privileges some kinds of experience and some kinds of explanations
over others.

In contrast to *The Sound and the Fury* and *As I Lay Dying*, in
Light in August there is a central, unifying narrator. Though not
characterized, he is concerned, obsessed, and continually attracts
our attention. He knows all the stories but cannot apprehend or
make sense of them. His desperation is reflected in the tone of his
voice when he speaks to us directly and when he translates or adds
his voice to the voice of a character. It is also reflected in the shape
of his endless sentences. But his inability to know and his need to
understand do not make him neutral. For he privileges the voices
of some storytelling characters, neglects or appropriates others,
and draws allegiance from those who should be antagonistic.
While reading the pertinent passages, carefully, we may be aware
that the question of Christmas's blood is open and that the killing
of Joanna Burden is in self-defense. But such careful reading may
take these passages out of their full narrative context, or ignore the
power of narrative authority.

Why is the question of Christmas's identity posed as a question
of his blood? Because we assent to the novel's most liberal
character-narrator, who is brought in to explain Christmas's
death, and who tells the most important part of Christmas's story
in a language that identifies black blood with violence and coward-
ice and white blood with reason. Some critics are careful to note
the inherent racism of the man whose line goes back to the original
fathers of Jefferson, and insist that his view is not the same as the
narrator's or the implied or real author's. But the "naive" reader
has good reason to be influenced by Gavin Stevens's explanation.
Indeed, the "naive" reader may be less naive than the close "critical" reader who fails to consider the power of Stevens's narrative
authority.

Gavin Stevens is introduced as a humane and patient character,
helping Mr. and Mrs. Hines onto the train. He is detached, not
having been involved in the Christmas story. He was educated at
Harvard and is the district attorney (at a time when district attor-

neys were valued in the popular imagination). He appears in other Faulkner novels as a man of intelligence and moderation, and an explainer. And he tells his story with rational conviction and breathless power. Gavin Stevens is implicitly identified with the traditional narrator. His sudden appearance has caused readers to criticize the novel's structure, but this does not diminish his power or authority. Nor does the recognition of the liberal lawyer's implicit racism. Nor does the assertion that he is not a spokesman for Faulkner.

Stevens may disturb us, once we gain a critical vantage, because of his inauthentic reliability, but let us look at what should be the least reliable set of narrators. We may accept the story of Christmas's death with skepticism (at least on hindsight), but it is surprising how easily we accept the story of his birth and early development, and at least give credence to the unfounded assertion that his father was black. For it is based on the evidence of a mad fanatic, who is Faulkner's most unsympathetic caricature. Once again, though, there is good reason for accepting his authority. While Hines has no empirical basis for knowing better than Milly that the man he had never seen was black, everything else we know of him establishes his judgment as infallible. He chases Milly and her lover in the dark, riding right up to the first buggy he sees, leaning down "without saying a word and without stopping his horse," and grabbing "the man that might have been a stranger or a neighbor for all he could have known . . . grabbed him by one hand and held the pistol against him with the other and shot him dead and brought the gal back home behind him on the horse" (414). And his infallibility is revealed as a terrible power when we hear how he sat in the corridor of the orphanage watching little Joe play, just watching, until the children started to call Christmas "nigger." Hines may look like a cartoon figure, he may be a fanatic, he may be mad, he may be incredible—but he establishes Christmas's identity as a black man on a level that makes the doubts of a close reader seem like nit-picking.

Thadious Davis establishes an important point: whether or not Christmas is biologically black, his life reflects the "myth and social reality of the black experience." His "odyssey is concerned with the social definition of Negro. He suffers aloneness and a crisis of identity as well as the trials of northern migration and life as an industrial laborer—all new experiences to the white Southerner during the Depression, but after the Civil War a familiar pattern in black life" (134). *Light in August* traces the formation of Christmas's social identity as a black man. Moreover, it demonstrates that biological facts are irrelevant; black identity is determined by social forces. Among these social forces is the poor white man who not only embraces the ideology that disenfranchises poor as well as black people but becomes its chief instrument. The power he has in shaping Christmas's life is reflected in his infallibility as a character—and in his relationship to the implied author-ity of the novel. Nor is his power diminished by his cartoon caricaturization.

One of the paradoxes of *Light in August* is that all the fanatics turn out to be right; indeed, the more fanatic they are, the more clearly they prove their infallibility. On one side of Hines is McEachern, who in comparison is almost benign. Though he had never committed lechery or listened to anyone who talked about it, "within thirty minutes of intensive thinking he knew almost as much of Joe's doings as Joe himself could have told him," and he galloped "in some juggernautish simulation of terrific speed" to the one-room schoolhouse, though "he had neither reason nor manner of knowing that there would be a dance held in it" (221–223).

On the other side of Hines is Percy Grimm, who has "a sublime and implicit faith in physical courage and blind obedience, and a belief that the white race is superior to any and all other races and that the American is superior to all other white races and that the American uniform is superior to all men," who chases Christmas "with the delicate swiftness of an apparition, the implacable undeviation of a Juggernaut or Fate," and who runs "straight to the kitchen and into the doorway, already firing, almost before he could have seen the table overturned and . . . the bright and glittering hands of the man who crouched behind it," who fires all five shots into an area that someone could cover with a folded handkerchief and then castrates Christmas with a butcher knife, crying, "Now you'll let white women alone, even in hell" (498, 508, 512f.).

Percy Grimm is introduced by the authorial voice, as it takes over from Gavin Stevens in describing Christmas's murder. Indeed, the authorial voice becomes omniscient, gives us a sketch of Percy Grimm's entire life, and reveals the fascist potential of a whole class of Southerners who were too poor to participate in the power structure and too young to have participated in the war (World War I) that had enabled the previous generation of poor whites to identify with their rebel forefathers. It also shows how Grimm and Christmas are both being moved around by "the Player," thereby absolving Grimm from blame and removing the situation from its historical, social, and political context. Finally, it provides us with an epilogue that transforms the vicious murder into a scene of resurrection and salvation—or turns it into a ritual sacrifice that will ultimately save the community. Given its omniscience, then, the authorial voice validates Stevens's story and the values of the community responsible for the tragedy of Christmas's life and death.

Which is not to say that the authorial voice is uncritical of McEachern, Hines, Grimm, and Stevens; we must remember that it caricatures the first three and distances the fourth. Nor should we forget the note of outrage in its reaction to the capriciousness of "the Player." Still, it speaks through them in a way that gives them authority. And it draws them into an odd combination of omnipotent father figures (Percy Grimm being the son who was born too late to be a father but who finally usurps his role)—all variations of God the Father and the omniscient author.

No wonder that *Light in August*, which traces the complex and barely comprehensible interrelationships of so many people from so many classes of society, focuses predominantly on the lives of Christmas, Byron, and Hightower—three male characters. Milly, Joanna, and Lena are important—Milly and Joanna are sacrificial victims whose tragedies may be as great as Christmas's—yet we hear very little of their stories. The structure of the novel reflects the social situation, where, like blacks, women are forced into serving and nurturing roles and become sacrificial victims: their voices are suppressed, their stories appropriated.

Milly is central to Christmas's biological story; she is literally its first cause. But she is removed from the center, first, because her story is removed from the story of his birth, and, second, because it is told as a result of mistaken identity—Mrs. Hines thinking that Lena's baby is Milly's grandchild. All we know of Milly is that she said her lover was a Mexican, but her father "knowed better" and killed him and then sat on the porch with his shotgun across his knees to keep her from getting any medical help and then watched her from the hall until she died. Her father appropriates both her story and her life.

While Milly is biologically the first cause of Christmas's tragedy, she is not a part of his experience, or of his psychological story. In his recollection, the first cause is the dietician—the woman who fed him in the orphanage and who provided ambivalent pleasure as he slowly devoured her sweet pink toothpaste among her clothes. As in *The Sound and the Fury* and *As I Lay Dying*, the source of tragedy is connected with women's sexuality, but here sexuality has wider implications and is more confusing. Little Joe Christmas cannot separate the sexual encounter he innocently witnesses from his stealing the toothpaste and devouring it among the womansmelling clothes or from his identification as a Negro. Nor can he separate the anger of the mother-dietician from her attempt to reward him with money or from his being expelled from what served as his home. Sexuality, race, and money are linked in the first cause of his psychological story. All evoking guilt, they add negative dimensions to the enigma of his birth and his identity. Moreover, all the women in the novel perpetuate the confusion and guilt. Mrs. McEachern rewards him with food after McEachern punishes him for not learning his catechism. McEachern's punishment may be heartless but it is satisfying—a way of balancing accounts. Bobbie Allen, who introduces him to sexual difference and betrays the secret of his race, is a waitress and a prostitute; now food and sex, women's nurturing and physicality, become commodities. He goes to Joanna Burden by climbing through the kitchen window, where he finds the "nigger food" laid out for him. She rewards him for gratifying her needs by offering to make him a rich Negro lawyer, who would embrace the very law that disenfranchised him. Indeed, she puts him in the position where he must either accept the role of nigger-lawyer-lover (a role combining all the confusing associations with sex, race, and money) or become a nigger-rapist-murderer in the eyes of society and undergo a ritual castration to exculpate the guilt projected upon him through the women of a sexist, racist, capitalist society.

In causing him to choose his identity, Joanna is central to Christmas's existential story. Unlike the other central women, she is given a voice through which to tell her own story. But it is constrained—in two ways. First is its context in the authorial pattern: we are introduced to her as the woman in the burning house, mysteriously murdered, her head nearly cut off. She is identified with the house and with her body. But more important, her death is a punishment for what the community agrees is wrong— and, because we are given no alternative account, we are drawn into that community. The house is burning and she is found "laying on her side, facing one way, and her head was turned clean around like she was looking behind her." As the countryman who found her said, "If she could just have done that when she was alive, she might not have been doing it now" (101).

Ironically, we discover, she was always looking behind her, though not in the sense the countryman meant. For, like so many of the characters in the novel, she was governed by the past. Which brings us to the second reason why Joanna Burden's story is constrained. She tells Christmas her story, and we hear it from Christmas's point of view: *his consciousness* governs the selection and ordering of facts in *her story*. Moreover, the authorial voice enhances Christmas's voice in its use of free indirect speech and soon takes over completely, now echoing the Chronicles, or original stories, of the Old Testament: "Calvin Burden was the son of a minister named Nathaniel Burrington. The youngest of ten children, he ran away from home at the age of twelve" (265). We may not notice the shift from limited to omniscient perspective—and therefore authoritative judgment—for good reason. Indeed, Hugh Ruppersburg tells us that Joanna describes her family history (49). What might be called a misreading only attests to the power of the traditional narrator. Like the power of all traditional authority, it seems natural.

The authorial voice situates Joanna in time and space, and begins her story with the original father. Her story is thoroughly patriarchal, tracing a lineage from Nathaniel to Calvin to Nathaniel to her half brother Calvin, who "had just turned twenty when he was killed in the town two miles away by an ex-slaveholder and Confederate soldier named Sartoris, over a question of negro voting" (273). Joanna was not born until fourteen years after Calvin was killed, after Calvin's mother died and her father wrote to his cousin in New Hampshire asking to send him "a good woman for a wife. I dont care who she is, just so she is a good housekeeper and is at least thirtyfive years old" (275).

We have a hard time keeping the Calvins and Nathaniels straight or in distinguishing one generation from the next—and in following their logic. "I'll learn you to hate two things . . . or I'll frail the tar out of you," says Calvin the original Burden, "And those things are hell and slaveholders" (267). And her own father Nathaniel tells her that her grandfather Calvin and brother Calvin were "murdered not by one white man but by the curse which God put on a whole race before your grandfather or your brother or me or you were even thought of. A race doomed and cursed to be forever and ever a part of the white race's doom and curse for its sins" (278). The confusion in both names and logic has a mimetic function. The authorial voice speaking through the omniscient narrator is conflating various strands of the dominant American heritage. Original sin is the first cause, which the father can blame upon the daughter just as the white man can blame the black. The Puritan heritage is compounded by the New England capitalist ethos where God became the Almighty Bookkeeper, and by the patriarchal ethos of the slave-owning South. The pervasive black and white conflict throughout the novel reflects the conflicts of blacks and whites, women and men.

But the conflict is turned into a causal explanation and a judgment: blacks and the women are to blame. And who provides the explanation and judgment? All the white father figures: McEachern, Hines, Grimm, Stevens, the main narrator, and, most notably, the Rev. Hightower. One of the most powerful father figures in the novel, Hightower is, ironically, the most passive, even impotent. He is pictured sitting in his study window "waiting for that instant when all light has failed out of the sky," thinking, "*soon, now*" (64). He listens to Byron telling about Lena Grove and then Joe Christmas. He listens to the confused appeal of Mrs. Hines. He is aroused to action when he delivers Lena's child and when he lies to save Christmas's life, but the lie is futile, even ignored, as Percy Grimm easily knocks him aside. Hightower's primary role in the main story is not as an actor but as a listener. As a minister of God, he is the omniscient ear, having heard all the stories, and is capable of drawing the conclusion: "Poor man," he says of Christmas, "Poor mankind"(109).

Hightower, of course, is a failure as a father figure, just as he is a failure as a husband to his wife and as a minister to his congregation. But this does not affect the importance of his role as central listener throughout the novel. Indeed, his very passivity leads all the major characters to be drawn to him. Moreover, his chapter, the story of his life, comes right after Christmas is killed. The Hightower chapter may seem anticlimactic, especially since his story is so hard to follow and understand, but it authorizes the Christmas story climax.

Christmas's story has just reached its end; so we can now draw a straight line from the moment of his birth to the moment of his death. The omniscient narrator may have parodied the voice of God the Father in McEachern, Hines, and Grimm, but now he speaks with solemnity and prophetic hopefulness:

For a long moment he looked up at them with peaceful and unfathomable and unbearable eyes. Then his face, body, all, seemed to collapse, to fall in upon itself, and from out of the slashed garments about his hips and loins the pent black blood seemed to rush like a released breath. It seemed to rush out of his pale body like the rush of sparks from a rising rocket; upon that black blast the man seemed to rise soaring into their memories forever and ever. They are not to lose it, in whatever peaceful valleys, beside whatever placid and reassuring streams of old age, in the mirroring faces of whatever children they will contemplate old disasters and newer hopes. It will be there, musing, quiet, steadfast, not fading and not particularly threatful, but of itself alone serene, of itself alone triumphant. (513)

Nothing in the novel so far, nothing in the world of Jefferson, gives rise to such hopefulness. The only peaceful valley has been the one in which Christmas sat reading stories of violence before killing Joanna. Nor do any characters seem as if they will sit beside "placid and reassuring streams of old age." But the message is validated by the Hightower chapter that follows—first, because the religious theme is reinforced by the story of a minister, and second, because Hightower's story is the story of recognition and conversion. Hightower reviews his life and takes responsibility for his wife's unhappiness and death. As a result, he can fully understand all he has seen and heard and done. His understanding is ultimately beyond words; he sees a mandala, the archetypal symbol of unity. It is composed of all the faces; in the center Christmas's and Grimm's strive to "free themselves from one another, then fade and blend again" (543).

Hightower ends the main story with a vision of unity. But the unity—with Christmas and Grimm becoming equals and creating the energy of the mandala—undermines the tragedy of Christmas's life. And so does the position of Hightower's chapter. Coming right after Christmas's death and symbolic resurrection, the chapter validates the prophetic imagery which pictures "the pent black blood" seeming to rush from his loins "like a released breath" (513), mythologizes the Christmas story—and undermines its specific social and historical reality. The overall pattern of the novel, then, turns the Christmas story into the story of Nathaniel Burden's sacrificial victim—the black burden that the white man will continually try to raise.

An important part of this pattern, for it seems to offer an alternative set of values, is the story of Lena Grove, as she travels to and away from Jefferson—having given birth to an illegitimate son—totally unaffected by the main, tragic line of action. Lena is like Dilsey. She is a figure of innocence, hope, and selfless love, though her love is more narrowly defined as the instinctive love of a mother for her child. If Dilsey is denied sexuality and made safe by her age, Lena is denied her sexuality and made safe by being defined as a mother. She is a sympathetic caricature of the immaculate conception, a male fantasy of the ideal mother.

Though she is identified with her body from the very start, the authorial voice pictures it only as "swollen" and "shapeless"; indeed, our first explicit image of her body comes from Winterbottom: "I wonder where she got that belly?" (9). Though she gave into her sexual impulses and bore an illegitimate child, all we hear is that she learned to open and close her window without making a sound and "she had not opened it a dozen times hardly before she discovered that she should not have opened it at all" (6). And the only indication of her feelings is when, "sucking the rich sardine oil from her fingers with slow and complete relish," she stops for a moment: "Her face has drained of color, of its full, hearty blood, and she sits quite still, *hearing and feeling the implacable and immemorial earth*" (31, my emphasis). In naturalizing Lena, the authorial voice denies her a social dimension—and a voice of her own. It is almost as if Faulkner needed to repress, or at least counterbalance, the threatening voice of motherhood that emerged when he let Addie loose two years earlier in *As I Lay Dying*.

Lena's story is set almost entirely in the frame that opens and closes the novel, outside of Jefferson. In the opening frame, the authorial voice describes her as pregnant and traveling with placid self-assurance toward the man who promised to marry her; the pastoral imagery and slow pace of her chapter contrast with the violence and breathless pace of the scenes that dominate the novel's central story. In the central story she gives birth, totally unaware of the tragedy taking place in Jefferson, or of her positive effect on Byron. In the closing frame, Lena sexually excites Byron Bunch, but the danger of her sexuality is neutralized by the furniture dealer telling a funny story to his wife with a view to proving himself a better man than his comic protagonist. He describes Byron walking "toward the truck . . . like he had eggs under his feet." When Lena wakes up she is only surprised, a little put out, but not frightened, "and she says, not loud neither: 'Why, Mr Bunch. Aint you ashamed. You might have woke the baby too'. . . . I be dog if I dont believe she picked him up and set him back outside on the ground like she would that baby if it had been about six years old" (554–555). Byron returns the next morning: " 'I be dog if I'm going to quit now.' 'Aint nobody never said for you to quit,' says Lena" (558). Her last lines are: " 'My, my. A body does get around. Here we aint been coming from Alabama but two months, and now it's already Tennessee' " (559).

Lena's innocent translation of time into space is amplified by an authorial voice aware of the pun that identifies Lena with her body, and that places her in a comic-pastoral frame where her sexuality is neither a threat nor a promise. Lena is outside of time and human history. Like Hightower, she denies the Christmas story its social and historical meaning. She leads us to forget it.

In contrast to Lena, Byron is a member of the Jefferson community, who becomes involved with all the major characters. He is the timekeeper at the planing mill and in the novel as well, for he tells most of Christmas's story. He is Jefferson's Calvinist conscience. He also establishes the beginning of the Christmas story on a Friday morning, initiating what will become an authorial pattern that identifies Christmas with Christ. Naive, selfless, honest, passive, detached, having no apparent stake in Christmas's story, he would seem a trustworthy narrator. It is just Byron's trustworthiness, though, that makes Hines's infallibility seem credible. For Byron tells Hightower—and therefore the reader—what Mrs. Hines told him about the mad old man riding out into the night and finding his daughter and the circus man. Nor can we distinguish Byron's voice from the authorial voice that told the story of McEachern riding out to find Christmas at the dancehall and Grimm chasing Christmas through the streets of Jefferson, in the same breathless tone and language. Byron author-izes Hines's credibility—and his story of Christmas's origin.

As representative of both the community of Jefferson and the main narrator, Byron reflects the confluence of their values. But Byron changes. He leaves Jefferson. And he changes from a passive man who uses his religion to insulate himself from the complexities of human intercourse to a man who commits himself, takes risks, acts. Significantly, when he becomes an actor, he ceases to be a storyteller. The last story he tells is motivated to arouse Hightower to action. He does not tell us about Christmas's death or about Hightower's conversion, or even about his decision to leave Jefferson with Lena. As a man of action, he may be ineffectual and foolish, but his change reflects a heroic kind of choice and renunciation. He renounces the Calvinism, which insulated him from life, which sharpened the division between black and white, which devalued women's sexuality, which underwrote the view of life as a ledger where lives and actions could be balanced—and which was a driving force in Christmas's tragedy. And he also renounces the authorial discourse.

Byron's ultimate renunciation—of authorial discourse—reflects the difficulty of not only telling but imagining alternatives to canonical storylines, that is, to the logic, forms of action, goals, and language authors inherit. For the price he pays for his choice and renunciation is to become a character in the story of a new character, who reduces him to "the kind of fellow you wouldn't see the first glance if he was alone by himself in the bottom of a empty concrete swimming pool" (546).

Like Byron, the main narrator has also stopped speaking. But he still chooses his replacement. He cannot abdicate his authority. He is responsible for Byron's comic reduction, just as he is responsible for redeeming the murder of Joe Christmas by patterning his story on the story of Jesus Christ, and just as he is responsible for ending the story of a man—destroyed by particular social forces at a particular point in history—with an epilogue that is ahistorical, apolitical, and hopeful.

I have developed my argument of the novel's conservative pattern to an extreme. We should not forget that the disruptions and violent dislocations are potent, even though they give way to a story that is both linear and logical. The disruptions are presences that challenge causality and linear explanation. The authorial voice is outraged and uncomprehending; it cannot come to grips with a past and present in which it is entangled. And it adds a dimension of parody to the voices of McEachern, Hines, and Grimm; that is, it adds a perspective and judgment on their stories. If some voices, explanations, and judgments are privileged, they are also only part of a heteroglossia and polylogue among voices that may be unequal but nonetheless compete. What emerges is a pattern of contending voices that reflects the forces of Faulkner's society.

And what does this pattern look like? Central to the pattern—to the story of Joe Christmas—is the hole, or enigma of his birth and race. Regardless of his biological identity, a social identity is imposed on him by the world of the South. And those who impose it most powerfully are the novel's storytellers and principal listener— the voices and conscience of Jefferson society: a poor, religious fanatic; his powerless wife; a liberal lawyer; a workingman who comes close to acting heroically and establishing his independence; a minister of the church; and an authorial voice that is sometimes troubled, sometimes amused, sometimes amazed, sometimes awed, but most often outraged. Despite its outrage, though, the authorial voice validates the stories that deny Christmas his identity by fitting them into an author-ized narrative pattern and by weaving his language into theirs—or reflecting what is common in the language of ministers of the church (whether fanatic or liberal), men of law, men who tell heroic stories, and men who turn history into myth.

7

Absalom, Absalom!

J oe Christmas's identity is on the one hand denied and on the other hand constructed by the character-narrators of *Light in August*, as they fit him into a social stereotype. Nonetheless, he is a character in the novel's diagesis. Christmas acts, talks, and thinks in a storyline running from his birth to his death—which is independent of those constructed by the character-narrators. Thomas Sutpen, on the other hand, is a fiction. He is never more than a construction of now one, now another of the character-narrators. All we see are his reported, imagined, or fantasized actions.

Nor can his truly legendary actions be pictured, realistically imagined, fully recalled. We do not know how he "went" to the West Indies (297), how he "subdued" the rebellious Haitians (317), how he "put . . . aside" his first wife (300), or how he got the slaves, the furnishings, and the French architect for Sutpen's mansion. He abrupts upon the peaceful and decorous scene and sits silently on his horse "immobile, bearded and hand palm-lifted" (5). And Rosa can only begin to sketch the scene that climaxes her story: *"he stood with the reins over his arm . . . and spoke the bald outrageous words exactly as if he were consulting with Jones or with some other man about a bitch dog or a cow or mare"* (210).

Sutpen is beyond picturing—just like Kurtz in Conrad's *Heart of Darkness*. He is beyond comprehension, beyond measure—because he is the progenitor, the source of value and measure. Granted, he is not literally or historically the first. The town fathers (who were also self-made aristocrats, having come out of the frontier just a generation earlier) were there before him. But Sutpen affronted them with a frank, though idealized image of what they were like—frank in reflecting their violence and acquisitiveness, but idealized by appearing aristocratic and larger than life. And when they lost the Civil War, they made him into a legend, a fictional father.[1] So he became the mythic source of the succeeding generations. Or he became a mythic source of the language in which the narrators think. This discourse has its roots in classical tragedy, the Bible, the Puritan heritage of New England, the heritage of European imperialism, the myth of the frontier, the story of the self-made man, and the romance of Southern patriarchy.

Since they think in his language, the narrators who create Sutpen are also his creatures. That is, they think of themselves in terms of his story, and are therefore under the control of his discourse. But the narrators, with the exception of Mr. Compson, are motivated to become free by at least understanding Sutpen, which leads to a conflict between them and the very images they construct of him.

There is also a conflict among the narrators. Rosa is a participant, but even more an outraged victim; her story has the most immediacy and urgency. Mr. Compson heard Sutpen's story directly from his father, who witnessed Sutpen's development from the perspective of an established town father, and who heard the first part of the story from Sutpen himself—so Mr. Compson is the bearer of the patriarchal legend. Quentin is called upon by Rosa to witness and bear her tale, which he can only hear through the screens of his father's story about why one of Sutpen's sons killed his brother, and of his own story about the relationship of Sutpen's son and daughter. Shreve is not from the South, or even the United States; he has the most remote perspective, but is also romantic and capable of imagining the ultimate act of a lover and Southern gentleman—replacing Judith's picture with one of his mistress and child so that she will not grieve for him. And when Quentin and Shreve weave the story between them, they highlight the relationship between Henry and Bon.

But besides the conflict of perspectives, there is a conflict of narrative power. Quentin's father is the bearer of the patriarchal legend; though his story is incomplete, we are not expected to question its authority. Quentin's story is privileged by the authorial voice, which focuses on him first and last, and makes him the central consciousness. It is through Quentin that we hear Rosa's and Mr. Compson's stories. Shreve attains another kind of authority because of his close relationship to Quentin, his questioning and parody giving way to what is commonly thought to be an empathic imagination. But his view of Bon's romantic self-effacement derives from a culturally shared youthful romanticism, and his final statement—about "the Jim Bonds . . . going to conquer the western hemisphere" (471)—reflects how much racism he has absorbed from Quentin.

Rosa Coldfield's function in the novel is central, for she calls for Quentin, arouses his interest, and leads him to the decaying Sutpen mansion where he actually meets Henry. Moreover, as Rosa tells it, she was not only a witness but a participant, and more important a victim. It is her voice to which we should primarily attend. But Quentin mediates and co-opts her story; even in the section where we hear it directly, we are influenced by the framework he has established. And Quentin's view is authorized by the authorial voice, speaking to us in free indirect speech, or moving in the opening lines from outside to inside his mind, and sharing the same discourse and tone.

From a little after two oclock until almost sundown . . . they sat in what Miss Coldfield still called the office because her father had called it that— a dim hot airless room with the blinds all closed and fastened for forty-three summers because when she was a girl someone had believed that light and moving air carried heat and that dark was always cooler, and which (as the sun shone fuller and fuller on that side of the house) became latticed with yellow slashes full of dust motes which Quentin thought of as being flecks of the dead old dried paint itself blown inward from the scaling blinds as wind might have blown them. (3)

The authorial voice establishes the mold. The afternoon is still, hot, weary, and dead. Miss Coldfield sits in what she continues to call the office *because* her *father* had called it that. So her story begins with her father. But the blinds are fastened "because when she was a girl *someone* . . ." And who was that superstitious someone who believed that "light and moving air carried heat"? Not her father, of course, but her mother, who is never mentioned, or her aunt, nameless because she does not count. And now Quentin sees Rosa: "in the eternal black which she had worn for forty-three years now, whether for sister, father, or nothusband none knew, sitting so bolt upright in the straight hard chair that was so tall for her that her legs hung straight and rigid as if she had iron shinbones and ankles, clear of the floor with that air of impotent and static rage like children's feet" (3–4).

She is a mad, old, frustrated, spinster, as well as a petulant child, commanding our attention as she does Quentin's—but not our confidence. Linda Kauffman points out that most critics follow Quentin. And she counters the established view of Rosa with an eloquent and persuasive reconstruction of her story as "a last cry from one who remembers not only her youth, her hopes, her capacity for love but her sexual desire; who is, moreover, capable of imagining a world of possibility beyond the one that has negated her, as Quentin negates her here" (245).

Kauffman situates Rosa in a tradition of amorous discourse that she traces back to Ovid's *Heroides*. Minrose Gwin, in a reading that is equally poignant and persuasive, sees Rosa's discourse as that of the hysteric, who has become the source of much attention in feminist psychology. Like Freud's Dora, Rosa embodies, exposes, and breaks through patriarchal repression. She has been denied her desire as a woman and as a female subject, as well as the langauge that could express them. "What makes her text so powerful and so beautiful—so madly seductive—is that, like the narrative of the hysteric, it follows the laws of its own desire and constitutes itself out of their free play" (99).

I want to build on both arguments (though I will make more use of Kauffman because she points out a vision in Rosa's story that goes beyond hysteria). But I also want to resituate Rosa within the arena of contending narrators, and argue that critics, and ordinary readers as well, have been swayed by more than Quentin. For Quentin's view is authorized by the authorial voice. Moreover, the male narrators form a community of storytellers where the conflicts in perspective are subsumed into a common discourse that derives from the very subject they are interrogating.

As Kauffman points out, Rosa tells a different story. Indeed, she does not tell a story at all but laments, pleas, demands, confronts an absent other. Moreover, her discourse is modeled on the loom rather than the ledger. She thinks in terms of relationship, interdependence, touch and feeling, rather than acquisition and abstraction. She "toils to give a gift of love to the woman who will marry the man she loves" (275). But it is important to add that, while her discourse is different, even revolutionary, it is not independent of the discourse shaping the male story.

Rosa's is a double-voiced discourse. The voice of amorous love does, as Kauffman says, affirm *"that-might-have-been,"* the possibility of love and faith, "despite the brutality of Sutpen's rejection, despite all the waste and grief and sorrow" (273). But it is also rooted in a tradition of romantic love that had become part of the Southern "aristocratic" male discourse. Rosa tells us she *"became all polymath love's androgynous advocate"* (182)—which is as abstract as anything Sutpen could conceive. She recalls *"the spring and summertime which is every female's who breathed above dust, beholden of all betrayed springs held over from all irrevocable time"* (178–179)—fitting herself into the pattern of the "universal" female constructed by male desire. She pictures herself as the *"dreamer clinging yet to the dream as the patient clings to the last thin unbearable ecstatic instant of agony in order to sharpen the savor of the pain's surcease*" (175)—romanticizing her passivity, identifying her love as a sickness, and limiting possibility to the dream.

In one voice, as Kauffman argues, Rosa follows the transgressive and defiant tradition where the heroine transforms herself "from the archetypal Woman Who Waits into the Woman Who Writes" (25), or in this case speaks. But in the other voice she speaks as a Woman Who Waits. Rosa is defiant, subversive, but in telling her story she struggles against a dominant discourse that retains its power even when it is being defied and subverted.

Her struggle against the dominant discourse is also reflected in the relation of her story to the dominant storyline. For while the dominant storyline is broken up, each section drives toward a dramatic climax, which seems to explain the previous series of events. Of course, the pattern results from the choices made by a master storyteller keeping us in suspense, but while the choices may be made for rhetorical or pragmatic reasons, they help create a pattern of values and meaning that exclude the values and meanings Rosa is trying to convey.

Rosa begins the narrative with Sutpen's arrival and leads up to the climax of the first chapter, where Ellen, Judith, and Henry witness his battle with a "wild negro." They are "both naked to the waist and gouging at one another's eyes as if their skins should not only have been the same color but should have been coloured with fur too." When Ellen arrives she sees "her husband and the father of her children standing there naked and panting and bloody to the waist and the negro just fallen evidently, lying at his feet and bloody too save that on the negro it merely looked like grease or sweat" (31).

This is what Joseph Boone insightfully calls a "primal scene" where "the act of parental copulation to which the young child is exposed is replaced, significantly, by an emblem of the homosocial, exclusively male, network of power that governs Sutpen's world" ("Creation," 223–224). Boone argues that because the father forces Henry to witness the ritual of male competition, and because the mother's intrusion has no effect, the homosocial replaces the heterosexual paradigm in forming male identity. But we should add that the "primal scene" is conveyed through Ellen's eyes, that the climax of this episode is Ellen's discovery of Judith, and that the ritual is central to Judith's identity since she witnesses it not just voluntarily but eagerly. Moreover, the episode is the culmination of Rosa's story in the opening chapter. The voice we hear reflects the frustration, outrage, and rebellion of a woman who has been excluded from the center of power. But the animal associations in her racist description of the "wild negro" derive from the conflicting voice that, while excluding her, nonetheless produces a repressed desire for the wild animal in Sutpen.

Of course, the climax is Quentin's, since it is his mind upon which we focus. Or it derives from the authorial voice, the central narrator, who ends the section and shifts his focus to create suspense, as well as to authorize Quentin's story. But now I want to emphasize the way Rosa's double voice is affected by the novel's pattern of development, and show how the ritual affects the female as well as male identity.

In the second chapter Quentin leads us to question Rosa's author-ity by beginning Sutpen's story again, now with his father's version of Sutpen's arrival. Mr. Compson focuses on Sutpen as a "public enemy" (50), building and furnishing Sutpen's Hundred, laying "deliberate siege" to Mr. Coldfield's cash and respectability (48), and courting his daughter. The first episode of his story climaxes with Sutpen's marriage—which is the ultimate outrage to the society where power relations and forms of acquisition are disguised in decorous forms. Sutpen is a barbarian, a threat to the religion, manners, family, and destiny of the Southern white race. He is a threat because he embodies the urges repressed by decorous manners, religious formalities, and the institution of the family in its public manifestation—the paternalistic rule of the plantation.

It is interesting that Ellen hardly figures in this part of the story, even though it is she who is getting married. Although Mr. Compson might ignore Ellen because she is a woman, he does foreground the aunt and turns her into a central character who pushes Sutpen into the background, insists on a big wedding, and forces the ceremony on the town. By shifting from Sutpen to the aunt, Mr. Compson shifts the blame to an unpredictable and unfathomable woman, who "being a woman . . . was doubtless one of that league of Jefferson women who on the second day after the town saw him . . . agreed never to forgive him for not having any past, and who had remained consistent." But who also probably thought that "any wedding is better than no wedding and a big wedding to a villain preferable to a small one with a saint" (61). The aunt is entirely Mr. Compson's construct; we hear of her only in his story. His fanatic spinster is implicitly blamed for forcing upon the town the aspiring patriarch, who, because of his blatant conduct, is the most virulent threat to the institution of the family.

Chapter Three begins with a non sequitur. We have just seen the townsfolk throwing garbage at Sutpen and learned that this did not keep those same people from "driving out to Sutpen's Hundred . . . to hunt his game and eat his food again and on occasion gathering at night in his stable while he matched two of his wild negroes against one another as men match game cocks or perhaps even entered the ring himself"—while Ellen weeps (68–69). And now we hear Quentin saying to his father, "If he threw [Miss Rosa] over, I wouldn't think she would want to tell anybody about it" (70).

But, though illogical, Quentin's assertion establishes a sequence that seems to link the two stories, and mislead us into thinking that Sutpen threw over Rosa, when, we will later learn, she made the decision not to play the role of "bitch dog or a cow or mare" (210). Mr. Compson reinforces Quentin's assertion by responding with " 'Ah' "—as if to say, "Well, you know these women." And he continues as if he were going to explain why. But he does not explain. He tells Rosa's story from the time she was born, focusing first on the role of the aunt, then on Bon's courtship of Judith and the relationship between Bon and Henry. He concludes the third chapter with a cliffhanger, as Wash Jones shouts "Air you Rosie Coldfield?" (107). And in the fourth chapter he turns the story away from Rosa, focusing on Henry and Bon's trip to New Orleans.

With no facts, he imagines a scene of the same psychological order as Sutpen's naked combat: the "primary blind and mindless foundation of all young male living dream and hope" (138). He pictures "the formal, almost ritual, preparations," with Bon "finicking almost like a woman," before entering "a place created for and by voluptuousness," where the "country boy with his simple and erstwhile untroubled code in which females were ladies or whores or slaves looked at the apotheosis of two doomed races presided over by its own victim—a woman with a face like a tragic magnolia, the eternal female, the eternal Who-suffers; the child, the boy, sleeping in silk and lace to be sure yet complete chattel of him who, begetting him, owned him body and soul to sell (if he chose) like a calf or puppy or sheep" (140–141).

Though less powerful, this is more complex than the "primal scene" of Sutpen's deadly battle with the "wild negro." This too is a homosocial ritual of initiation, with no women witnesses, but with a woman—Bon's octoroon mistress—at the center, and with his son, "sleeping in silk and lace," owned body and soul by the father, who could sell him as a whim.

The first ritual scene takes place in the male world of the father's stable; it centers on the manly act of naked battle, where the white man virtually kills the black man. It is a ritualization of homosocial relationships, a celebration of violence, a demonstration of the father's power, and a valorization of racism as well as the master-slave relation. The second scene also ritualizes the power of the homosocial community, sublimates the violence of male prerogative, and relates heterosexual desire and the patriarchal family to imperial conquest and slavery. But it takes place in the mother's dark voluptuous world—what Freud called the "dark continent"—that the white man must conquer and turn into a commodity. The white man victimizes, commodifies, and even packages an idealized black woman ("taken at childhood, culled and chosen and raised more carefully than any white girl" [144]) to produce an androgynous mulatto, not to be loved but used or sold at whim. The two interrelated tableaux, as we will see, are central to the discourse of which Sutpen is the symbolic father.

Mr. Compson has shifted the focus of Rosa's story by constructing a scene that is, on the one hand, beyond the limits of Rosa's imagination and, on the other, central to the "self" image she tries to achieve. But he is not through. He now focuses on Judith and the letter she receives from Bon. Indeed, he creates a framework where every reader and critic I know sees an arrogant declaration as a lyric expression of love. "*We have waited long enough*," says Bon. And then, imposing himself upon her: "*You will notice how I do not insult you either by saying I have waited*" (162). Finally, Mr. Compson returns to Henry and Bon as they approach the gate. He climaxes his story by finishing the speech Wash began at the end of the last chapter: " 'Air you Rosie Coldfield? Then you better come on out yon. Henry has done shot that durn French feller. Kilt him dead as a beef' " (165). Through this suspense and repetition Mr. Compson has displaced Rosa and established the goal of the male story: to answer the question of why Henry killed Bon. By turning Rosa's quest for recognition into the quest for a rational answer, or Rosa's lyric cry into a detective story (which Poe called "a tale of ratiocination"), he has established the basis for rationalizing the historical facts of violent acquisition, slavery, incest, and murder.

"*So they will have told you*" (166), begins Rosa, intruding herself into the male story and recognizing her role in the public legend. "*But they cannot tell you how I on went up the drive*" (168). They could not have told Quentin that her story begins with the "Sutpen coffee-colored face" of Clytie, who bars the stairs but recognizes her—"*she did me more grace and respect than anyone else I knew; I knew that from the instant I had entered that door, to her of all who knew me I was no child*" (172). Rosa's story begins with an initiation into adulthood (she was fourteen at the time) and an act of recognition, or with an act of mutual recognition, since, in barring the way, Clytie also touches her: *"there is something in the touch of flesh with flesh which abrogates, cuts sharp and straight across the devious intricate channels of decorous ordering."* But Rosa, reacting as a jealous and abandoned lover, establishes her identity as a white gentlewoman and puts Clytie in her place: *"Take your hand off me, nigger!"* (173).

Rosa's initiation into adulthood, then, implicates her in the system that denies blacks and women identities of their own. Her story has two foci. She becomes *"all polymath love's androgynous advocate,"* where the voice of feminine desire or that of the repressed hysteric struggles against the voice of internalized male desire. And she suffers Sutpen's *"bald outrageous words"* that sounded *"as if he were consulting with Jones or with some other man about a bitch dog or a cow or mare,"* that declare her a commodity of exchange, and that deny her desire and subjectivity.[2] But it is wrong to call her monologue a story. Indeed, Gwin shows how it refuses to be contained in a story. And Kauffman points out that she does not tell what happened; she shows the effects. "Her discourse . . . disrupts the dichotomies of diegesis and mimesis, of present and past, for what Quentin hears is not a mere story but its repercussions" (244–245). And the repercussions vary as, "torn by a thousand conflicting emotions, she oscillates from love to hate, forgiveness to revenge, pathos to despair" (247).

Rosa is far more complex than the monomanical Sutpen, the predictable Mr. Compson, even the ambivalent Quentin, as she rebels against the male story, strives for recognition, and tries to give voice to the absence she embodies in a frankly idealized Bon. For the discourse in which she thinks and dreams is part of the same Southern, male discourse that excludes her—or turns her into a mad, old spinster. It also turns her into an accomplice in her own self-effacement—when, first she pictures herself as the passive lover in a futile love plot, and then imagines that Sutpen could salvage her dream or at least give her some identity. He was *"my best my only chance in this: an environment where at best and even lacking war my chances would have been slender enough since I was not only a Southern gentlewoman but the very modest character of whose background and circumstances must needs be their own affirmation"* (211).

Rosa will not allow herself to be contained in the male story, for she refuses to tell us Sutpen's *"bald outrageous words."* But she nonetheless gives way to the public story: *"They will have told you how I came back home.*" And the public story becomes part of the repertoire of nursery rhymes and childhood taunts: "*Rosie Cold- field, lose him, weep him; caught a man but couldn't keep him*" (210). She continues to assert herself, but her voice ceases to command much attention. She forgives Sutpen and recognizes her kinship with Ellen, and Wash Jones's "*fatherless daughter*" (214). Indeed, her story continues right up to the death of Thomas Sutpen. But Quentin is no longer listening. He upstages Rosa and brings her chapter to an end, imagining Henry "with his shaggy bayonet-trimmed hair, his gaunt worn unshaven face, his patched and faded gray tunic, the pistol still hanging against his flank" speaking with his sister "in short brief staccato sentences like slaps, as if they stood breast to breast striking one another in turn, neither making any attempt to guard against the blows." And Quentin's italicized passage displaces the italics that marked Rosa's voice in her chapter:

Now you cant marry him.
Why cant I marry him?
Because he's dead.
Dead?
Yes, I killed him. (215)

Then Rosa dies—and her story is lost. Suddenly we find ourselves in Cambridge, Massachusetts. Quentin is looking at the letter from his father telling him that "*Miss Rosa Coldfield was buried yesterday*" (217). Shreve fills in Sutpen's "*bald outrageous words.*" Quentin tells how he was killed by Wash Jones for the insult to his daughter when she failed to bear Sutpen a son. But in the next chapter he begins all over again, establishing the second pole of the novel's dialogic center. He tells the story Sutpen told his grandfather—about his origin in the mountains of West Virginia, and how his family slid "back down out of the mountains" (278), and of the outrage he suffered when the "monkey nigger" would not let him in the front door of the big house, up to his "innocent" question: "You see, I had a design in my mind. Whether it was a good or a bad design is beside the point; the question is, Where did I make the mistake in it" (329).

In two structurally central chapters, Rosa and Sutpen are presented in their own words. Rosa's chapter is short, italicized, intense, and direct;[3] Sutpen's is long and indirect, though authoritative since it comes from his reliable mentor, General Compson. At the center of this novel then—at the center of the arena of contending voices—is a dialogue, or agon, between Rosa and Sutpen. Unlike Addie in her struggle with the community of male storytellers, Rosa loses. For, while Addie had to tell her story in the language of the fathers, she could violate it, turn the story of a heroic journey into a joke, intrude a disturbing view of "motherhood," and expose the discourse that constructed her identity. Rosa tries to tell an independent story, but she can barely make herself heard because she embraces the language of the fathers, of which Sutpen is the symbolic source. This is not to say that Rosa does not have a profound impact, that her hysteria does not break through and expose the male discourse, or that she does not embody the discourse of feminine desire and a world of possibility beyond that of her auditors. Only—as the history of Faulkner criticism attests—the voice of feminine desire had to contend with the internalized voice of male desire, which is enhanced by the male narrators and the narrative design.

She also loses because Quentin stops listening—because the problems inherent in her story are not as important to Quentin and Shreve, who go on to imagine, or construct, the story of Henry and Bon. Rosa's need for recognition is replaced by Henry's need to be independent of his father and Bon's need to be recognized by him.[4] Rosa's amorous discourse gives way to Bon's final romantic gesture.

And Thomas Sutpen gives way to Henry, who holds the answer to what has become the novel's driving question: why he shot Bon. It is not because of the bigamy, we learn, and not because of the incest—but because of the miscegenation. This is what Quentin heard from Henry. This is what he was able to tell his father. As John Irwin points out, Quentin wins the struggle for authority with his father ("Dead Father," 156). But we only learn of this indirectly, when Shreve wonders about Mr. Compson getting "an awful lot of delayed information awful quick" (332). All we see of the dramatic scene where Quentin confronts Henry is:

And you are——?
Henry Sutpen.
And you have been here——?
Four years.
And you came home——?
To die. Yes.
To die?
Yes. To die.
And you have been here——?

Four years.
And you are——?
Henry Sutpen. (464–465)

Quentin cannot finish the scene that reflects his victory over his father. So his victory, his liberation, is incomplete. This is not because his father is so powerful, but because his absent, symbolic father is the source of the language in which Quentin must think.

When young Sutpen was denied entrance to the front door of the white house, not by the white man who owned all the land and "niggers" but by the "monkey nigger" dressed in the white man's livery, he thought: "If you were fixing to combat them that had the fine rifles, the first thing you would do would be to get yourself the nearest thing to a fine rifle. . . . But this aint a question of rifles. So to combat them you have got to have what they have that made them do what he did. You got to have land and niggers and a fine house to combat them with" (297).

But this was not young Sutpen's lesson. Nor should we be misled by Mr. Compson and his father into thinking he was innocent. "Innocence," when used this way, is a form of vindication and recognition by the privileged class. Ab Snopes is not considered innocent in *The Hamlet*, when he walks through the front door of the white house, wipes the manure off his shoes on to Major de Spain's hundred dollar white rug, and has one of his strapping daughters wash it with something like "brickbats instead of soap" (15). And Rosa is not considered innocent in her reaction to Sutpen. Sutpen may be a threat to the established class, but he recognizes its authority, and General Compson was secure enough to recognize him.

The lesson young Sutpen learned was how to get from the idealized frontier to the realistic world of the American South. And in defining the passage, he defined their common ground. In the idealized frontier, men were equal—except in strength. Women were not equal to men, though "his pap" had said something about how his mother, that "fine wearying woman" who never appears in the story, had got him "even that far West" (278). But strength and aggressiveness counted: the man who ruled was the strongest man, or the man who could get the finest rifle. The idealized frontier, then, was founded upon male strength, violence, and aggression. What Sutpen had to learn was that intangible symbols of respectability were more powerful than objects, even fine rifles. Even more, he had to learn acquisitiveness, not of goods (the basis of Coldfield's motivation and Northern capitalism), but of land, slaves, a fine house, and a family with a male heir.

Sutpen is threatening not because he does not understand the values of Southern tradition and the meaning of family relations but because he does. For as a self-made father he is not so different from the historical fathers who bought slaves, broke up their families for their profit, satisfied their lusts on black women, and, though they considered slaves as their children, fit them into the design of their destiny. Nor is his logic any different, based, as Linda Kauffman points out, on the ledger, the "list of Negroes bought, bred, and sold," which reveals "how fundamental the equation of sex and money is in the false economy of the Sutpen's design and, alas, in the entire South" (267)—indeed, the entire country.

Even more important, when Sutpen found out that he needed "land and niggers and a fine house to combat them with," he "went to the West Indies." If one part of Sutpen's story connects the frontier with the Southern plantation, another part connects the history of America with the history of European imperialism. And it connects the American myths of achievement with the discourse of African conquest.

Martin Green argues convincingly for the continuum between British imperialism and America's penetration into the frontier:

The case of Daniel Boone and the invasion of Kentucky shows how local and popular, how American, the imperialist dynamic was, even before 1776. In pouring through the Cumberland Gap, and driving the Indians out of their lands, the settlers were going against the treaties and wishes of the government in London. The frontier—not the court—was where one saw the empire in action. And American high culture, though reluctantly, followed and reflected that action. As the U.S. gradually became the leading edge of the modern [imperialist] system, so did its literature develop the leading form of adventure. (129)

The myth of Thomas Sutpen is based on the myth of the frontier, a virgin space but also a dark continent, where a strong enough man could penetrate and take what he wanted. It is also based on the myth of the self-made man, who could rise above his father's class if he was strong enough to take what he wanted. It is based on the myth of the patriarch, the symbolic father, the source of law, value, and the language that valorizes conquest. It is based on the myth of his son, who needs to gain authority from his father. And the myth of incest, which is one way the son can gain authority. And the story of male bonding, which establishes the dominant male community. And the story of the romantic hero, who embodies male aspirations in decorous forms.

Of course Sutpen fails. Joseph Boone demonstrates how the father's story in *Absalom, Absalom!* contains the seeds of its own deauthorization. "Sutpen's self-proclaimed authority" is founded upon deep anxieties about male identity and the status of fatherhood. He cannot ultimately control the threatening difference, the otherness of women, blacks, and his own children, who undermine his design. "As Shreve's prophecies on the last page warn of Sutpen's dynastic dreams, there is always the nigger who gets away: all those fractious, marginal, excrescences of plot, all those emblems of 'nonmaleness,' of otherness, that refuse to mirror the father or confine their desires to his preformulated masterplot" ("Creation," 232).

But Sutpen's failure and the deauthorizations of his story occur within the central, white male storyline, which turns black people and women into marginal characters, which persists despite Rosa's attempt to tell another story, and which must be told in the language of which Sutpen is the symbolic source. The discourse does contain the seeds of its own deauthorization, but it is nonetheless capable of marginalizing and co-opting voices that oppose it.

FAULKNER SHARED Joyce's ambivalence about history and language, but he had much greater reverence for what Bakhtin called the "absolute past." He undermines the unitary language and disrupts the authoritative plotline in ways that challenge causal explanation. He parodies the mythic quest and depicts the poignant struggle of a woman telling a revolutionary story of motherhood against the hegemony of male storytellers. He creates a carnival of contending voices that crosses the lines of gender, race, and class. He interrogates history and heroism and treats them comically. But he does not draw what was sacrosanct and beyond question into "a zone of crude contact," finger it familiarly on all sides, turn it upside down, inside out, peer at it from above and below, take it apart, dismember, lay bare, and expose it (Bakhtin, 23). His most ambitious novel interrogates "a world of 'beginnings' and 'peak times' in the national history, a world of fathers and of founding of families, a world of 'firsts' and 'bests.' " But the epic and absolute past of the American South is inaccessible to its interrogators—the authorial voice and his character-narrators. For, despite their common outrage and different perspectives, they share the language of a "reverent . . . descendent" (Bakhtin, 13–15). Despite the range of contending narrators, the dominant narrative community is white, male, and established, or has at least internalized that view; it draws in the reader who identifies with their need for order. And the comic tall-tale that Faulkner tells so well reveals itself as an ambitious text, a story that valorizes the myth of success even as it illuminates its failure, that celebrates the patriarch even as it rages against his tyranny, and that extends the form of imperialist adventure even as it deplores its consequences.

Virginia Woolf:
An Other
Modernism

8

Woolf's Struggle with Author-ity

Joyce struggled against the author-ity of the Catholic Church, the British Empire, and a literary canon that denied him an authentic voice. But he was the oldest son, and his father had enough money for James's "educational fund"—or at least to start him off with an upper-class, Jesuit education. He may have been alienated by his lower social standing at Clongowes but he was nurtured there; at Belvedere and University College he took to the canon, learned it systematically—and was not only encouraged but rewarded by the very authorities he would reject.[1]

He rebelled at least as early as the beginning of *Dubliners*— declaring "I will not serve" in forms that become more and more iconoclastic. But "I will not serve" is a performative speech act (like "I thank you" or "I promise," where saying performs the act of thanking or promising). And to say "I will not serve" performs the act of echoing Satan in Genesis; it invokes and perpetuates the very Father and the very line of author-ity it repudiates. Joyce may parody, undermine, bring the canon into what Bakhtin calls the "zone of crude contact," but he requires that we recall or more often learn the canon, put it to active use in our reading, and even teach it to a new generation of readers. Furthermore, he requires that we admire the way he parodies and undermines canonical writers. I do not mean to imply that Joyce was dominated by the canon he parodied, undermined, overturned, and extended. Rather, I am arguing that Joyce was less alienated from the canonical author-ity, he was more at ease with it—after all, he finally became the father of modern fiction—just because he was a man. And Virginia Woolf was more alienated from the canon just because she was a woman, and her novels do not depend on it.

Woolf, of course, came from a much higher social class than either Joyce or Faulkner. She moved in a social circle they could never enter and had continual access to the social and literary power structure of England. Though she lectured to working-class women, and related them to women of the middle class in being mutually enslaved by the patriarchy,[2] she depended on her servants and extended little sympathy to the lower classes in her novels. More-over, the voice in her *Times Literary Supplement* book reviews is hard to distinguish from those of her male colleagues, who had been educated in the public schools and the universities. And, as Gillian Beer has shown, her novels are filled with echoes of Victorian au-thors, though they are parodied and arranged in pastiche.

Woolf received a good education from her father's library, which is pictured in *To the Lighthouse*. Sitting in the boat on the way to the lighthouse, Cam recalls her father's study—where, "if he saw she was there, reading a book, he would ask her, as gently as any one could, Was there nothing he could give her?" (282). Nonetheless, the study was a world presided over by old men who sat in armchairs, reading *The Times*, who took up her eager ques-tions "with their clean hands (they wore grey-coloured clothes; they smelt of heather) and they brushed the scraps together, turn-ing the paper, crossing their knees, and said something now and then very brief" (281). Cam pictures her father, and the old men presiding over the library, as benevolent but nonetheless forbid-ding; she was excluded by their manners, their cleanliness, their movements, and their discourse. Moreover, she sensed the ease with which their power was disguised by their manners, cleanli-ness, movement, and discourse.

Louise DeSalvo gives us two important insights into this power, as it manifested itself in the Victorian family and deeply affected Virginia Woolf. The first is indirect but major: the Victorian family was a site of physical abuse, incest, and sexual violence. Virginia was traumatically molested by her half brother Gerald Duckworth at age six or seven and continually molested and probably raped by George Duckworth during the most trying years of her adolescence—and the Stephen family abetted such action not only through neglect but by its general support of its several violent men.

The second is direct: about the time of Virginia's birth, her half sister Laura was having problems reading, or she was not reading well enough to suit her father. Leslie prescribed various forms of punishment, increasing in severity, and was outraged when she whined or cried or worked herself into a fury—that is, when she did not submit without response. His final solution was to move her into a different part of the house, where she lived for six or seven years, throughout Virginia's childhood. At nineteen or twenty, Laura was sent away from the family; at twenty-one she was sent to an asylum. "Seen in the light of Laura's treatment," DeSalvo con-cludes, "Virginia Woolf's childhood and adolescent habit of reading voraciously—'Gracious, child, how you gobble,' her father would say—becomes terrifyingly comprehensible. Laura had been locked away, it must have seemed, for not having read well enough, for having stumbled over her words. Every time that Virginia knocked on the door of her father's study, and asked him to hand down yet another volume, she was proving that she was not Laura: she was keeping herself from being called perverse; she was buying the right to live a life within the family; she was keeping herself from being locked up, from being locked away, from being sent to an asylum" (34).

Nor, DeSalvo demonstrates, was this kind of treatment unusual in the Victorian family, where the father ruled supreme, where though standing for discipline he could rage and whimper, where the mother was idealized and overworked, where children were supposed to brighten the lives of their parents but nonetheless had to be broken in and taught obedience, where the sons would be able to vent their feelings and indulge their passions, where the daughters were taught to be subservient and repress their feelings, where the dark private world of the home was insulated from public view, where child abuse was a logical result of the family structure, where incest was common—indeed, where Virginia's sexual abuse by her half brothers throughout her childhood and adolescence, as well as the effects on her unhappy life, could go unnoticed.

Cam took pleasure in "watching her father write, so equally, so neatly from one side of the page to another" (282). But, as Elizabeth Abel points out, she never attempted to decipher the meaning of what he wrote: both the father as text and the father's texts remain "hermetic" to Cam. Woolf, on the other hand, learned to read both the father's texts and the father as text (and DeSalvo describes her heroic struggle). So she shared Joyce's ambivalence about history and language, though for a very different reason, and this ambivalence is reflected in her book reviews, her early pronouncements about politics and literature, and in all of her novels. But as she developed into a self-conscious woman writer, she developed a different relationship to the authority of the epic and absolute past, the world of fathers and founding families, and traditional literary discourse. Indeed, because she understood that traditional author-ity is gendered, she developed an alternative form of author-ity and founded an independent line of modern fiction. In her struggle with author-ity, she gives us a perspective on Joyce's and Faulkner's achievements—and leads us to a fuller understanding of the politics of narration.

Two Voyages to the Lighthouse

Let me begin to examine Woolf's struggle with author-ity by taking a cue from her *A Room of One's Own*, turning her invention of Shakespeare's sister on its head, and asking: how would Virgil Woolf, Virginia's unborn brother, have written *To the Lighthouse*? For, after all, Virgil would have had a journey-man's experience. Virgil would have followed in the footsteps of Odysseus, who journeyed round the world for ten years but had to come home to prove he was a father, husband, warrior, king. He certainly would have identified with Aeneas, whose journey led to the founding of Rome. And he would have identified with his own namesake, who led Dante on a journey through Hell and Purgatory to the founding (oops) vision of Heaven.

Journeys—voyages of discovery, intrusions into the unknown, the acquisition of fortune, the establishment of family-kingdom-empire, the appropriation of mystery—had been a means by which men established their identities. The goal of a journey was not just a place but mastery, power, and a self unified by its achievement. When male writers came to write the middle-class novel, they invented the *Bildungsroman*, the *Entwicklungsroman*, the *Künstlerroman*, where journey-men leave home, learn, develop, and finally achieve a social identity and a position of power in a less glamorous business world. But their heroines—with the telling exception of Moll Flanders—would have to stay home, or become servants in another home, and marry or die. Nor could women, when they came to write novels, authentically fashion their heroines on the models of journey-men.

But Virgil was no woman. So writing *To the Lighthouse* would be easy. He would focus on James Ramsay, beginning with the young boy cutting out a picture of a refrigerator from the illustrated catalog of the Army and Navy Stores, while his mother knitted a reddish brown stocking and imagined him all red and ermine on the Bench or directing a stern and momentous enterprise in some crisis of public affairs. James would be excited, anticipating a voyage to the lighthouse, if the weather would only be fine tomorrow. "But," his father would say, "it won't be fine." Were there an ax handy, or a poker, any weapon that would have gashed a hole in his father's breast and killed him, there and then, James would have seized it. Mr. Ramsay, lean as a knife, narrow as a blade, would grin sarcastically, not only with the pleasure of disillusioning his son and casting ridicule upon his wife, but also with some secret conceit at his own accuracy of judgment. (Passages from *To the Lighthouse* are liberally play-giarized in this section. Note what happens when Virginia's voice and story are mediated by Virgil's.)

"But it may be fine—I expect it will be fine," his mother would say, assuringly. His father would be right, of course, it would not be fine the next day. And it would take ten years before James would undertake his journey to the lighthouse. His mother would be dead, and so would his sister Prue. He would go in Mr. Macalister's boat with his father and his younger sister Cam. James would steer, still wary of his father's judgment as he headed for the stark tower on the bare rock. Mr. Macalister would point out the spot where three men had drowned. His father would sit reading, though he would still preside over the journey. James would dread the moment when his father would look up and speak sharply to him about something or other. And if he did, James would think, then I shall take a knife and strike him to the heart. Yes, he would repeat the very words he had said to himself when he sat at his mother's feet cutting out pictures, but he would not be thinking of her, not once on this last lap of his journey. Nor would he view his father as the enemy. He too would realize that the lighthouse was a stark tower on a bare rock after all, and feel that it satisfied him, confirming some obscure feeling about his own character. Indeed, he would be sharing his father's knowledge, repeating fierce lines half aloud, exactly as his father had said them. Now James would be steering a steady course alongside the rocks where waves broke in white splinters like smashed glass. And now his father would look up, take out his watch, make some mathematical calculation, and say triumphantly: "Well done! You steered us like a born sailor."

Virgil would have shown James freeing himself from his mother's apron strings, and coming through the Oedipal battle with his father. He would give the story of an ordinary young man's development epic resonance. He would have a fine beginning and a resounding climax. But what about the middle? How could he fill in those ten years? It wasn't a journey like that of Odysseus or Aeneas or Dante. His hero had not even ventured out into the world; he had only gone through the ordinary rounds of adolescent domestic life. What kind of journey was that? Granted, James Joyce had filled the journey of his *Ulysses* with details from contemporary domestic life, but he had limited the wanderings of Leopold Bloom to a single day. Virgil was no piker. He'd have laid his money on Homer any day: he had committed himself to ten years. What was he to do? Where was he to turn? He had sworn he wouldn't ask his sister. He wouldn't even tell her what he was doing, why he had been keeping her out of the little storage room, which he'd cleaned up and called his own. He had never been able to keep his mind on her little books, as they switched from here to there and never focused on anything really important, where all he could feel was an incessant shower of atoms. But all the while he must have known that he'd have to turn to Virginia.

Virginia, of course, had solved the problem years before. She had devoted almost two hundred pages to the evening when Mrs. Ramsay sat in front of the drawing-room window with her little son James, while Lily Briscoe painted their picture and Mr. Ramsay intruded with his facts about the weather. But her story encompassed so much more than the agon between a father an a son. It included a whole set of relationships—in a household of seven other children and the house guests, Lily Briscoe, Charles Tansley, Augustus Carmichael, William Banks, Minta Doyle, and Paul Rayley—over which Mrs. Ramsay presided. And the point of view had shifted from character to character, so we could never know any one of them as a unified self but only as she or he saw or was seen by another character at a particular moment in a particular situation.

And there was another hundred pages that focused on the voyage to the lighthouse. But that voyage was continually interrupted by the story of Lily Briscoe finishing her painting. Lily finally realized her independence from both Mr. and Mrs. Ramsay and was able to imagine the father and son landing on the rocks. Then she "looked at her canvas . . . with a sudden intensity" and "drew a line there, in the centre. It was done; it was finished. Yes, she thought, laying down her brush in extreme fatigue, I have had my vision" (310).

Virginia's problem was different from Virgil's, for her story did not have a simple focus and was not primarily linear. It was about a set of relationships, focused on in a new way. James Naremore coins the term "multipersonal subjectivity"; he sees Woolf composing a "total emotional life" that connects the feelings of her different characters (122). The narrative voice provides continuity, relates one character's view to another's, and links two temporally separated views of the same characters—sometimes within the same sentence. But while the narrator is omniscient, "she lacks the tone of certainty that one finds, for example, in George Eliot" (126). It is not what she lacks, though, but what she gains that is important: an openness to the differences and conflicts among the different subjects, including the narrator, which makes the "multipersonal subjectivity" truly multiple, heterogeneous, polylogic—and not unified as Naremore implies. And what she lacks—or gives up—is the very certainty that characterizes the traditional authorial voice, that imposes unity upon its plot and characters.

Woolf was developing an authorial voice that gains authority without domineering—that is, without imposing her order (proportion) on the others, and without co-opting (converting) them. She was striving for an inclusiveness of all the points of view and changes of mood or self, which takes place or is newly positioned in each moment. In the next chapter I will show how she stretched the traditional sentence, or developed a new narrative unit, to achieve maximum inclusiveness. Now I will just point out, or enumerate, what takes place in the first few flickering seconds of Virginia's novel. An argument develops among three characters: 1) Mrs. Ramsay says, " 'Yes, of course, if it's fine tomorrow.' " 2) Mr. Ramsay says, " 'But . . . it won't be fine.' " 3) Mrs. Ramsay says, " 'But it may be fine—I expect it will be fine.' " 4) Mr. Tansley echoes his mentor Mr. Ramsay, " 'It's due west,' " implying that it was "the worst possible direction for landing at the Lighthouse." 5) And Mrs. Ramsay says, " 'Nonsense.' " Yet the focus shifts far more often, picturing the scene from a series of vantage points that are both discontinuous and overlapping: 6) We see James a short distance away, sitting on the floor, cutting out pictures. 7) We enter his mind guided by the narrator to see him endowing the picture of a refrigerator with "heavenly bliss." 8) He appears "stark and uncompromising" to "his mother, watching him guide his scissors neatly round the refrigerator." 9) She imagines him "all red and ermine on the Bench or directing a stern and momentous enterprise in some crisis of public affairs." 10) James wishes for an axe or a poker, "any weapon that would have gashed a hole in his father's breast and killed him." 11) He thinks that his mother is "ten thousand times better in every way." 12) Mrs. Ramsay realizes that what her husband said was true. "It was always true. He was incapable of an untruth; never tampered with a fact; never altered a disagreeable word to suit the pleasure or convenience of any mortal being, least of all his own children"; 13) and now Mr. Ramsay's voice takes over, "who, sprung from his loins, should be aware from childhood that life is difficult; facts uncompromising; and," 14) the narrator adds, "the passage to that fabled land where our brightest hopes are extinguished, our frail barks founder in darkness (here Mr. Ramsay would straighten his back and narrow his little blue eyes upon the horizon), one that needs, above all, courage, truth, and the power to endure." 15)

Mrs. Ramsay punctuates her response with a twist of the stocking she is knitting. 16) She thinks of the Lighthouse keeper and his little boy "who was threatened with a tuberculous hip" and how hard it must be living "upon a rock the size of a tennis lawn." And 17) she asks or thinks of asking her daughters, "How would you like that?" After Tansley joins in the argument, 18) she thinks of how "she would not let them laugh at him," 19) for Rose, Prue, Andrew, Jasper, and Roger mocked him. They called him "the little atheist." 20) And "even old Badger without a tooth in his head had bit him" (9–13).

Woolf's narrator may provide continuity, but her shifts in perspective deny the unity of time, space, character, the traditional English sentence, and the way they are laid end to end to form a traditional narrative. They expose the basis of traditional unity as forms of force, intrusion, and violation. And the continuity that develops results in relationship, or connection, without unity. I want to emphasize the difference. For there is good reason to see Woolf as trying to achieve unity in the fragmented world of her novels. I am not referring to what has been misconceived as the modernist urge to unify. As I argued in my discussion of Joyce, the major modernists may have begun with that goal in mind, and critics may have searched for unity out of habit, need, and their underlying ideology. But Joyce, Faulkner, and Woolf (and others as well) were open to what their experiments were realizing: a field of relations where different voices could argue as independent others, some empowered by tradition, some by revolutionary energy, now one, now the other gaining ascendancy—though Woolf placed more emphasis on the interrelations.

There is also good reason to think of Woolf as striving for unity, though, after reading "A Sketch of the Past." There she differentiates the "cotton wool" of ordinary experience from the "moment of being" where "we—I mean all human beings—are connected" (72). And her characters sometimes experience this "moment of being." But Louise DeSalvo compels us to reassess it. Woolf's first "moment of being" is her memory of "lying half asleep, half awake, in bed in the nursery at St. Ives . . . hearing the waves breaking, one two, one two, and sending a splash of water over the beach . . . hearing the blind drawing its little acorn across the floor . . . feeling, it is almost impossible that I should be here; of feeling the purest ecstasy I can conceive" ("Sketch," 64–65).

"It is almost impossible that I should be here." This phrase—and its implications of disbelief, dislocation, disconnection, or as DeSalvo says, of questioning her very right to exist—suddenly comes into focus when we understand that Woolf is recollecting not a pure experience of idyllic childhood, but an exceptional moment during a traumatic summer at St. Ives. For it is linked to the moment when Gerald Duckworth lifted her onto the ledge in the dining room that was used to lay out the family meals, and put his hands under her dress while she watched what was happening to her in a mirror across the room.

DeSalvo's re-vision is important not just for the insight it gives us in to Woolf's life, but for creating a new social and literary frame of reference in which to read her novels, and for showing how the old frame—limited to psychology and aesthetics, or separating the private from the public—was a product of the very ideology responsible for her neglect, violation, and repression. The "moment of being," then, is not a mystical moment beyond historical time; it is an ecstatic moment linked to moments in historical time. It is not a glimpse into the underlying unity of life; it is an experience of unity contaminated by the reality of violence, powerlessness, and disconnection.

This new understanding leads us to shift the focus from Woolf's unities to her discontinuities, her leaps in perspective, the holes in her stories—where she reflects and exposes the violence, or the kind of power, that has imposed its order on the family as well as the Empire. Lily Brisoe's epiphany and liberation result from the line she draws down the center of her painting that *divides* rather than unifies it. Woolf's unifying characters—Mr. Ramsay as paterfamilias, Mrs. Ramsay as "Angel in the House," and (as I will show) Peter Walsh, Percival, and Bernard—are like the twin goddesses of Proportion and Conversion, and the Policeman directing traffic in *Between the Acts*, agents of the Empire. She recognized that the urge to unify was an urge to dominate, suppress, and exclude. And she developed a strategy to include, to open her novels, to seek relationships.

But, while Virginia's story is far more inclusive than her brother Virgil's, it would be unfair to say that it is *completely* different. There is a storyline; it is established by the very title. "To the lighthouse" requires a subject (a character or characters) and a verb that connotes journey, traveling, linear movement through time and space, and the achievement of a goal. Nor should we forget, despite the variety of meanings critics have attached to the lighthouse—seeing it as an eye, a guiding light, a unifier, associated with the mother sea—it is phallic. The lighthouse stands alone on bare rock in the middle of the sea. The lighthouse is associated with the father, who as a historian and a philosopher, governs not only the family but all that society considers important and meaningful, and who will pass on his power to his son. And the lighthouse is the goal that, the novel's title promises, must be reached. So Virginia too was confronted by the problem of what to do in the ten-year middle stretch.

Her brilliant solution was to make the center into a hole, an absence, that interrupts the journey, denies it its power to achieve control and unity, but gives form and meaning to what the traditional journey leaves out. In the twenty-five-page chapter called "Time Passes," the characters we have come to know are absent from the summer house. The lamps are put out, the moon sinks, an immense darkness begins; hinges rust, woodwork swells, wallpaper fades, dust collects. And Mrs. McNab, a "toothless, bonneted care-taking woman," lurches, rolls "like a ship at sea" (196), and sings an old tune as she dusts, wipes, closes the house and then, ten years later, returns with Mrs. Bast. "Slowly and painfully, with broom and pail, mopping, scouring, Mrs. McNab, Mrs. Bast, stayed the corruption and the rot; rescued from the pool of Time that was fast closing over them now a basin, now a cupboard; fetched up from oblivion all the Waverley novels and a tea-set one morning; in the afternoon restored to sun and air a brass fender and a set of steel fire-irons" (209). The family we have come to know so well is replaced by the house. And the house is seen from the point of view of eternity, or, more precisely, (Mother) Nature and the cleaning women.[3]

All the important events in the story occur elsewhere, and in square brackets. Indeed, the most important event occurs in a parenthetical clause: "[Mr. Ramsay, stumbling along a passage one dark morning, stretched his arms out, but Mrs. Ramsay having died rather suddenly the night before, his arms, though stretched out, remained empty]" (194). We also learn that "[Prue Ramsay, leaning on her father's arm, was given in marriage]" and "[. . . died that summer in some illness connected with childbirth]" (198, 199). We learn that "[A shell exploded. Twenty or thirty young men were blown up in France, among them Andrew Ramsay, whose death, mercifully, was instantaneous]" (201). And we learn that "Mr. Carmichael"—who said nothing, whom the children said took opium and stained his beard yellow with it, who lived alone in what Mrs. Ramsay felt was a horrid little room— "[brought out a volume of poems . . . which had an unexpected success. The war, people said, had revived their interest in poetry]" (202).

The death of Mrs. Ramsay, the death of her daughter in childbirth, a world war, a change in fortune and public taste are evoked not as events but as absences, as holes in a chapter that while itself parenthetical is the most powerful chapter Virginia Woolf ever wrote. And I want to make three points about this absence, or hole in the journey-men's story.

The first is that Woolf makes absence into a presence. Every reader I know feels the loss of Mrs. Ramsay, the tragedy of a young woman who dies in childbirth, the shock of a war that not only takes lives of young men without reason but reduces them to one among numbers. Indeed, to return to one argument I have been developing, it is just this hole that makes the story inclusive rather than exclusive—or makes it seem whole.

The second is that, though most critics have labeled Woolf as a novelist concerned with states of mind rather than issues of state, she was very concerned about the effect of World War I. Lee Edwards demonstrates how *Mrs. Dalloway* reflects a world still recovering and obsessed with the memory of The Great War. She shows how almost every character has an experience, memory, or association with the war, and that the associations—which include the marching soldiers encountered by Peter Walsh and the explosion of the motor into the very structure of the narrative—are pervasive and central. If modern readers have a problem making the associations, it is because our image of World War I has been overshadowed by the experience and representations of World War II, or because the very notion of those world wars is nostalgic. It is also because Woolf was trying to write a novel where there was "no plot, no comedy, no tragedy, no love interest or catastrophe in the accepted style" ("Modern Fiction," 212). And our sense of "the real world" may still be conditioned by the "accepted style."[4]

But it is also more complicated. For, as James Haule has shown, Virginia Woolf generalized and euphemized the strong images of war that were in her original holograph manuscript of "Time Passes," and then effaced the remaining allusions from the typescript. The changes suggest that in this autobiographical exploration Woolf was coming too close to her traumatic experiences—and it would take until *Three Guineas* and *Between the Acts* before she could articulate the relationship between the patriarchal family and war.[5]

Nonetheless she was able to evoke the violence. *To the Lighthouse* has far fewer references to the war, and the few are rendered in parentheses. But the shell that exploded between parentheses—blowing up twenty or thirty young men, "among them Andrew Ramsay"—reverberates more than it would in a battle scene just because it evokes the absence and loss, and because it sets this absence within the context of the journey-men's story of adventure and conquest.

The third point I want to make about this hole in the plotline is that Woolf connects the senseless violence of World War I to the impulse toward mastery and domination that governs journey-men's novels. According to Martin Green, "the adventure tales that formed the light reading of Englishmen for two hundred years and more after *Robinson Crusoe* were, in fact, the energizing myth of English imperialism. They were, collectively, the story England told itself as it went to sleep at night; and, in the form of its dreams, they charged England's will with the energy to go out into the world and explore, conquer, and rule" (3). In *To the Lighthouse* Woolf disrupts, or deconstructs, the traditional journey with an untraditional view of its logical conclusion: loss, absence, waste. Moreover, she connects the violence of war with the death of a woman who has struggled in a role of the "Angel in the House"—or mother, nurturer, and unifier—and of a daughter who, like so many young women, died giving birth to her child. Now we can begin to understand why in the central section (or central hole in the novel) the authorial voice gives way to (Mother) Nature and the cleaning women. Indeed, Jane Marcus argues that the cleaning women, suppressed by both gender and class, erupt into the novel as a voice of the semiotic (*Languages of Patriarchy*, 7). This is a woman's story that is suppressed by the traditional journey.

Nonetheless, it is important to realize that Mrs. Ramsay's story is completed in Mr. Ramsay's sentence; that Prue's story is completed in a sentence dominated by her father; that the novel compels us to go beyond the hiatus, to reach the lighthouse; that the tragedy of young Andrew, who died before he could even glimpse his potential, is relieved by the victory of young James. And that the novel concludes with the promise of patriarchal succession. " 'Well done!' " says Mr. Ramsay. "James had steered them like a born sailor" (306). Mr. Ramsay's voice signals the union of father and son and the completion of the journey. Lily Briscoe's thoughts may continually interrupt this journey. She may (as Rachel Blau DuPlessis cogently argues) undermine the men's journey with the forming of a pre-Oedipal community of parent-child relationships, "geniality, sisterhood, motherhood, brotherhood" and "bisexual oscillation" (60–61). She may have liberated herself by gaining the capacity to understand and feel for Mr. Ramsay and to imagine James and his father reaching the lighthouse. But the fact that she must complete the journey-men's story before she can finish her own is a mark of its power to co-opt the female artist. And this may be why every reader and critic I know sees the line Lily draws down the center of her painting as uniting—rather than dividing—the family.

In the last section of the novel, the narrator reflects the struggle for author-ity between the man's and woman's story by cutting back and forth between the journey to the lighthouse (where, as Elizabeth Abel argues, Cam learns to accommodate her independence to her father's and brother's authority) and Lily finishing her picture. Lily's story engages us not by its goal but by a developing and shifting network of interrelationships. It centers for the most part on Mrs. Ramsay, to whom she relates as adoring lover, admiring daughter, and emancipated woman. This shifting set of positions and interrelationships is due to more than a shifting of perspectives; it derives from a notion that character—the self—is not unified but multiple. And the multiplicity is reflected in Lily's relationship not only with Mrs. Ramsay but with Mr. Ramsay (to whom she can finally give something of herself without giving it all), with Mr. Bankes (who fulfills the role of a friend), and to the other characters in the extended family. Indeed, Lily's multiple relationships include even the institution of the family itself. She imagines "an old-fashioned scene" of Mr. Ramsay's proposal and Mrs. Ramsay's laconic reply (295). And she completes the story of the family at the same moment she emancipates herself from it.

Ten years earlier Lily "had been looking at the table-cloth, and it had flashed upon her that she would move the tree to the middle, and need never marry anybody, and she felt an enormous exultation" (262). Now she decides, not to move the tree, but to draw a line down the center of the painting—to divide the family, and in so doing to divide herself from it.

What does the dividing line say about her development? And what does it say about her vision? Did she reflect the "extraordinary transformation of the ideals of marriage and family life" that Alex Zwerdling describes so well (145)? Did she understand the patriarchal marriage that Jane Lilienfeld illuminates? Did she intimate the violence, neglect, and violation that Louise DeSalvo uncovers in the Stephens family and that was common at the time? Did she come to realize that marriage was more than "a man and a woman looking at a girl throwing a ball" (110)? Did she sense why Mrs. Ramsay needed to be by herself? That by wanting to shed the "attachments" to "this self," Mrs. Ramsay was not necessarily being metaphysical or mystical but giving vent to repressed feelings about her social role (95)? Mrs. Ramsay may have been experiencing a "moment of being," but this was a rare moment that reflected her disconnection rather than her connection with life. Indeed, when Mrs. Ramsay thought about "this self having shed its attachments," she shifted into the discourse that governed her husband's fantasies: she would now be "free for the strangest adventures," and the first adventure would be to "the Indian plains" (95–96).

Mrs. Ramsay, Lily might also have intimated, repressed a great deal in her enthusiasm for marriage. When she reflected too long about Minta and Paul, she felt "life rather sinister." And she had to rationalize, "because whatever she might feel about her own transaction, she had had experiences which need not happen to every one (she did not name them to herself)" (92). It is important that she calls her marriage a "transaction." It is even more important that she cannot name the experiences to herself—and that by feeling these experiences need not happen to everyone she implicitly blames herself.

At the end of the day, as she talks with her husband about Minta and Paul's engagement, Mrs. Ramsay comes dangerously close to seeing what she has repressed and sublimated in an annihilating light. "Slowly it came into her head, why is it then that one wants people to marry? What was the value, the meaning of things?" And she wishes that her husband would say something, anything, "for the shadow, the thing folding them in was beginning, she felt, to close round her again. Say anything, she begged, looking at him as if for help." All he says is, " 'You won't finish that stocking tonight.' " But "that was what she wanted. . . . 'No,' she said, flattening the stocking out upon her knee, 'I shan't finish it' " (183–184).

She capitulates, but then rallies her powers of independence. He wants her to tell him that she loves him. And the day that began with a quarrel about going to the lighthouse, ends with a battle of wills. "A heartless woman he called her; she never told him that she loved him." She walks to the window, turns, looks at him, and smiles. Finally she says, " 'Yes, you were right. It's going to be wet tomorrow. You won't be able to go.' And she looked at him smiling. For she had triumphed again. She had not said it: yet he knew" (185–186).

Of course, this is a reconciliation that makes them both feel good, a transaction between adults that enables them not only to go on but to do so in a way that is mutually supportive. But what is the price of reconciliation and who pays? What is the nature of the transaction? And what is Mrs. Ramsay's triumph?

She is able to *not* say that she loves him by saying " 'Yes, you were right.' " She is able to bring about a happy ending by repressing thoughts that would threaten the family romance. And what does it mean for her to have triumphed? To have *not* said she loved him? Or why, we might first ask, does the woman who can make Charles Tansley feel "an extraordinary pride" (25), who triumphs at dinner by acting like the chairman of a meeting—why should this woman who has such control over social discourse have trouble expressing her feelings? Unless she was trying not to express but repress them.

Lily might have glimpsed this image of Mrs. Ramsay, from which she needed to gain independence. And she does liberate herself from Mrs. Ramsay's tyrannical hold by affirming herself as a single woman and an artist, and by finishing her picture with a line that divides the family. But despite her liberation—and despite the way her story interrupts, indeed undermines, the journey to the lighthouse—she unifies the family by finishing their picture at the end of the novel, and she author-izes the journey-men's story by telling us the end.

Virgil Woolf could not finish his version of *To the Lighthouse*; he could not imagine—or had to suppress—a woman's story that is so central to the classical journey, the story of adventure, the quest for independence, identity, and power. Virginia could not ultimately inhibit the momentum of the classical journey, or the power of the father's voice. But she could give a woman the last word. Moreover, she could disrupt the traditional narrative line— as she does through the hole of "Time Passes" and by intercutting Lily's story with that of the journey-men's. The struggle between Virgil's and Virginia's stories—or between the classical journey and the story of disruption and relationship—reflects Woolf's struggle with author-ity.

9

Stretching the Sentence: *Mrs. Dalloway*

Woolf came to recognize that language—or the way words are organized (ordered) in sentences and then "laid end to end" (*Room*, 80)—is not natural or neutral. Discourse is largely shaped by cultural forces, specifically by institutions: governments, churches, schools and the great books they promulgate, the family, the press, and the publishing industry. It is shaped, more specifically, by those who have the power to govern (we listen to them with special attention), the power to preach (we listen to them with reverence), the power to teach (we listen to them with respect for their knowledge), the power to rule the family (we obey them with love and respect), the power to report the news (we read them with the desire to know what happened), and the power to publish what we accept as important or interesting.

Even more specifically, Woolf recognized that down through history, those who had the power to govern, preach, teach, rule, report, and publish were men. And inevitably language—even the very structure of the English sentence—was shaped to fit their perspectives, capture their experiences, reflect their values, suit their needs. In *A Room of One's Own* she says:

All the great novelists like Thackeray and Dickens and Balzac have written a natural prose . . . taking their own tint without ceasing to be common property. They have based it on the sentence that was current at the time. The sentence that was current at the beginning of the nineteenth century ran something like this perhaps: "*The grandeur of their works was an argument with them, not to stop short, but to proceed. They could have no higher excitement or satisfaction than in the exercise of their art and endless generations of truth and beauty. Success prompts to exertion; and habit facilitates success.*" That is a man's sentence; behind it one can see Johnson, Gibbon and the rest. It was a sentence that was unsuited for a woman's use. (79–80, my emphasis)

But what is it exactly that characterizes the man's sentence? According to Susan Leonardi, it is "a certain posture—this 'com-

144

manding' gesture, this 'grandeur,' this 'higher excitement'—which Woolf would depict over and over in her novels as the male mode toward the world. Mr. Ramsay in *To the Lighthouse*, for example, who 'never altered a disagreeable word to suit the pleasure or convenience of any mortal being,' tried to inspire the children 'sprung from his loins,' with 'courage, truth, and the power to endure.' This posture finds appropriate expression in highly subordinated sentences—the man is the main clause" (150–151).

Leonardi also points out that Woolf chose to coordinate, or join, rather than subordinate—like many modernists who rejected ordered relationships and strove for a language that could reflect the fragmentation of modern life and the disintegration of values.[1] But, she argues, Woolf's rejection of the hierarchical sentence is specifically feminine. Leonardi develops this point thematically in an illuminating discussion of *Night and Day*. But she does not show us exactly how Woolf's basic sentence is different from Joyce's or the other male modernists. Nor does Joan Lidoff, who compares Woolf's "female sense of fusion, lack of separation, boundary or division" to Nancy Chodorow's point that girls develop a greater sense of relationship than boys because they do not have to sever relations with their mothers to establish gender identities (44). Nor does Makiko Minow-Pinkney, though she develops the argument further by bringing to bear the insights of postmodernism.

Sandra Gilbert, on the other hand, offers a way out: Woolf's ideal woman's sentence is a "fantasy," a "utopian linguistic structure" that defines or perhaps disguises "*not woman's language but woman's relation to language.*" Woolf wanted to overturn the "sentence-as-'definitive-judgment,' the sentence-as-decree-or-interdiction, by which woman has been kept from feeling that she can be in full command of language. The utopian concept of woman's grammatical sentence is thus a sort of mask for the more practical idea of woman's legal sentence" (209).[2]

Gilbert's point about male sentencing is important (though her assumptions and argument lead her to ignore the voices in Joyce's *Ulysses* that, I have tried to show, subvert the power structure). But in shifting away from grammar, and calling Woolf's ideal sentence a fantasy, she undermines Woolf's insight into the relationship between sentences and sentencing, or between the structures of language and the power governing those structures. Moreover, she minimizes Woolf's literary accomplishment. She also gives us an easy way out of the dilemma—how to define a sentence that we recognize as distinctive, but that is designed to resist definition, or "definitive judgment."

Woolf's sentence resists definitive judgment in part because it resists traditional grammar. I do not mean to say that her sentences are ungrammatical—though, as we will see, she makes strong and complex use of the sentence fragment. I mean that we must look at her sentence, not just as a grammatical unit but as a basic unit of expression and representation, and the building unit of narrative.

Mrs. Dalloway said she would buy the flowers herself.
For Lucy had her work cut out for her. The doors would be taken off their hinges; Rumpelmayer's men were coming. And then, thought Clarissa Dalloway, what a morning—fresh as if issued to children on a beach.
What a lark! What a plunge! *For so it had always seemed* to her, when, with a little squeak of the hinges, which she could hear now, she had burst open the French windows and plunged at Bourton into the open air. How fresh, how calm, stiller than this of course, the air was in the early morning; like the flap of a wave; the kiss of a wave; chill and sharp and yet *(for a girl of eighteen as she then was)* solemn, feeling as she did, *standing there at the open window*, that something awful was about to happen; looking at the flowers, at the trees with the smoke winding off them and the rooks rising, falling; standing and looking *until* Peter Walsh said, "Musing among the vegetables?"—was that it?—"I prefer men to cauliflowers"—was that it? *He must have said it at breakfast one morning when she had gone on to the terrace*—Peter Walsh. *He would be back from India one of these days*, June or July, she forgot which, for his letters were awfully dull; it was his sayings one remembered; his eyes, his pocket-knife, his smile, his grumpiness and, when millions of things had utterly vanished—how strange it was!—a few sayings like this about cabbages.
She stiffened a little on the kerb. (my emphasis).

In the opening passage of *Mrs. Dalloway*, Woolf laid the groundwork for a new kind of sentencing. She stretched the sentence across periods and paragraph breaks from the beginning to the end of the scene. She created a basic narrative unit, where the narrator could intrude into her character's thoughts, or where both the character's thoughts and narrator's intrusion are included, where no one clause is more important than any other, where past and present interpenetrate, where metaphors mix and similes tumble into incongruous mixtures.

In the opening two lines she literally stretches the sentence across two grammatical breaks, a period and a paragraph. More often, of course, she stays within the bounds of grammar, but her opening move reflects an urge to expand the basic unit that builds stories and represents thought. In the fragmentary second sentence she undermines hierarchical grammar, but by emphasizing the subordinate clause, she reflects the hierarchical relationship of the mistress and her servant. This may reflect the double voice in the novel's free indirect speech, or Woolf's ambivalence toward the established order. But it is also a way of breaking away from the established order and, at the same time, including it in a new form. Breaking and including, I hope to show, are marks of Woolf's new sentence, where (like Bakhtin's carnival) heterogeneity—or inclusion—is the key, where multiple voices can be heard, including the voice of authority and the voices that disrupt and decenter it, but where (unlike Bakhtin's carnival) interconnection is as important as confrontation.

Woolf's narrator uses free indirect speech. That is, she uses Clarissa's language, restricts herself to Clarissa's view, and indicates her presence only in her use of the third person and the past tense. But we might wonder how much of this is Clarissa's language when we encounter the second strong sentence fragment—"What a lark! What a plunge! For so it had always seemed. . . ." Our uncertainty is increased when we discover how often "for" is used to break as well as link sentences—and when we discover that this connective does not always do the job of linking or explaining.

James Naremore, in his sharp analysis of the novel's style, lists "for" as one of several transitional devices that "dissolve the boundaries" between characters. The narrator, he argues, interprets her character's stream of thoughts and draws it into a seamless flow. But if "for" helps create a seamless flow, it is also an intrusion of the narrator into her character's thoughts, and it breaks the flow. It also breaks our perspective. While the narrator still mediates between us and the characters, she also enters their field. And this is a new development in Woolf's writing. In *Jacob's Room* and the short story "Mrs Dalloway," which was intended to be the novel's opening chapter, the narrator leaps from one perspective to another, but not within the same paragraph. She does not intrude but remains apart.

Another intrusion is the parenthetical phrase: "(for a girl of eighteen as she was then)." Harvena Richter recalls how Woolf asked herself, "Could I do it in a parenthesis? So that one had the sense of reading two things at the same time?" (*Diary*, September 5, 1926). And she describes how Woolf's parenthetical phrases evoke the simultaneity of thoughts, feelings, speech, and actions—not only of one but sometimes of two different characters. But we encounter even more than the representation of simultaneous physical and psychological experiences. We encounter an intrusion

of the physical parentheses—the typography calling attention to
itself and undermining the realistic illusion that depends on the
transparency of the print. The parentheses will become much more
intrusive and problematic when Richard comes home after Lady
Bruton's lunch.

What a surprise! In came Richard, holding out flowers. She had failed
him, once at Constantinople; and Lady Bruton, whose lunch parties were
said to be extraordinarily amusing, had not asked her. He was holding
out flowers—roses, red and white roses.
    (But he could not bring himself to say he loved her; not in so many
words.)
    But how lovely, she said, taking his flowers. She understood without
his speaking; his Clarissa. (178–179)

Who thinks the thoughts in the parenthetical paragraph? Is it
Richard, as he thinks about what he cannot say? Is it the narrator,
as she says what he cannot say, or think? Is it Clarissa, implying
how well she knows Richard? And who thinks "she understood
without his speaking"? Is it Richard, rationalizing his failure and
then reestablishing his authority with "his Clarissa"? Is it Clarissa,
who understands Richard so well she knows how he speaks to
himself? Or who, understanding without his speaking, feels herself
to be "his Clarissa"? Do they both think and feel all this, the
parenthesis reflecting a mutual understanding? Or do the parenthetical thoughts escape from authorial control? We encounter an
overlap but at the same time a destruction of perspective—the
result of stretching the sentence to include multiple possibilities.
    I want to emphasize the difference between the open-ended multi-
plicity I am trying to describe and the multiplicity that follows from
Richter's well-grounded psychological approach. For Richter, the
discontinuities in thought ("its lack of organization, its sudden
breaks and shiftings, which create a certain bewilderment as does
the data of consciousness which thrusts itself upon us each moment") are ultimately resolved as "we automatically sort and sift [it]
out for ourselves" (43). Woolf's style and characterization of the
self, then, reflect a "multiplicity-within-unity" (44). Richter has
good reasons for viewing Woolf through the intellectual and artistic
lenses of her period, and a good basis in Woolf's own reflections—
especially about the "moment of being." But this was before Louise
DeSalvo provided the violent context for Woolf's moments of being
and convincingly argued that they reflected her disconnection
rather than connection. Moreover, when we look back at Woolf

from a postmodern perspective, we can see how she was far in advance of her times—or how she was going beyond psychological representation to discover possibilities of thought and language that were only beginning to be discovered by the postimpressionists, Bergson, William James, and Freud.

Among the possibilities is a conflation of experiences—and of possible experiences. We encounter this in the simple merging of the past and present, when the little squeak of the hinges takes Clarissa back to her youth at Bourton. And we encounter a more radical leap and displacement when Clarissa (a girl of eighteen) is standing at the open window thinking that something awful is about to happen, "until" Peter Walsh says something like " 'Musing among the vegetables'." For we soon discover he must have said it "at breakfast one morning when she had gone on to the terrace." Then we move back to the present as Clarissa thinks, "He would be back from India one of these days." And suddenly we find ourselves on the kerb. But how did we get there? Have we been walking with Mrs. Dalloway along the street all the time, her thoughts being more important, or "real," than the "real" world of the streets? Or have we been standing on the kerb with her, the thoughts all streaming in at the moment she stiffened?

Woolf stretches the sentence, or the basic narrative unit, to include grammatical gaps, physical gaps, narrative intrusions, conflations of experiences and possible experiences, leaps in time and space, and leaps from the mental to the physical world. And her sentence will also come to include the mixing of metaphors, or similes that suddenly transform themselves and succeed one another helter-skelter.

When Clarissa returns with her flowers, the hall is as cool "as a vault." She feels "like a nun who has left the world . . . blessed and purified." But she experiences the next moment as one of the "buds on the tree of life, flowers of darkness . . . (as if some lovely rose had blossomed for her eyes only)" (42–43). The cloistered vault has become a garden, the tree a rose bush, and the feeling of blessed purity an experience of lovely darkness. Then Lucy tells her that Mr. Dalloway will be having lunch at Lady Bruton's and takes the parasol "like a sacred weapon" (43). Clarissa shivers like a "plant on the river-bed" (44). She fears "time itself" and reads it "on Lady Bruton's face, as if it had been a dial cut in impassive stone," and then experiences the hesitation, "an exquisite suspense, such as might stay a diver before plunging while the sea darkens and brightens beneath him, and the waves which threaten to break, but only gently split their surface, roll and conceal and encrust as they just turn over the weeds with pearl" (44). In the next moment "the appalling night" is seen more accurately as "this matter-of-fact June morning; soft with the glow of rose petals." And in a few lines she feels "like a nun withdrawing, or"—and now a final leap—"a child exploring a tower" (45). The narrator may be tracing the subtle shifts in mood in these three pages, but she does so through a galloping incongruity of the images.

We encounter an even greater incongruity in her portrayal of Clarissa's and Peter's reunion. At the most poignant moment Peter's grief rises "like a moon looked at from a terrace, ghastly beautiful with light from the sunken day." But the moon is soon reduced to two dimensions, looking more like a disk hanging against the painted canvas of a stage set:

as if in truth he were sitting there on the terrace he edged a little towards Clarissa; put his hand out; raised it; let it fall. There above them it hung, that moon. . . . Then, just as happens on a terrace in the moonlight, when one person begins to feel ashamed that he is already bored, and yet as the other sits silent, very quiet, sadly looking at the moon, does not like to speak, moves his foot, clears his throat, notices some iron scroll on a table leg, stirs a leaf, but says nothing—so Peter Walsh did now. For why go back like this to the past? he thought. (62–63)

Of course, we have been taken back to the past, for the terrace is like the terrace at Bourton. But we are also taken out of Clarissa's sitting room into a second-rate romantic stage set that upstages the actors, who register their feelings in a series of delicate movements.

The incongruities multiply in the scene where Peter and Clarissa, who have been fencing with pocket-knife and knitting needles on the blue sofa, suddenly become two horses, pawing the ground and tossing their heads before a battle begins (66), and when Septimus and Evans, attracted to one another in the trenches of France, become "two dogs playing on a hearth-rug; one worrying a paper screw, snarling, snapping, giving a pinch, now and then, at the old dog's ear; the other lying somnolent, blinking at the fire, raising a paw, turning and growling good-temperedly" (130).

Virginia Woolf's ideal sentence was not a fantasy. In her early work she implied and later she articulated the connections between language and power. She transgressed, undermined, or toppled its structures, sometimes tentatively, sometimes boldly, sometimes playfully, sometimes defiantly. She created a basic narrative unit open to experiences of relationship denied by the male hierarchy of thought. Her new unit of expression breaks hierarchic order of grammar, space, time, logic, and literary convention—and strives for ultimate inclusion.

Woolf's sentence is like the scene of a film—made up of many shots, where the camera moves from one shot to another, sometimes seamlessly, sometimes erratically, sometimes through a dissolve, sometimes through a technique that calls attention to itself. The transitions may be smooth, as when Clarissa or Peter or Richard or Elizabeth walk through the streets. They may be abrupt, as when the motorcar backfires, or the airplane lifts us to a bird's-eye view of London. Or they may abrogate time, as when Big Ben strikes noon while Clarissa lays out her green dress and the Smiths walk toward Dr. Bradshaw's.

And at the end of the novel her sentence is stretched to capture the entire climactic party. The narrative eye (anticipating Renoir's traveling camera) glides around the ballroom, between the columns, through archways, up and down staircases, pulling back to take in a group of ladies in the cloakroom, closing in to capture a couple in conversation, following Clarissa as she flits from one guest to another and then up into the little room where the prime minister had sat with Lady Bruton, moving in to frame her thoughts about the young man who had killed himself, following her back to the party where "she must find Sally and Peter," then dissolving to Sally and Peter, and climaxing the party as it closes in on Peter, filled with extraordinary excitement.

"The idea of a party always excited" Virginia, wrote Leonard Woolf. "She was very sensitive to the actual mental and physical excitement . . . the rise of temperature of mind and body, the ferment and fountain of noise" (98). And on 27 April, 1925 she wrote in her diary that she "should like to investigate the *party consciousness*," which she then considered to be a "frock consciousness . . . where people secrete an envelope which connects and protects them from others."

Woolf experimented with ways to convey the frock consciousness in the stories that Stella McNichol collected in *Mrs Dalloway's Party*. In the title story a shallow Mrs Dalloway turns each failure of relationship among her guests into a romance. But when Woolf developed the story into a novel, we get a different picture of the party and an expanded view of party consciousness. Mrs. Dalloway has become a much more complex character, capable of feeling a deep relationship with the lonely old woman in the window across the way, and with Septimus at the moment he committed suicide.

Party consciousness reflects the forms that enable people to establish polite connections, but it is also a release of repressed energy, a "rise of temperature of mind and body," a "ferment and fountain of noise"—and a search for connection and inclusiveness, proscribed by social form. The party was a social institution that may have reflected the male hierarchy when honoring the prime minister, but it was within the woman's domain. In *Mrs. Dalloway* Woolf was discovering the potential of party consciousness for women's narrative. She would focus some of the ambiguities in *To the Lighthouse*: Mrs. Ramsay's guests would feel "conscious of making a party together in a hollow, on an island; had their common cause against that fluidity out there" (147)—but Lily makes us aware that the cause is not that common. In *The Waves*, Bernard would see all the characters at Percival's last supper, as "a single flower . . . to which every eye brings its own contribution" (127); but, as I hope to show, Woolf questions the authority of both Bernard and Percival. *The Years* would culminate in an all-night party bringing together yet revealing the fissures among three generations of Pargiters. And all of *Between the Acts* would be a party, indeed a carnival, that brings all the periods of English history into "a zone of crude contact," to be fingered familiarly, turned it upside down, inside out, taken apart, dismembered, laid bare, and exposed.

Mrs. Dalloway's party culminates as Clarissa returns from the little room where she identified with Septimus, stands at the top of the staircase, and fills Peter with terror, ecstasy, extraordinary excitement. The new authorial voice has stretched and overturned what Gilbert called "the sentence-as-'definitive-judgment,' the sentence-as-decree-or-interdiction, by which woman has been kept from feeling that she can be in full command of language" (209). In the novel's final section the new authorial voice has achieved an inclusiveness that reflects not only the actions and thoughts of her many guests as they see one another, but a disturbing connection between Mrs. Dalloway and Septimus Smith. But this is not to say the new authorial voice is in full command. For the traditional authorial voice has generated a counterforce in the shape of an old-fashioned romance plot—or the courtship of Peter Walsh.

Granted, Peter is indecisive and ineffectual and can only play the role of a lover in his fantasies. Granted, he does not get Clarissa physically, emotionally, or dramatically. Their meeting is a failure. Clarissa realizes that marriage to Peter would be suffocating. Nonetheless, it is Peter who appears first in Clarissa's thoughts on that splendid spring morning, who intrudes into her bedroom and causes her to "hide her dress, like a virgin protecting chastity"(59), whom she still found "enchanting" (61)—and whom we follow as he forms a major narrative line through the novel. He walks through the park past Septimus and Rezia, takes us through the London streets, first away from Clarissa and then back, and becomes a major focal point at her party. Most important, he has the culminating vision, the last word: "It is Clarissa, he said." And then the narrator author-izes his sentence: "For there she was."[3] Peter Walsh literally gets Mrs. Dalloway into his sentence, which—being the final sentence in the diegesis, or story proper, and then being authorized by the narrator—becomes the point toward which a strong narrative line, the romantic plot, has been leading.

But what about Peter's rival, Sally Seton? Clarissa's moments with Sally are the most highly charged moments in the novel.

She could remember standing in her bedroom at the top of the house . . . and saying aloud, "She is beneath this roof. . . . She is beneath this roof!"
. . . .
. . . .
She could remember going cold with excitement, and doing her hair in a kind of ecstasy . . . and going downstairs, and feeling as she crossed the hall "if it were now to die, 'twere now to be most happy" . . . all because she was coming down to dinner in a white frock to meet Sally Seton!
. . . .
. . . .
Then came the most exquisite moment of her whole life passing a stone urn with flowers in it. Sally stopped; picked a flower; kissed her on the lips. The whole world might have turned upside down! (51–52)

Clarissa suppresses her love for Sally to marry Richard—and Emily Jensen illuminates the repressive forces of "proportion" and "conversion" that lead to Clarissa's "respectable suicide." But Sally is also suppressed by the romance plot. Between Peter's entrance into Clarissa's bedroom and the final scene (or for two-thirds of the novel), the only glimpse we get of Sally is in Peter's thoughts. And when Sally bursts in at the party, Clarissa thinks, "One might put down the hot water can quite composedly. The lustre had gone out of her" (260). Sally has lost not only her "lustre," she has lost her role as a major character in the novel. Despite her highly charged presence in Clarissa's story, she gives way to Peter in the novel's overall structure. Sally had Clarissa in the beginning of the novel, Peter has her at the end. Indeed—since Sally is sitting with Peter as he captures Clarissa in his final line—he has them both.

But what are we to make of Peter's authority? He has proven himself overbearing, intolerant, and unreliable—continually imposing his views on others. " 'Star-gazing'?" he asks, coming upon Clarissa and Sally after their ecstatic kiss (53). "Lovers squabbling under a tree," he thinks, as he passes Septimus picturing "legions of men prostrate behind him" and Rezia feeling so alone and unhappy (106–107). And, when he hears the siren of the ambulance taking Septimus to the hospital, he marvels at the wonders of civilization.

Peter is not just overbearing, intolerant, and unreliable: just back from India, he reflects the mentality—and author-ity—of imperialism. Reflecting the kinds of stories by which England went to sleep, he pictures himself as "an adventurer . . . a romantic buccaneer" (80)—as he followed a young woman down the street. Clarissa Dalloway is independent and elusive. She flits from place to place, time to time, and indeed, from self to self. She escapes the hierarchy and logic of not only the plotline but the traditional English sentence. But (to use Gilbert and Gubar's phrase) she is finally "sentenced"—by the hero of the romance plot and a failed civil servant of the Empire who imagines himself an adventurer.

I do not mean to depreciate the insights of feminist critics who have taught us to read the suppressed and subversive stories in *Mrs. Dalloway*. Given the power of traditional authorial forms, it is important to know, as Jane Marcus points out, that Caroline Stephen, Woolf's aunt, wrote a history of sisterhoods—including the order of Clarissan nuns, "who were married but signed vows of celibacy with their husbands, lived at home, and were secret nuns. They performed good works without threatening the family by living in groups" ("Niece of a Nun," 10). Marcus reminds us that the vow of celibacy was one of the few ways that women could rebel against the Victorian patriarchy and what for many was a prison house of the family. And she recalls that Woolf not only identified chastity with integrity in *Three Guineas*, but eroticized chastity and sexualized politics, as had St. Teresa, Joan of Arc, and Christabel Pankhurst ("Niece of a Nun").

It is also important to understand the story of Clarissa's failure, of what Emily Jensen calls her "respectable suicide," which is suppressed not only by Clarissa but by the conventions of author-ity that, despite Woolf's success in undermining them, maintain a residual power over readers and critics. Mitchell Leaska recognizes the nature of Clarissa's identification with Septimus, who suppressed his love for Evans. But he sees her as finally relieved and released: "By refusing to deny her deficiency in marriage, by acknowledging her deceptions, by admitting in private and safeguard-ing in memory her love for another woman, Clarissa is prepared to go on living, even if ever more inwardly." In what is otherwise a sensitive study, Leaska privileges marriage, accepts society's view of Clarissa's guilt, and sees her as saved. Indeed, he declares that "the *new* Clarissa" has "emerged from the perilous depths, chas-tened, finally at one with herself, more fully conscious, and per-haps more enduring" (117).

By privileging the most exquisite moment of Clarissa's life, or lesbian union as opposed to marriage in a patriarchal society, Jen-sen leads us to see how Leaska's view is not much more enlight-ened than that of Dr. Bradshaw. Through illuminating analyses of the novel's "verbal network" and Clarissa's responses to the other characters, she demonstrates that "Clarissa's approval of Septi-mus's literal suicide reveals the extent to which she understands the self-destruction involved in her own life. She recognizes that she has committed her own kind of suicide: she has in fact commit-ted one of the most common suicides for women, that respectable destruction of the self in the interest of the other, firmly convinced that in this world where the dice fall with the white on top, 'that is all' that is possible" (178).

But despite the subversive and suppressed stories, the disrup-tions of the traditional storyline, the sentences that are stretched beyond limit, Peter Walsh has the final word. He imposes his order, his image of unity, on the multiple and even contradictory strands of the novel. And it is up to resisting critics and teachers to unknot them and put Peter Walsh in his place. But to ignore Peter's power is to ignore the context of Woolf's subversive and sup-pressed stories, her struggle with author-ity, and the politics of narration. Woolf stretches her sentences to embody the trans-gressive energy and interconnections of party consciousness. She undermines authority. She tells stories that could not be told in traditional forms. She challenges traditional habits of reading, ex-pectations, and assumptions—and she has changed them for many readers. But she contends with the residual power of convention and habit. Indeed, her novels embody and expose the dialogic, or struggle for author-ity.

10

The Waves

*T*he Waves has no storyline. In fact, it has no narrator, no description of the characters or the setting, no summaries of the action, no commentary—only dialogue with minimal attribution. " 'I see a ring,' said Bernard. . . . 'I see a slab of pale yellow,' said Susan. . . . 'I hear a sound,' said Rhoda" (9). Moreover, the dialogue is not really dialogue. For the six characters, we soon learn, are not talking to each other. Nor is it monologue, for they are not even talking to themselves. What we hear are thoughts, that, given the quotation marks, would seem to come directly from the children's minds. Except that all the voices sound the same.

What we hear then is Woolf's most successful realization of female author-ial voice—which does not separate itself from the narrative to tell the story but em-bodies it. I want to distinguish this voice as female because her story is, to use Nancy Miller's terms, an erotic rather than an ambitious text. It does not strive to achieve a goal but to em-body relationships. And it does so through what Julia Kristeva calls the semiotic: a fluid, wild, and polyvalent language that transgresses denotation, syntax, logical order, and develops in the pre-Oedipal and prelinguistic stage, when we find our source of pleasure and value in the mother's body. Garrett Stewart has illuminated the novel's semiotic rhythm with great precision and persuasiveness, adding a psycholinguistic dimension to what I am calling the stretched sentence. He also makes an important point by recognizing the problem of biological determinism, or essentializing women, and argues that the semiotic is "maternal in orientation—that is, pre-social—without being female in essence" (442). But it is also important to recognize that while writing *The Waves* Woolf was consciously struggling with male author-ity and seeking ways to alter the assumptions, perspectives, and possibilities of traditional narration. She teaches us to be wary of dualisms, which perpetuate hierarchical relations; but we must acknowledge the historical fact of gender relations in order to recognize the ground of Woolf's struggle.

Since the female authorial voice em-bodies her story, we might rather call it the em-bodying source. For this indeed is what we encounter in the creation myth, the myth of Aurora, that opens the novel. "*The sun had not yet risen. The sea was indistinguishable from the sky, except that the sea was slightly creased as if a cloth had wrinkles in it.*" Then, instead of a male voice declaring "Let there be light," "*the arm of a woman*" raises a "*lamp and flat bars of white, green and yellow, spread across the sky like the blades of a fan.*" As she raises her arm higher, the sea slowly becomes transparent, the light strikes the trees in the garden, the birds begin to chirp, and the blind of a bedroom window begins to stir (7–8).

In *To the Lighthouse*, a woman's story was also told from—or embodied in—the point of view of nature and eternity. And it disrupted the story of the journey-men. But the story in "Time Passes," and the story of Lily's liberation as well, were limited to disruptions—or to holes in the ambitious text. And we might reflect that the women's story in Dinesen's "The Blank Page" required its separate space, that Molly's story in Joyce's *Ulysses* was separated from the journey-men's story by a hole in the text, that Addie's story in Faulkner's *As I Lay Dying* was limited to its hole in the text, and that Rosa Coldfield's discourse of desire is felt in its disruptions. In *The Waves*, the woman's story comes out of the hole and pervades the entire novel. The creation myth continues in the italicized interchapters to focus on nature rather than human lives, and traces the course of the sun throughout a single day. And out of this grows the story—or set of changing interrelationships—among Bernard, Susan, Rhoda, Neville, Jinny, and Louis from childhood to old age.

Their story is embodied in the language of the authorial voice. But soon a conflict arises between the embody-ing source and the author-ity of her three male characters. Louis, the first child to become individuated, tells the story of his initiation: a devastating encounter with Jinny. Feeling alienated by his nationality and class, he stands alone by the wall, watching "Bernard, Neville, Jinny and Susan (but not Rhoda) skim the flower-beds with their nets." He wants to be unseen and stands "rooted to the middle of the earth," peering through an eyehole in the hedge. But now Jinny's eyebeam slides though the chink. "She has found me. I am struck on the nape of the neck. She has kissed me. All is shattered" (12–13).

But Jinny has a different story—which, as far as I know, has gone unnoticed. She sees the leaves moving in the hedge and thinks it is a bird in its nest. But there is no bird in the nest, and the leaves go on moving, and she is frightened. "I ran past Susan, past Rhoda, and Neville and Bernard in the tool-house talking" (13). Note that in her story Rhoda is with the children, who are not skimming the flower beds with their nets, as Louis reported, but in and around the tool-house. Once we recognize that Louis and Jinny are telling different stories, we can begin to understand that we are witnessing a struggle for narrative control, and we may see Jinny's reaction in a different light.

"I cried as I ran, faster and faster. What moved the leaves? What moves my heart, my legs? And I dashed in here, seeing you green as a bush, like a branch, very still, Louis, with your eyes fixed. 'Is he dead?' I thought, and kissed you, with my heart jumping under my pink frock like the leaves" (13). Jinny's "speech" is in the second person; she is speaking directly to Louis. And why does she kiss him? Because of her sensuality, which, especially considering her later thoughts and action, has been labeled as aggressive and narcissistic. But perhaps we have not been alert to the story she is trying to tell. And recent changes in psychological theory may help us understand what this story might entail.

Irene Stiver (Director of Psychology at McClean Hospital in Massachusetts and Principal Associate in Psychiatry at the Harvard Medical School) tells of a young woman who developed a psychotic condition after her stepfather had a stroke. She talked of wanting to sleep with him. Not content to draw a Freudian conclusion, Stiver questioned her more closely. She found out that the stepfather had been a powerful businessman, contemptuous of weak people like her mother, but very kind to her as a child. After his stroke, he became terrified: he was afraid to close his eyes for fear he would die. The young woman was not motivated by incestuous desire, as male-stream psychology would have it. She simply could not bear to see this powerful man become so vulnerable. "I thought . . . if I slept with him, if I put my arms around him, comforted him, he would be less afraid, that he would sleep, and he would stay alive" (26).

Irene Stiver provides another frame of reference in which to see Jinny. She is a physical person, and will develop into a woman who "can imagine nothing beyond the circle cast by my body" (128–129). But her instinct toward Louis is neither sexual nor aggressive. It is simply caring. She is sensitive to Louis's devastating feeling of isolation and inadequacy, which is like death. And her instinct is to nurture him, to make him feel warm and wanted, to physically revive him. Moreover, her later refusal to be "attached to one person only . . . to be fixed, to be pinioned" (55), may now be seen, not as narcissistic, but as a need to connect with everyone. This need, as Jean Baker Miller and Carol Gilligan point out, is devalued in a culture dominated by male values of independence—and is continually misinterpreted and therefore frustrated by the men Jinny meets.

Jinny's kiss initiates both Louis and Jinny into the threatening world of sexuality—or gender and power. Jinny intrudes into Louis's haven when, due to his colonized status and class, he is feeling powerless. But, his gender gives him power, and privileges his story over hers. And her gender causes him to see her as a threat identified with the very power structure that excludes her. Susan, having already internalized the stereotype that leads to competitiveness between girlfriends, reinforces Louis's reaction through her agony and rage. And her response is reinforced by Bernard, who recognizes her anguish, takes her away, and comforts her with the story of Elvedon. Louis, Susan, Bernard, and by implication the other children, form the social mirror through which Jinny begins to define herself. They also form a narrative power structure that suppresses Jinny's story and shapes our view of her.

Neville becomes an author-ial figure because he is a poet, but, more important, because he introduces and continually invokes Percival, the silent but central character. Moreover, he concludes every other section until Bernard's final monologue. Neville competes with Rhoda, who concludes all the other sections. But, we should ask, why doesn't she have as much narrative power?

"Louis writes; Susan writes; Neville writes; Jinny writes; even Bernard has now begun to write. But I cannot write. I can see only figures," says Rhoda in her early school days (21). Nor can she look at herself in the mirror—"That is my face . . . in the looking-glass behind Susan's shoulder. . . . But I will duck behind her to hide it, for I am not here. I have no face" (43). Garrett Stewart, working within a Lacanian frame of reference, points out that Rhoda emerges "into voice at precisely the moment of her exclusion from written discourse." She sees "only graphic shapes . . . not their possible meaning. Here is the otherness of language stressed as the language of others, an accession to the symbolic whose rite of passage, whose writing, Rhoda alone among her peers cannot achieve" (433–434). She cannot say herself in language, just as she cannot see herself in the mirror. According to Lacan, the mirror offers the child its first opportunity to see a unified image of itself. But, since the child does not feel unified, what it sees is an image of an "other."

The mirror phase is a step on the way to the acquisition of

language, which also unifies the self and transforms subjectivity into otherness, by constituting it in the symbolic pronoun "I." Language, then, is an expression of lack, of a gap between the self and the world, and indeed, within the self. Woolf, according to Stewart, offers an "alternative, a new way of hearing the lexical void." But not for Rhoda, for whom the gaps become "remorseless, disruptive, and incapacitating" (432).

Neville anguishes but articulates the gap, and establishes his narrative power by invoking the silent and absent Percival as an object of desire and authority. "Now I will lean sideways as if to scratch my thigh. So I shall see Percival. There he sits, upright among the smaller fry. He breathes through his straight nose rather heavily. His blue, and oddly inexpressive eyes, are fixed with pagan indifference upon the pillar opposite. He would make an admirable churchwarden. He should have a birch and beat little boys for misdemeanours. He is allied with the Latin phrases on the memorial brasses. He sees nothing; he hears nothing. He is remote from us all in a pagan universe" (35–36).

It is significant that Percival does not appear until the boys have separated from the girls; indeed, we never learn how the girls get to know him. Percival arises out of the male world of the public school—where all three men excel in language. And this world is governed, as Woolf tells us, by a curriculum that trains men not only in good manners and the classics but in "the arts of dominating other people . . . of ruling, of killing, of acquiring land and capital" (*Three Guineas*, 34). Eve Kosofsky Sedgwick illuminates another dimension of this world by showing how social and political power was engendered in the public schools by a set of male homosocial relations: friendship, mentorship, entitlement, rivalry, and homosexuality. The term "homosocial" was designed to distinguish male bonding from homosexuality in a society characterized by its homophobia. But Sedgwick makes a good argument for considering homosocial relationships along a continuum, not as Adrienne Rich does to valorize homosexual love and demonstrate the continuity of feeling among women, but to illuminate the set of relations—the hegemony—that secured and perpetuated male power in social and literary institutions. Sedgwick focuses on eighteenth- and nineteenth-century English literature. When we apply her argument to a twentieth-century novel that undermined character and action, the very forms responsible for this hegemony in fiction, we discover that the male hegemony was inscribed not just in representation but in a more elemental level of narration.

It is interesting that the original Welsh Percival did not reflect the male hegemony; in fact, the power he comes to represent in *The Waves* is reflected in the way his story was appropriated by the (male) storytellers of the late Middle Ages, or transformed to deny the importance of women and even the female meaning of his story. As Barbara Walker points out, the ithyphallic demigod named Peredur Paladrhir (Spearman with a Long Shaft) was initiated by the witches of Caer Loyw. Each day for twenty-one days in the woman's "great court," Peredur watched the women kill a man, bathe him in the "Cauldron of Regeneration," and bring him back to life. And he was instructed by his ladylove, "the most beautiful damsel in the world."

Women figured importantly even in Chrétien de Troyes's twelfth-century *Roman de Perceval,* for, Walker continues, he was hidden and brought up in secret by his mother, as in most versions of the "Divine Child." Moreover, a lady prophesied his destiny, an instructress taught him the secret meaning of chivalry, and at the Grail Castle he saw a vision of the holy vessel in the hands of Queen Repanse de Joie. Later versions of the story first vilified his instructress by depicting her as a Jew and as Satan's mistress who gave birth to the Antichrist, and then displaced her—as well as the feminine meaning of his quest (784–786). Indeed, even Chrétien de Troyes's story gets transformed in the authoritative 1972 *Encyclopedia Britannica:* "Perceval's father and brothers having been killed in pursuit of chivalry, he is brought up by his mother in isolation from the world and complete ignorance of knighthood." Note how the mother is sentenced through grammatical tactics that subordinate her to the father and deny her a crucial role.

Percival's historical appropriation by male author-ity is reflected in the novel's narrative hegemony, first by his emerging at the male public school, and then by the men carrying the narrative that makes him central to the novel. True, Jinny announces his entrance at the Hampton Court (122) and sees him as central to the moment they all want to hold forever (145). And Rhoda responds to him in a way that makes us think of Blake's fearful Christ the tiger (126, 130). But the men dominate. They "speak" far more often and their "speeches" are far longer. Recent studies show that men still speak more frequently and for longer periods of time—in most conversations, coeducational classrooms, and even in meetings among enlightened men and women.[1] And in most of *The Waves* the men narrate while the women react—or form a chorus. Indeed, it is Bernard who tells us that Percival loves Susan and that "when he takes his seat by Susan, whom he loves, the occasion is crowned" (123). Susan thinks about the smell of carpets and furniture (which she hates), about the fields of her farm and her children (which she loves), and about Jinny by whom she is torn by jealousy—but never about Percival, not even in the section announcing his death.

Within the world of the story, the men relate to Percival through different forms of desire. Neville's is homoerotic and charges the hegemony with sexual energy that is at least implicit in the thoughts of the other men. Louis, coming from a British colony and from a lower class, "resent[s] the power of Percival intensely," but feels that "it is Percival I need; for it is Percival who inspires poetry" (39–40). That is, he relates to Percival through a desire for a form of beauty and permanence to which he is socially denied. Bernard is inspired to describe the last supper with Percival as a "communion" (126), and in the end to be aroused by "a new desire"—as he identifies with Percival the knight and flings himself against death. His desire is the most complex and will require further examination.

Percival is the source of male desire and the focal point of narrative hegemony. His role in the novel is to unite both the men and the women through a male ideal shared by the pagan hero, the wise fool, the Christian martyr, and the imperial conqueror. He is the silent figure who unites the six friends in a last supper, the foolish knight who is killed when his horse trips, and the romantic knight who gallops with his hair flying in the wind and his spear couched—inspiring Bernard as he approaches death.

Which brings us to Bernard, who becomes a professional writer and is the dominant storyteller. Early in the novel, he follows Susan—"gently . . . to be at hand, with my curiosity, to comfort her when she bursts out in a rage and thinks, 'I am alone' " (14). And he tells her a story. In the story of Elvedon, Bernard leads Susan—and the reader—past a thorny hedge that the ladies clip each noon with scissors, through a ringed wood with its rank and poisonous undergrowth where they hear the flop of a giant toad, and up to a wall. Peering cautiously over the wall, they watch the gardeners, who sweep with giant brooms, who would shoot the children if they saw them, who would nail them like stoats to the stable door. And in the center of this menacing world, between two long windows, is the lady writing.

Elvedon, as Maria diBattista says, is the displaced center of the novel—though I would describe its displacement differently to illuminate the struggle for author-ity. On the one hand, the lady writing rules the manor. And the menacing world that Bernard describes reflects his fear of female author-ity. Indeed, we might consider Elvedon to be what Kristeva calls the "chora," from the Greek word for enclosed space, or womb, which houses the wild and threatening semiotic rhythm that runs beneath controlled, symbolic expression. Throughout Western history, the woman's body, especially her womb, has been represented as mysterious and incomprehensible; the language associated with her body has been threatening to male author-ity because it is "other," contradictory, uncontrollable, and cannot be fixed in language. The menacing walls and woods and gardeners, which Bernard creates in his story, not only threaten him. They not only keep him out. They keep the lady writing in. Bernard's story may express his fear of the lady writing, but it is also designed (to use Gilbert's term) to "sentence" her, imprison her between the windows of her mansion—to keep her in her place.

Bernard's story is so convincing that Susan collaborates in telling it. It is so successful that we accept him as an author-ial figure even though he is a child. Although he is pompous and ineffectual and often parodied by the authorial voice, most readers and critics take what he says as author-itative in passages that dominate every section of the novel. They take him at his word when he tells us that he is androgynous. And they attend to him with great anticipation in his chapter-long monologue, which begins, "Now to sum up" (238). And, while many resisting readers are not drawn to him at all, to ignore his authorial power is to ignore the power of the male hegemony, the space he takes up in the novel, the role he plays as a storyteller, the way he is positioned in narrative sequence, the way he is empowered through an identification with Percival. Indeed, it is to ignore the textual, cultural, and historical context, the power of the dominant interpretive community—and the politics of narration.

What we encounter in the final section is not a stylized soliloquy, like all the other monologues. It is Bernard's actual speech to a stranger sitting across the dinner table, probably at his club: " 'Since we do not know each other (though I met you once I think on board a ship going to Africa) we can talk freely' " (238). The trip to Africa may remind us that Bernard is a member of the ruling class of the British Empire. Moreover, since he rarely addresses his companion directly, the implied "you" in this dramatic monologue gradually becomes the reader. And we become implicated, as we did in *Heart of Darkness*, when we were drawn to identify with the community of listeners on the *Nellie*. Bernard addresses us directly. He cannot arouse the interest of his companion, but he arouses our interest and holds our attention. For we have come to

care about him. But more important, we have come to rely on him
for guidance in this experience of shifting viewpoints and intricate
relationships. And here he is telling us: " 'Now to sum up. Now to
explain to you the meaning of my life' " (238).

But note the shift. Summing up becomes finding the meaning of
his life. As Bernard reviews the story of each character, he fits the
fragmentary incidents of the past into a pattern that gives *his* life
meaning. In appropriating their stories—as he appropriated the
story of the lady writing—he displaces the female author, or the
em-bodying source. Indeed, he literally takes on the paternalistic
role of an omniscient narrator—" 'So now, taking upon me the
mystery of things, I could go like a spy without leaving this place' "
(291). Moreover, he co-opts the female myth of creation. For,
drawing his story to an end, he tells us, " 'Day rises; the girl lifts
the watery fire-hearted jewels to her brow: the sun levels *his* beams
straight at the sleeping house' " (291, my emphasis). That is, he
appropriates the language of the lady writing (whose "*girl couched
on her green-sea mattress tired her brows with water-globed jewels*" [148]). He transfers the girl's power to a male sun god. And he
reduces the female creator to the kind of figure that adorns the
men's club where he is probably dining.

In the end Bernard feels "beat and done with it all" (296). Then
he becomes "aware . . . of a new desire," and identifies with
Percival—but not with the Percival of the last supper or the Percival
who fell to his death when his horse tripped. Bernard rides against
death "with my spear couched and my hair flying back like a young
man's, like Percival's when he galloped in India" (297).

There is no question that Bernard is a complex character, continually questioning the language in which he thinks and writes,
changing as we see him through the eyes of other characters, thinking of himself as multiple rather than single, believing that he is
androgynous. Nonetheless, in the end he takes on the combined
role of omniscient narrator and phallic hero. He is driven by the
desire for unity and urge toward mastery. And, fantasizing himself
as Percival who gallops in India with his spear couched, he is
aroused by a thirst for violent adventure, military invasion, and
imperialist glory.

Now these are just the drives that Virginia Woolf attacked and
parodied in *Mrs. Dalloway,* when the narrator broke through her
highly controlled narrative to rail against imperialism, or the Goddess of Conversion. And this is just the dual fantasy satirized in *To
the Lighthouse,* when Mr. Ramsay realizes that he might never
reach R., but would go on with the struggle. "He would find some

crag of rock, and there, his eyes fixed on the storm, trying to the end to pierce the darkness, he would die standing." And the searchers would find him "dead at his post, the fine figure of a soldier" (55, 56).

It is important to remember that Woolf had just written *A Room of One's Own,* where she identified the power of male sentencing. Moreover, she had also just finished *Orlando*—which begins, as Jane Marcus reminds us, with the paragon of a young man, "slicing at the head of a Moor which swung from the rafters," a head that his father or grandfather had struck "from the shoulders of a vast Pagan."[2] They "had ridden in fields of asphodel, and stony fields, and fields watered by strange rivers, and they had struck many heads of many colours off many shoulders and brought them back to hang from the rafters. So too would Orlando, he vowed." But since he was too young "he would steal away from his mother and the peacocks in the garden and go to his attic room and there lunge and plunge and slice the air with his blade"—before settling down to spend an hour composing his Tragedy in Five Acts (13). The parody links the imperialist warrior with the voice of traditional author-ity. And, while in *Orlando* Woolf turned her young hero into a woman, in *The Waves* she would turn him into Percival.

But then why do we take Percival seriously? Why don't we laugh at what is more of a pratfall than the death of an idealized hero or martyr? Why do we see him as a unifying force? Why do we glorify his innocence? Why do we invest his silence with meaning? Why, when Jinny is so lonely and Rhoda commits suicide, do we see *him* as representing the loss of human possibility? And why do we accept Bernard's author-ity? Why, when we only have his own self-serving word for it, do we trust his sympathy? Why, when he fantasizes a biographer to tell us, do we accept his androgyny? Why, after seeing what he actually writes—the romantic sketch of a back street where "a girl stands waiting. For whom?" And the story of "a purple lady swelling, circumambient, hauled from a barouche landau by a perspiring husband" with a small crane fixed to the top of a wall (115)—why do we even believe in him as a writer? And why don't we give full weight to the waves that break on the shore—the novel's final line that silently undermines Bernard's heroic gesture against Death?

In the beginning of *The Waves* we are drawn to the woman's story—the female creation myth and the voice that embodies the evolving interrelations of six friends. But soon we are drawn to the authorial voices of the male characters, who have mastered the language, whose thoughts are most sustained and aggressive, who take on the substantial roles for which they were trained, and who can count on readers' needs for traditional forms of order and unity. And the narrative hegemony carries what gradually emerges as a narrative.

Moreover, the embodying source conceives her characters as multiple, and all the characters articulate their multiplicity. For, as Stewart points out, the semiotic is maternal but not limited to female experience, and Woolf has created a narrative idiom that enables both her male and female characters to express feelings that cannot be mirrored in the dominant, symbolic discourse. But as the narrative power shifts, as the male narrators take over, and especially as Bernard sums it all up, the characters take on unitary roles in what is more like a storyline.

Which is not to say that the female authorial voice gives way to the voice of traditional authority. The characters never rest in unitary positions. The story does not harden into a storyline. The female authorial voice does have the first and the last words. The waves will continue to break on the shore. Figure and ground continually shift. The novel is always dialogic. In *The Waves* Woolf eliminates all the "appalling narrative business of the realist: getting on from lunch to dinner," all the conventions so that there is "no plot, no comedy, no tragedy, no love interest or catastrophe in the accepted style and perhaps not a single button sewn on as the Bond Street tailors would have it" ("Modern Fiction," 212). There is no history, nothing of what Alex Zwerdling calls the "real world." She eliminates, we might say, all the traditional conventions of fiction and history, or fiction as his-story. But what emerges is a historical expression of the ruling-class mind and the woman's struggle—as she develops alternative forms of author-ity.

THE LADY writing em-bodies the shifting interrelationships of three men and three women, who were all members of the ruling class in England in the early twentieth century. The three men emerge with positive forms of identity. Bernard is a professional writer, a husband, and a father. Louis is the successful manager of a shipping business. Due to his social position, Neville can afford to be a poet and a homosexual; and he gains power through his association with Percival.

Besides having positive forms of identity, the men form a narrative hegemony—which, like the ruling class of the British Empire, is hierarchical. Though we attend to Louis's authority, Bernard and

Neville dominate, reflecting the power of their birthright. Bernard is privileged because he is a professional storyteller, identified with the literary tradition, and traditionally conceived as a sympathetic, worldly, and rational guide. He tells the most dramatically important parts of the story—indeed, he turns the developing field of interrelationships into a story and gives it "meaning" by fitting it into the pattern of his life. Neville is also privileged, though less so, because he is identified with the Latin poets. His narrative authority derives partly from his relationship to Percival. It also derives from his being given the final word, the power to "sentence," or close every chapter with the exception of Bernard's final monologue.

The women, on the other hand, lose their connections as soon as they leave the school of the six friends' childhood; they go their separate ways and live their separate, limited lives. While Susan is happy in her role of farm-wife and mother, she is also a depersonalized archetype of the eternal female. And Louis identifies her as a threat during the supper at Hampton Court, when he thinks in images out of Bernard's Elvedon: "To be loved by Susan would be to be impaled by a bird's sharp beak, to be nailed to a barnyard door" (120). Jinny, identified with her body, pays for being a threat; she runs from one man to the next until she loses her looks. And Rhoda, who could never accommodate, commits suicide. So we can see how the ruling-class mind sentences its women by limiting both their options and their powers of expression.

Despite her failure in what Bernard sums up as the novel's story, Rhoda is able to identify the power from which the dominant discourse springs. When Percival arrives at the supper, Rhoda feels that "the tiger leapt, and the swallow dipped her wings in dark pools on the other side of the world" (126). And later she thinks, "If I could believe . . . that I should grow old in pursuit and change, I should be rid of my fear: nothing persists. One moment does not lead to another. The door opens and the tiger leaps" (130). Louis may see Percival as destructive, "as he blunders off, crushing the grasses" (40), but Rhoda identifies him as menacing, as Christ the tiger without Blake's overtones of awe, as responsible for the gaps in time and language, as the source of intolerable discontinuity in a self she cannot see. And, on a historical level, she identifies him as the tiger who causes the swallow to dip "her wings in dark pools on the other side of the world," or as the righteous, romantic, imperial journey-man, who—in his quest for adventure, salvation, identity, power, domination—imposes himself and disenfranchises, dispossesses, isolates, and appropriates what he makes into the other.

Martin Green shows how popular tales of adventure "charged England's will with the energy to go out into the world and explore, conquer, and rule" (3). And Patrick Brantlinger goes further to show that journeys of adventure dominate " 'serious' domestic realism," as well as the light reading, the two being "seemingly opposite poles of a single system of discourse, the literary equivalents of imperialist domination abroad and liberal reform at home." Imperialism was "a pervasive set of attitudes and ideas, closely interwoven with racism and sexism," that "influenced all aspects of Victorian and Edwardian culture" (8, 12).

Because the romance plot was so deeply inscribed in the form of the novel, Peter Walsh was able to establish his author-ity in Mrs. Dalloway's story if not in her life. That he was also a civil servant of the Empire reflects the power of the ideology that the narrator blatantly condemns. It also relates the ideology of imperialism to the conventions of romance—which includes not only the conquest of a lady but the journey of adventure. For Peter—who unifies *Mrs. Dalloway* by imposing his view on Clarissa—pictures himself as "an adventurer . . . indeed . . . a romantic buccaneer" as he followed a young woman down the street (80). And Mr. Ramsay—who unites the family and Woolf's next novel by landing at the lighthouse—pictures himself as soldier leading his family on an expedition to a mountain "across the icy solitudes of the Polar region" (54). And Percival—who unifies the characters in *The Waves*—is pictured galloping in India with his hair flying back and his spear couched.

Joyce was conscious of himself as a colonized subject of the British Empire; he realized the attraction of the adventure story to his young narrator in "An Encounter" and its power over Eveline's imagination, and he brought the popular adventure story of Ulysses into the "zone of crude contact" and fearless laughter. Nonetheless, *A Portrait of the Artist* is a quest for identity and power. And however much the Homeric myth is undermined, it compels us to see *Ulysses* as dominated by a father's and a son's quests for identity. Faulkner illuminates the racism and sexism interwoven in the myth of the frontier, the story of the self-made man, the romance of the Southern patriarch—which are the American forms of imperialist adventure. But *As I Lay Dying* takes the form of a mythic journey and *Absalom, Absalom!* centers on the quest of a self-made man, and Faulkner's central, controlling characters (who are all male) all quest for meaning and identity.

So Joyce and Faulkner continually fracture and undermine forms of traditional authority and order, parody the traditional quest, create fields of relationship that allow stories of the marginalized and suppressed to be told, and picture the self as multiple. But what drives their central (male) characters is the quest for individual identity and meaning—which are forms of domination that require the imposition of order, the reduction of multiplicity, and the appropriation of the other. And these quests are enhanced by canonical myths and allusions even when they are parodied and interrogated.

Woolf, on the other hand, came to understand and argue that the kinds of mastery—or author-ity—that valued order and unity were central to the male-dominated curriculum and related to "the arts of dominating other people . . . of ruling, of killing, of acquiring land and capital." And that the image of adventurous manhood led to what were "called in German and Italian Führer or Duce; in our own language Tyrant or Dictator" (*Three Guineas*, 34, 142). She could not avoid the forms of domination that were so deeply inscribed in narrative discourse. But she could identify them and engage them on a field that undermined their power and engendered other kinds of stories. And most important, she could, as Patricia Waugh argues, construe "human identity in terms of relationship and dispersal, rather than as a unitary, self-directing, isolated ego" (12).

In *Mrs. Dalloway* Woolf learned to stretch the (male) sentence to achieve maximum inclusiveness and interconnection. In *To the Lighthouse* she countered the journey-men's story head on with a woman's story of relationships. In *Orlando* she played with authorial gender in a way that challenged the unity of character, plot, and history. In *The Waves* she developed a new authorial voice that em-bodied her characters as multiple, existing only in their shifting relations with one another. In *The Years* she wrote in a more traditional mode but indicted the family as a major source of imperial male author-ity. We do not know how *Between the Acts* would have turned out, for, despite her husband's assurance, it was incomplete. But it was a frightening and angry novel, and Woolf was breaking new ground. One source of her fear and anger we can now understand is the news article that haunts Isa throughout the day: "As her father-in-law had dropped the *Times*, she took it and read: 'A horse with a green tail . . . ' which was fantastic. Next, 'The guard at Whitehall . . . ' which was romantic and then, building word upon word, she read: 'The troopers told her the horse had a green tail; but she found it was just an ordinary horse. And they dragged her up to the barrack room where she was thrown on a bed. Then one of the troopers removed part of her clothing, and she screamed and hit him about the face . . .' "(20).

Whitehall, we should remember, is a palace housing the British Government. And *The Times,* Cam Ramsay remembered, was what the old men read, sitting in armchairs, presiding over the study, and taking up her questions "with their clean hands (they wore grey-coloured clothes; they smelt of heather) and they brushed the scraps together, turning the paper, crossing their knees, and said something now and then very brief" (*To the Lighthouse,* 281). And in *The Years* another memorable *Times* article contained a picture of Mussolini gesticulating. It caused the elderly Eleanor to shout "Damned," as "she tore the paper across with one sweep of her hand and flung it on the floor," the word on her aunt's lips shocking Peggy, the noise of the tear sending a shiver over her skin (330).

The romantic imperial guard, a violent rape, *The London Times,* the father's library, a gesticulating fascist, and then the husband, Giles—who picks up a stone and, remembering the rules of the game he had learned as a child, kicks it to the goal, which is a snake choked with a toad in its mouth. "It was birth the wrong way round—a monstrous inversion. So, raising his foot, he stamped on them. The mass crushed and slithered. The white canvas on his tennis shoes was bloodstained and sticky. But it was action. Action relieved him. He strode to the barn, with blood on his shoes" (99).

Afraid that the Nazis were about to invade England and fighting her last depression, Woolf was bringing to consciousness the full realization that fascist domination, like her own sexual violations, was a logical outcome of the patriarchal family, a school system that engendered violence in the guise of good fellowship and sports, the adventure of imperialism, and the author-ity relfected in the historical pageant of English literature.

We do not know how *Between the Acts* would have come out. But *The Waves* is certainly an achievement. Here Woolf develops the potential of party consciousness and replaces the traditional voice of author-ity with an em-bodying force. She undermines all the author-ial conventions, decenters the novel form, replaces the journey-men's story or ambitious text with an erotic text, brings the semiotic rhythm to the surface, and exposes the historical source of political, social, and linguistic author-ity. But she also gives full expression to the dialogic of power relations—in which the semiotic and symbolic always contend, and the lady writing continually struggles against the author-ity of the male sentence.

Epilogue: An Open End

I have been trying to show that what distinguishes modern fiction—especially the fiction of James Joyce, William Faulkner, and Virginia Woolf—are disruptions, discontinuities, silences, absences, holes. And as our experience comes to include the holes, their stories become more inclusive, or (w)hole. For the holes derive from or reflect the mediation of language, the materiality of the text, our separation from what was supposed to have happened, the limitations of subjectivity, and the fact that we cannot fully know the subjectivity of the "other." To affirm not only the necessity but the value of holes is to affirm the value of difference.

All three writers were struggling against a tradition that maintained its author-ity by disguising the way it mediated and imposed its order on experience, and by ignoring, co-opting, or suppressing what it did not value or found threatening. Therefore, another kind of hole, or absence, is generated by the power of the authorial voice—in its linear plots, stories of development, ambitious texts, quests for identity and power, but also in the echoes of canonical writers, and the regenerated myths of male power, the hierarchy of characters, and the imposition of unity.

I tried to show how in Joyce's *A Portrait of the Artist* a rebellious voice argues with the authorial voice. In *Ulysses* the rebellious voice disrupts the authorial voice, leaps across time and space, impedes our view of central events, draws revered myths into a zone of crude, comic contact, undermines the ambitious story of development, and asserts the physicality of its own text— to em-body a story of relationships where voices can relate to each other as independent subjects. But the authorial voice has a residual power built into the discourses of our culture, inscribed in the forms of our stories, ingrained in our habits of reading, inured to the full impact of disruption and parody, and fostered by critics and teachers in their need for stability, mastery, and authority.

Faulkner's novels contain a great variety of storytelling voices that cross the lines of gender, race, and class. By intercutting among them, he disrupts the authoritative plotline in ways that challenge causal, or authorial, explanation. He parodies the mythic quest and interrogates history and heroism. But he is more susceptible to the power of the authorial voice—which arranges the storytellers to its own advantage, co-opts the voices of its opposition, compels us to reassert chronology and causality, or become its accomplice in restoring authorial order. Nonetheless, Faulkner leads us to understand the many strategies by which the authorial voice maintains its authority. Moreover, he makes us feel the power of his absent, suppressed, and repressed characters. We can hear the echoes of Caddy's love and feel the impressions of her absence. We can hear the anger of Addie Bundren and her subversive story of motherhood. We can attend Rosa Coldfield's discourse of desire.

More alienated from author-ity because of her gender, Woolf identifies the sources of power, illuminates the inherent violence, and traces the history. She establishes an independent line of modern fiction by identifying what has denied women and other marginalized people their identity—and by developing a female sentence and an authorial voice that realize forms of multiplicity and relationship that cannot be achieved in Joyce and Faulkner. For, despite the heterogeneity of their worlds, their shifting points of view, and the multiple selves that emerge, their novels are dominated by characters searching for singular identity, and questing for singular meaning. But Woolf too must contend with the voice of traditional author-ity, for, even though she em-bodies shifting relationships, the quest or the journey of adventure is so deeply inscribed in the storytelling tradition that it empowers some of the very kind of characters she mocks or condemns.

I have tried to line up the voices, describe the strategies, and define the struggles for author-ity. Moreover, I have argued that while we need to discover and recover the power of rebellious leaps and gaps and subversive voices and stories, we should not ignore the power of the authorial voice. For this would be to ignore textual context and cultural history. As a result, however, I have polarized the heterogeneity of these rich texts, and reduced inclusiveness to dualism, and multivalence to essentialism. And in my enthusiasm for semiotic disruption and fullness, and the erotic as opposed to the ambitious text, I have run the danger of essentializing women and advocating psychological empowerment at the expense of political achievement and power.

The problem of polarization became clear to me in a recent dialogue with Pamela Caughie on authority in teaching Virginia Woolf. I was trying to demonstrate how Jinny in *The Waves* was shaped by the male story, how readers had accepted Louis's author-ity and not even recognized that Jinny's version had different facts. Moreover, by tuning in on her story and viewing it through a frame of feminist psychology, we could see her kiss not as aggressive or sexual but as caring—as a recognition of Louis's vulnerability and devastation, as an attempt to nurture and revive him. But, Caughie responded, however much I wanted to show that Jinny was shaped by the male story, and however much we might want to resist seeing her kiss as an aggressive sexual act, it is just this view that exposes Louis's fear of female sexuality and its threat to his independence as a male. "That is, as a woman, I might still want to read Jinny as a woman who isn't afraid to live out her sexual desires, not as a woman who represents female nurturing."[1] Nor did Caughie want to stop with this convincing alternative; she wanted to show Woolf as a writer who was continually opening new possibilities, denying closure, breaking out of dualistic thinking.

Yet Caughie herself was forced back into a dualistic position, and not simply to counter my argument. It was because the politics of narration leads from heterogeneity to polarization, from multiplicity to dualism, from the carnival to the agon. The power of the authorial voice derives from tradition—the ways of teaching, learning, reading, and writing established by the class whose authority the authorial voice reflects and perpetuates. It reduces the multiplicity of voices, or positions, to two: those that enhance its power, either deliberately or by co-optation, and those that oppose it. And it does so not only because that is the nature of hegemonic relations, but because aggression, competition, and dualism are so ingrained, or, as Walter Ong points out, the tradition is agonistic.

Fortunately, the tradition is also unstable—especially, as Bakhtin argues, the tradition of the novel with its propensity toward carnival. Joyce, Faulkner, and Woolf have contributed to its instability. Our task as scholars, critics, and teachers—with our ambiguous relationship to the authority of the dominant discourse—is to generate awareness of the politics of narration, and maintain the instability of rebellious texts. And what are the prospects for the future? Pretty good I would say, considering that the modern (and postmodern) canon in the United States alone is coming to include writers like Toni Morrison, Maxine Hong Kingston, and the remarkable collaboration of Louise Erdrich and Michael Dorris—who create vast decentered and intersubjective fictions of African-American communities, Chinese-American families, and Native-American generations. Moreover, a new generation of scholars and teachers is restructuring and reopening the canon, teaching strong and resisting ways to read, and creating collaborative classrooms. Of course, we will have to be alert to new problems of canonization, marginalization, author-ity. And we may have to define a new field in which to engage the politics of narration.

Notes

Introduction

1. See Andreas Huyssen, *After the Great Divide*, and Maarten van Delden, "Modernism, the New Criticism, and Thomas Pynchon's *V*," for their insightful discussions of New Criticism. Poirier adds an important historical note to the period in which the New Criticism flourished.

2. My argument about modernism and postmodernism is developed in "What Joyce After Pynchon?" For a fuller discussion of Joyce as a postmodernist, see Christine van Boheemen, *The Novel as Family Romance*.

3. Turner, Ladurie, and Davis are quoted in Mary Russo's "Female Grotesques: Carnival and Theory."

4. Wawrzycka's point was made in a paper delivered at the 1987 James Joyce Symposium in Milwaukee, Wisconsin.

Chapter 2. *A Portrait of the Artist as a Young Man*

1. My thanks to Morris Beja for suggesting that I compare the opening epiphany in *A Portrait* with the epiphany in the original manuscript.

2. See Morris Beja, "Epiphany and the Epiphanies."

3. "The quick light shower is over but tarries, a cluster of diamonds, among the shrubs of the quadrangle where an exhalation arises from the black earth. In the colonnade are the girls, an April company. They are leaving shelter, with many a doubting glance, with the prattle of trim boots and a pretty rescue of petticoats, under umbrellas, a light armoury, upheld at cunning angles" (Scholes and Kain, *The Workshop of Daedalus*, 35).

4. For further discussion of this paragraph, see my *Novel in Motion*.

5. See Mary Ewens, *The Role of the Nun in Nineteenth Century America*, for the history of American nuns . I also learned about them from conversations with James Keneally, who has long been a historian of Catholic women.

6. He would have to reject traditional religious and aesthetic conventions to reflect what R. B. Kershner and Mary Lowe-Evans say is Havelock Ellis's "new spirit," which relates awakening sexuality to artistic creation. Kershner argues convincingly that Ellis's *New Spirit* should be read dialogically with *A Portrait* (*Joyce, Bakhtin, and Popular Culture*, 231–232), and Lowe-Evans makes an important case for considering Stephen as being personally liberated from the Church's repression of sexuality (*Crimes Against Fecundity*, 49). But I would argue that, in what Kershner astutely describes as a dialogue and what Lowe-Evans illuminates as a major struggle, Stephen is governed by the superior power of author-ity.

CHAPTER 4. *ULYSSES*

1. It is interesting to note that many classical scholars have been troubled by the story of Ulysses' return, and attribute it to a different author (Wender, *The Last Scenes of the Odyssey*).

2. Fritz Senn proposed the notion in a symposium; Hugh Kenner developed it in *Joyce's Voices*, 87.

3. I am taking Restuccia's point out of a context. Indeed, she develops a contradictory argument (based on Sacher-Masoch's and Deleuze's paradigm of masochism) that Molly is used by Joyce to exorcise the fathers.

4. See Cheryl Herr, Joseph Heininger, Kimberly Devlin, and others in *The Historical Molly Bloom*, ed. Richard Pearce, forthcoming.

CHAPTER 5. CAN A WOMAN TELL HER STORY?

1. See Wesley Morris's important discussion of Faulkner's writing as revision, repression, perversion, but also recovery, in *Reading Faulkner.*

2. I would argue for the power of the authorial voice over that of prevailing scholarly opinion on the appendix—at least for most readers between 1946 and 1987. Faulkner wrote the appendix for Malcolm Cowley's *Portable William Faulkner.* It became the forward to the 1946 Modern Library double volume of *The Sound and the Fury* and *As I Lay Dying*, and in 1967 Modern Library printed it as an appendix. Many, perhaps most, critics agreed with André Bleikasten, who in his important study warned that the appendix should not be considered an "organic part" of the novel (*Most Splendid Failure*, 243). But this is to overlook the power of the authorial voice—especially after creating a need for order in most readers of this novel.
In 1987 Vintage issued the first corrected edition since the novel was published, deciding that the original manuscript was more authentic than what became a revision in 1946—and therefore dropping the appendix. I should say that in 1988 my argument may not have carried as much weight, when, after noticing the quizzical looks on my students' faces, I discovered my edition to be out of date. So the scholarly establishment may be more powerful, and have more author-ity, than the author. And my argument about the appendix may soon be a historical statement of reader response.

3. Quentin's grandfather is modeled on William Clark Falkner, whom Wesley Morris describes as Faulkner's "First Ancestor"—a "great-grandfather, a legendary figure whose authority in family history rests on his role as founder, as originating force" (*Reading Faulkner*, 89). Morris describes the role of the First Ancestor in Faulkner's works, as well as that of "The Descendant"—who "inherits [the great-grandfather's] stories as well as the function of retelling them. It is an ambiguous power involving a test of wills, the one a legend's bequest, the other a present desiring" (89).

4. For an analysis of Dilsey's opening image see *The Novel in Motion*, 28f.

5. Dorothy J. Hale analyzes the language of the characters in *As I Lay Dying* to show the relation of private to public self and to extend our understanding of them. She also goes beyond earlier critics in defining Faulkner's use of interior monologue ("*As I Lay Dying's* Heterogeneous Discourse").

6. See my discussion of the "hovering narrator" in *The Novel in Motion*.

CHAPTER 6. WIDENING THE GYRE

1. André Bleikasten makes a similar point in his important argument for an ideological criticism of Faulkner that is not limited by Marxism ("For/Against an Ideological Reading of Faulkner's Novels").

CHAPTER 7. *ABSALOM, ABSALOM!*

1. Robert Con Davis uses "the fictional father" as the title of a collection of essays based on Lacan's concept of "the symbolic father," or "the name-of-the-father." I have been influenced by André Bleikasten's essay "Fathers in Faulkner" and John Irwin's "The Dead Father in Faulkner," but my focus is more social than psychological.

2. Minrose Gwin compares Rosa to Dora, whose hysteria resulted from her father reducing her to "a commodity of exchange in an economy generated by male desire," allowing "Herr K. access to his daughter in return for acquiescence in his affair with Herr K.'s wife" (*The Feminine Faulkner*, 74).

3. For a good discussion of Rosa's language, see Phillip Weinstein, "Meditations on the Other: Faulkner's Rendering of Women."

4. André Bleikasten argues that Henry tries to break "out of the iron circle of paternal rule," but ends by becoming his "appointed avenger" ("Fathers in Faulkner," 141).

CHAPTER 8. WOOLF'S STRUGGLE WITH AUTHOR-ITY

1. Kevin Sullivan describes Joyce's education in *Joyce among the Jesuits*.

2. Jane Marcus argues that "the salient subtext in every Woolf novel is the voice of the working-class women"(*Virginia Woolf and the Languages of Patriarchy*, 138).

3. Michael Tratner develops the point very convincingly that, while the cleaning women had to stay behind the kitchen door dividing the classes at the dinner party, or the great scene of social unity, now they come out and become agents of social change. His paper, comparing Woolf and Joyce on gender and class, was delivered at the twelfth International James Joyce symposium during the last editing stage of this book.

4. Kate Flint argues that Woolf's sense of the "real world" did not extend beyond her class. She points out that besides the Great War, "Time Passes" may reflect the General Strike of the British mine workers that seriously upset the established order and that took place at the very time Woolf was writing this section. While Woolf pictures "the destructive forces of patriarchy and the dangers of impersonality [being] countered by female effort," she also reestablishes the hierarchy of classes ("Virginia Woolf and the General Strike," 332).

5. Haule presented his evidence at the 1989 meeting of the Modern Language Association in a pamphlet reproducing the manuscripts, entitled "*To the Lighthouse* and the Great War: The Evidence of Virginia Woolf's Revisions of 'Time Passes.' " In a later conversation with me he made a strong case for Woolf's motivation, based on his correspondence with DeSalvo during her research.

Chapter 9. Stretching the Sentence

1. Leonardi builds her argument on Liisa Dahl's notion of the "rounded impressionistic sentence," and on David Tallentire's computer study that tabulates Woolf's abundant use of the coordinate conjunction "and" ("Bare Places and Ancient Blemishes").

2. Gilbert's essay was later published in Gilbert and Gubar's *No Man's Land* and may now be attributed to both authors.

3. Some resisting readers emphasize the change in tense from "is" to "was" in the final sentence. They argue that the narrator is contradicting Peter and saying that the real Clarissa was in the room thinking of the old woman and Septimus. But I would argue that author-ity dominates in the explanatory "for."

Chapter 10. *The Waves*

1. See Catherine G. Krupnick, "Women and Men in the Classroom: Inequality and Its Remedies."

2. In a paper delivered at the 1987 Modern Language Association meeting.

Epilogue

1. Richard Pearce and Pamela Caughie, "Resisting 'The Dominance of the Professor': Gendered Teaching, Gendered Subjects" (Paper presented at the annual meeting of the Modern Language Association, December 1989).

Works Cited

Abel, Elizabeth. "Cam the Wicked: Woolf's Portrait of the Artist as Her Father's Daughter." In *Virginia Woolf and Bloomsbury: A Centenary Celebration*, ed. Jane Marcus, pp. 170–194. Bloomington: Indiana University Press, 1987.

Adams, Henry. *The Education of Henry Adams*. New York: Random House, 1931.

Angeli, Diego. "Extract from *Il Marzocco*" (12 August 1917). In *A Portrait of the Artist as a Young Man*, ed. Chester G. Anderson, p. 327. New York: Viking Press, 1968.

Bakhtin, Mikhail M. *The Dialogic Imagination: Four Essays by M. M. Bakhtin.* Edited by Michael Holquist. Translated by Caryl Emerson and Michael Holquist. Austin: University of Texas Press, 1981.

Bazargan, Susan. "Monologue as Dialogue: Molly Bloom's 'History' as Myriorama." *Works and Days 10* 5 (1987): 63–78.

Beauvoir, Simone de. *The Second Sex*. Translated by H. M. Parshley. New York: Vintage, 1983.

Beck, Warren. *Joyce's Dubliners: Substance, Vision, and Art*. Durham: Duke University Press, 1969.

Beer, Gillian. "The Victorians in Virginia Woolf: 1832–1941." In *Arguing With the Past: Essays in Narrative from Woolf to Sidney*, pp. 138–158. London and New York: Routledge, 1989.

Beja, Morris. "Epiphany and the Epiphanies." In *A Companion to Joyce Studies*, ed. Zack Bowen and James E. Carens, pp. 707–725. Westport, Conn.: Greenwood Press, 1984.

Benstock, Shari. "The Dynamics of Narrative Performance: Stephen Dedalus as Storyteller." *ELH* 49 (Fall 1982): 707–738.

Benstock, Shari, and Bernard Benstock. "The Benstock Principle." In *The Seventh of Joyce*, ed. Bernard Benstock, pp. 10–21. Bloomington: Indiana University Press, 1982.

Bleikasten, André. "Fathers in Faulkner." In *The Fictional Father: Lacanian Readings of the Text*, ed. Robert Con Davis, pp. 115–146. Amherst: University of Massachusetts Press, 1981.

———. "For/Against an Ideological Reading of Faulkner's Novels." In *Faulkner and Idealism: Perspectives from Paris*, ed. Michel Gresset and Patrick Samway, S.J., pp. 27–50. Jackson: University Press of Mississippi, 1983.

———. *The Most Splendid Failure: Faulkner's The Sound and the Fury.* Bloomington: Indiana University Press, 1976.

Boone, Joseph Allen. "Creation by the Father's Fiat: Paternal Narrative, Sexual Anxiety, and the Deauthorizing Designs of *Absalom, Absalom!*" In *Refiguring the Father: New Feminist Readings of Patriarchy*, ed. Patricia Yaeger and Beth Kowaleski-Wallace, pp. 209–237. Carbondale and Edwardsville: Southern Illinois University Press, 1989.

———. *Tradition Counter Tradition: Love and the Form of Fiction.* Chicago: University of Chicago Press, 1987.

Booth, Wayne. *The Rhetoric of Fiction.* Chicago: University of Chicago Press, 1961.

Brantlinger, Patrick. *Rule of Darkness: British Literature and Imperialism, 1830–1914.* Ithaca: Cornell University Press, 1988.

Brown, Richard. *James Joyce and Sexuality.* Cambridge: Cambridge University Press, 1985.

Budgen, Frank. *James Joyce and the Making of Ulysses.* Bloomington: Indiana University Press, 1960.

Chatman, Seymour. *Story and Discourse: Narrative Structure in Fiction and Film.* Ithaca: Cornell University Press, 1978.

Cixous, Hélène. "Sorties: Out and Out: Attacks / Ways Out / Forays." In Hélène Cixous and Catherine Clément, *The Newly Born Woman.* Translated by Betsy Wing, pp. 61–132. Minneapolis: University of Minnesota Press, 1986.

Conrad, Joseph. "The Heart of Darkness." *Heart of Darkness: An Authoritative Text, Background and Sources, Criticism.* Edited by Robert Kimbrough. New York: W. W. Norton, 1971.

Davis, Natalie Zemon. "Women on Top." In *Society and Culture in Early Modern France,* pp. 124–52. Stanford: Stanford University Press, 1975.

Davis, Robert Con, ed. *The Fictional Father: Lacanian Readings of the Text.* Amherst: University of Massachusetts Press, 1981.

Davis, Thadious M. *Faulkner's "Negro": Art and the Southern Context.* Baton Rouge: Louisiana State University Press, 1983.

DeSalvo, Louise. *Virginia Woolf: The Impact of Childhood Sexual Abuse on Her Life and Work.* Boston: Beacon Press, 1989.

Devlin, Kimberly. "The Romance Heroine Exposed: 'Nausicaa' and *The Lamplighter.*" *James Joyce Quarterly* 22 (Summer 1985): 383–396.

DiBattista, Maria. *Virginia Woolf's Major Novels.* New Haven: Yale University Press, 1980.

Dinesen, Isak. "The Blank Page." *Last Tales.* New York: Random House, 1957.

DuPlessis, Rachel Blau. *Writing Beyond the Ending: Narrative Strategies of Twentieth-Century Women Writers.* Bloomington: Indiana University Press, 1985.

Duvall, John N. "Murder and the Communities: Ideology in and Around *Light in August.*" *Novel* 20 (Winter 1987): 101–122.

Edwards, Lee. "War and Roses: The Politics of *Mrs. Dalloway.*" In *The Authority of Experience: Essays in Feminist Criticism,* ed. Arlyn Diamond and Lee Edwards, pp. 160–177. Amherst: University of Massachusetts Press, 1977.

Eisenstein, Sergei. *Film Form: Essays in Film Theory.* Edited and translated by Jay Leyda. New York: Harcourt, Brace & World, 1949.

Ellmann, Richard. *James Joyce.* New York: Oxford University Press, 1982.

Ewens, Mary. *The Role of the Nun in Nineteenth Century America.* New York: Arno Press, 1978.

Faulkner, William. *Absalom, Absalom!* New York: Random House, 1987.

———. *As I Lay Dying.* New York: Random House, 1957.

———. *The Hamlet.* New York: Random House, 1956.

———. *Light in August.* New York: Random House, 1987.

———. *Selected Letters of William Faulkner.* Edited by Joseph Blotner. New York: Random House, 1978.

———. *The Sound and the Fury.* New York: Random House, 1956.

Fetterly, Judith. *The Resisting Reader: A Feminist Approach to American Fiction.* Bloomington: Indiana University Press, 1978.

Flint, Kate. "Virginia Woolf and the General Strike." *Essays in Criticism* 36 (October 1986): 319–334.

Fowler, Doreen, and Ann J. Abadie, eds. *Faulkner and Women: Faulkner and Yoknapatawpha, 1985.* Jackson: University Press of Mississippi, 1986.

Freud, Sigmund. "The Question of Lay Analysis." *The Standard Edition of the Complete Psychological Works of Sigmund Freud,* vol. 20. Translated by James Strachey in collaboration with Anna Freud. London: Hogarth Press, 1959.

Garnett, Edward. "Reader's Report." In *A Portrait of the Artist as a Young Man,* ed. Chester G. Anderson, pp. 319–320. New York: Viking Press, 1968.

Gifford, Don. *Joyce Annotated: Notes for Dubliners and A Portrait of the Artist as a Young Man.* Berkeley: University of California Press, 1982.

Gilbert, Sandra M. "Woman's Sentence, Man Sentencing: Linguistic Fantasies in Woolf and Joyce." In *Virginia Woolf and Bloomsbury: A Centenary Celebration,* ed. Jane Marcus, pp. 208–224. Bloomington: Indiana University Press, 1987.

Gilbert, Sandra, and Susan Gubar. *No Man's Land: The Place of the Woman Writer in the Twentieth Century,* vol. 1. New Haven: Yale University Press, 1987.

Gilbert, Stuart. *James Joyce's Ulysses.* New York: Vintage, 1955.

Gilligan, Carol. *In a Different Voice: Psychological Theory and Women's Development.* Cambridge and London: Harvard University Press, 1982.

"Glasgow Herald." In *A Portrait of the Artist as a Young Man,* ed. Chester G. Anderson, p. 335. New York: Viking Press, 1968.

Gombrich, E. H. *Art and Illusion: A Study in the Psychology of Pictorial Representation.* Princeton: Princeton University Press, 1969.

Green, Martin. *Dreams of Adventure, Deeds of Empire.* New York: Basic Books, 1979.

Gubar, Susan. " 'The Blank Page' and the Issues of Female Creativity." *Critical Inquiry* 8 (Winter 1981): 243–262.

Gwin, Minrose C. *The Feminine and Faulkner: Reading (Beyond) Sexual Difference.* Knoxville: University of Tennessee Press, 1990.

Hale, Dorothy J. "*As I Lay Dying*'s Heterogeneous Discourse." *Novel* 23 (Fall 1989): 5–23.

Harlow, Barbara. *Resistance Literature.* New York and London: Methuen, 1987.

Hart, Clive. "Wandering Rocks." In *James Joyce's Ulysses: Critical Essays,* ed. Clive Hart and David Hayman, pp. 181–216. Berkeley: University of California Press, 1974.

Haule, James M. "*To the Lighthouse* and the Great War: The Evidence of Virginia Woolf's Revisions of 'Time Passes'." Printed for talk at 1989 Modern Language Association meeting; forthcoming.

Hayman, David. "The Joycean Inset." *James Joyce Quarterly* 2 (1986): 157–172.

———. *Ulysses: The Mechanics of Meaning.* Madison: University of Wisconsin Press, 1982.

Heath, Stephen. *The Sexual Fix.* New York: Schocken, 1984.

Herr, Cheryl. " 'Penelope' as Period Piece." *Novel* 22 (Winter 1989): 130–142.

Herring, Phillip F. *Joyce's Uncertainty Principle.* Princeton: Princeton University Press, 1987.

Homer. *The Odyssey.* Translated by E. V. Rieu. Baltimore: Penguin, 1946.

Humphrey, Robert. *Stream of Consciousness in the Modern Novel.* Berkeley: University of California Press, 1965.

Huyssen, Andreas. *After the Great Divide: Modernism, Mass Culture, Postmodernism.* Bloomington: Indiana University Press, 1986.

Irwin, John T. "The Dead Father in Faulkner." In *The Fictional Father: Lacanian Readings of the Text,* ed. Robert Con Davis, pp. 147–168. Amherst: University of Massachusetts Press, 1981.

———. *Doubling and Incest / Repetition and Revenge: A Speculative Reading of Faulkner.* Baltimore: Johns Hopkins University Press, 1975.

James, Henry. *The Ambassadors.* Edited by Leon Edel. Boston: Houghton Mifflin, 1960.

Joyce, James. *Dubliners.* Edited by Robert Scholes and A. Walton Litz. New York: Viking Press, 1969.

———. *A Portrait of the Artist as a Young Man.* Edited by Chester B. Anderson. New York: Viking Press, 1968.

———. *Ulysses: The Corrected Text.* Edited by Hans Walter Gabler with Wolfhard Steppe and Claus Melchior. New York: Vintage, 1986.

Jensen, Emily. "Clarissa Dalloway's Respectable Suicide." In *Virginia Woolf: A Feminist Slant,* ed. Jane Marcus, pp. 162–179. Lincoln: University of Nebraska Press, 1983.

Kauffman, Linda S. *Discourses of Desire: Gender, Genre, and Epistolary Fictions.* Ithaca: Cornell University Press, 1986.

Kenner, Hugh. *Joyce's Voices.* Berkeley: University of California Press, 1978.

———. *Ulysses.* London: George Allen and Unwin, 1980.

Kershner, R. B. *Joyce, Bakhtin, and Popular Literature: Chronicles of Disorder.* Chapel Hill: University of North Carolina Press, 1989.

Kolodny, Annette. *The Land Before Her: Fantasy and Experience of the American Frontiers, 1630–1860.* Chapel Hill: North Carolina University Press, 1984.

Kristeva, Julia. *Desire in Language: A Semiotic Approach to Literature and Art.* Edited by Leon Roudiez. Translated by Thomas Gora, Alice Jardine, and Leon Roudiez. New York: Columbia University Press, 1980.

———. *Revolution in Poetic Language.* Translated by Margaret Waller. New York: Columbia University Press, 1984.

Krupnick, Catherine G. "Women and Men in the Classroom: Inequality and Its Remedies." *On Teaching and Learning* 1 (May 1985): 18–25.

Ladurie, Emmanuel. *Carnival in Romans.* Translated by Mary Feeney. New York: Braziller, 1979.

Lawrence, Karen. *The Odyssey of Style in Ulysses.* Princeton: Princeton University Press, 1981.

Leaska, Mitchell A. *The Novels of Virginia Woolf: From Beginning to End.* New York: John Jay Press, 1977.

Leonardi, Susan J. "Bare Places and Ancient Blemishes: Virginia Woolf's Search for New Languages in *Night and Day.*" *Novel* 19 (Winter 1986): 150–163.

Levenson, Michael. "Stephen's Diary in Joyce's *Portrait*—the Shape of Life." *ELH* 52 (Winter 1985): 1017–1035.

Lidoff, Joan. "Virginia Woolf's Feminine Sentence: The Mother-Daughter World of *To the Lighthouse.*" *Literature and Psychology* 32 (1986): 43–59.

Lilienfeld, Jane. "Where the Spear Plants Grew: The Ramsays' Marriage in *To the Lighthouse.*" In *New Feminist Essays on Virginia Woolf,* ed. Jane Marcus, pp. 148–167. Lincoln: University of Nebraska Press, 1981.

"Liverpool Daily Express." In *A Portrait of the Artist as a Young Man,* ed. Chester G. Anderson, p. 336. New York: Viking Press, 1968.

Lowe-Evans, Mary. *Crimes Against Fecundity: Joyce and Population Control.* Syracuse: Syracuse University Press, 1989.

MacCabe, Colin. *James Joyce and the Revolution of the Word.* New York: Harper & Row, 1979.

Mahaffey, Vicki. *Reauthorizing Joyce.* Cambridge: Cambridge University Press, 1988.

Marcus, Jane. "The Niece of a Nun: Virginia Woolf, Caroline Stephen, and the Cloistered Imagination." In *Virginia Woolf: A Feminist Slant,* ed. Jane Marcus, pp. 7–36. Lincoln: University of Nebraska Press, 1983.

———. *Virginia Woolf and the Languages of Patriarchy.* Bloomington: Indiana University Press, 1986.

———, ed. *New Feminist Essays on Virginia Woolf.* Lincoln: University of Nebraska Press, 1981.

———, ed. *Virginia Woolf: A Feminist Slant.* Lincoln: University of Nebraska Press, 1983.

———, ed. *Virginia Woolf and Bloomsbury: A Centenary Celebration.* Bloomington: Indiana University Press, 1987.

McGee, Patrick. *Paperspace: Style as Ideology in Joyce's Ulysses.* Lincoln: University of Nebraska Press, 1988.

Miller, Jean Baker. *Toward a New Psychology of Women.* Boston: Beacon Press, 1976.

Miller, Nancy K. "Emphasis Added: Plots and Plausibilities in Women's Fiction." *PMLA* 96 (1981): 36–48.

Minow-Pinkney, Makiko. *Virginia Woolf and the Problem of the Subject.* New Brunswick, N.J.: Rutgers University Press, 1987.

Morris, Wesley, with Barbara Alverson Morris. *Reading Faulkner.* Madison: University of Wisconsin Press, 1989.

Naremore, James. *The World Without a Self: Virginia Woolf and the Novel.* New Haven: Yale University Press, 1973.

Naylor, Gloria. "The Myth of the Matriarch." *Life* (Special Issue: *The Dream Then and Now*) 11 (Spring 1988): 65.

O'Brien, Mary. *The Politics of Reproduction.* Boston: Routledge & Kegan Paul, 1981.

Olsen, Tillie. *Silences.* New York: Delacorte Press, 1978.

Ong, Walter. "Agonistic Structures in Academia: Past to Present." *Daedalus* 103 (Fall 1974): 229–238.

Pearce, Richard. *The Novel in Motion: An Approach to Modern Fiction.* Columbus: Ohio State University Press, 1983.

———. "What Joyce After Pynchon?" In *James Joyce: The Centennial Symposium,* ed. Morris Beja, Phillip Herring, Maurice Harmon, and David Norris, pp. 43–46. Urbana and Chicago: University of Illinois Press, 1986.

Pearce, Richard, and Pamela Caughie. "Resisting 'The Dominance of the Professor': Gendered Teaching, Gendered Subjects." Paper presented at the annual meeting of the Modern Language Association, December 1989.

Pecora, Vincent P. " 'The Dead' and the Generosity of the Word." *PMLA* 101 (1986): 233–245.

Pitavy, François. *Faulkner's Light in August.* Bloomington: Indiana University Press, 1973.

Poirier, Richard. "Hum 6, or Reading before Theory." *Raritan* 9 (Spring 1990): 14–31.

Restuccia, Frances L. "Molly in Furs: Deleuzean/Masochian Masochism in the Writing of James Joyce." *Novel* 18 (Winter 1985): 101–116. Revised in *Joyce and the Law of the Father*, pp. 124–176. New Haven: Yale University Press, 1989.

Richter, Harvena. *Virginia Woolf: The Inward Voyage.* Princeton: Princeton University Press, 1970.

Riquelme, John Paul. *Teller and Tale in Joyce's Fiction: Oscillating Perspectives.* Baltimore and London: The Johns Hopkins University Press, 1983.

Ross, Stephen M. *Fiction's Inexhaustible Voice: Speech and Writing in Faulkner.* Athens: University of Georgia Press, 1989.

———. "Voice in Narrative Texts: The Example of *As I Lay Dying.*" *PMLA* 94 (1979): 300–310.

Roudiez, Leon. "Introduction." In *Desire in Language: A Semiotic Approach to Literature and Art* by Julia Kristeva. Edited by Leon Roudiez. Translated by Thomas Gora, Alice Jardine, and Leon Roudiez. New York: Columbia University Press, 1980.

Ruppersburg, Hugh M. *Voice and Eye in Faulkner's Fiction.* Athens: University of Georgia Press, 1983.

Russo, Mary. "Female Grotesques: Carnival and Theory." In *Feminist Studies / Critical Studies*, ed. Teresa de Lauretis, pp. 213–229. Bloomington: Indiana University Press, 1986.

Scholes, Robert. "Stephen Dedalus, Poet or Esthete." In *A Portrait of the Artist as a Young Man*, ed. Chester G. Anderson, pp. 468–480. New York: Viking Press, 1968.

———. *Textual Power: Literary Theory and the Teaching of English.* New Haven: Yale University Press, 1985.

Scholes, Robert, and Richard M. Kain. *The Workshop of Daedalus: James Joyce and the Raw Materials for A Portrait of the Artist as a Young Man.* Evanston: Northwestern University Press, 1965.

Schwartz, Lawrence H. *Creating Faulkner's Reputation: The Politics of Modern Literary Criticism.* Knoxville: University of Tennessee Press, 1988.

Scott, Bonnie Kime. *James Joyce.* Atlantic Highlands, N.J.: Humanities Press, 1987.

———. *Joyce and Feminism.* Bloomington: Indiana University Press, 1984.

———, ed. *New Alliances in Joyce Studies: "When it's Aped to Foul a Delfian."* Newark: University of Delaware Press, 1988.

Sears, Sallie. "Theater of War: Virginia Woolf's *Between the Acts.*" In *Virginia Woolf: A Feminist Slant*, ed. Jane Marcus, pp. 212–235. Lincoln: University of Nebraska Press, 1983.

Sedgwick, Eve Kosofsky. *Between Men: English Literature and Male Homosocial Desire.* New York: Columbia University Press, 1985.

Stein, Jean. "William Faulkner: An Interview." In *William Faulkner: Three Decades of Criticism*, ed. Frederick J. Hoffman and Olga Vickery, pp. 67–81. New York: Harcourt Brace & World, 1963.

Stewart, Garrett. "Catching the Stylistic D/rift: Sound Defects in Woolf's *The Waves.*" *ELH* 54 (Summer 1987): 421–461.

Stiver, Irene. "Beyond the Oedipus Complex: Mothers and Daughters." *Work in Progress.* A publication of the Stone Center for Developmental Services and Studies, Wellesley College, Wellesley, Massachusetts, No. 26, 1986.

Straus, Nina Pelikan, "The Exclusion of the Intended from Secret Sharing in Conrad's *Heart of Darkness.*" *Novel* 20 (Winter 1987): 123–137.

Sullivan, Kevin. *Joyce among the Jesuits.* New York: Columbia University Press, 1958.

Thomas, Brook. "Not a Reading of, But the Act of Reading." *James Joyce Quarterly* 16 (Fall/Winter 1979): 86.

Tilly, Louise A., and Joan W. Scott. *Women, Work, and Family*. New York: Holt, Rinehart and Winston, 1978.

Tobin, Patricia. *Time and the Novel: The Genealogical Imperative*. Princeton: Princeton University Press, 1978.

Turner, Victor. "Frame, Flow, and Reflection: Ritual and Drama as Public Liminality." In *Performance in Postmodern Culture*, ed. Michel Benamou and Charles Caramello. Center for Twentieth Century Studies, Theories of Contemporary Culture, vol. 1. Madison, Wis.: Coda Press, 1977.

Valente, Joseph. "The Politics of Joyce's Polyphony." In *New Alliances in Joyce Studies: "When it's Aped to Foul a Delfian,"* ed. Bonnie Kime Scott, pp. 56–72. Newark: University of Delaware Press, 1988.

Van Boheemen, Christine. *The Novel as Family Romance: Language, Gender, and Authority from Fielding to Joyce*. Ithaca: Cornell University Press, 1987.

Van Delden, Maarten. "Modernism, the New Criticism, and Thomas Pynchon's *V.*" *Novel* 23 (Winter 1990): 117–136.

Wagner, Linda W. "Language and Act: Caddy Compson." *Southern Literary Journal* 14 (1982): 49–61.

Walker, Barbara G. *The Woman's Encyclopedia of Myths and Secrets*. San Francisco: Harper & Row, 1983.

Waugh, Patricia. *Feminine Fictions: Revisiting the Postmodern*. London and New York: Routledge, 1989.

Weinstein, Philip M. "Meditations on the Other: Faulkner's Rendering of Women." In *Faulkner and Women: Faulkner and Yoknapatawpha, 1985*, ed. Doreen Fowler and Ann J. Abadie, pp. 81–99. Jackson: University Press of Mississippi, 1986.

Wells, H. G. "James Joyce." *The New Republic* (10 March 1917). In *A Portrait of the Artist as a Young Man*, ed. Chester G. Anderson, p. 331. New York: Viking Press, 1968.

Wender, Dorothea. *The Last Scenes of the Odyssey*. The Netherlands: Brill, 1978.

Woolf, Virginia. *Between the Acts*. New York: Harcourt Brace Jovanovich, 1969.

———. *Jacob's Room*. New York: Harcourt Brace Jovanovich, 1978.

———. "Modern Fiction." *The Common Reader I*, pp. 184–195. London: Hogarth Press, 1962.

———. "Mr. Bennett and Mrs. Brown." *The Captain's Deathbed and Other Essays*, pp. 94–119. New York: Harcourt, 1950.

———. *Mrs. Dalloway*. New York: Harcourt Brace Jovanovich, 1953.

———. *Mrs Dalloway's Party: A Short Story Sequence*, ed. Stella McNichol. New York: Harcourt Brace Jovanovich, 1972.

———. *Orlando*. New York: Harcourt Brace Jovanovich, 1956.

———. *A Room of One's Own*. New York: Harcourt Brace Jovanovich, 1957.

———. "A Sketch of the Past." *Moments of Being*, ed. Jeanne Schulkind, pp. 61–160. New York: Harcourt Brace Jovanovich, 1985.

———. *Three Guineas*. New York: Harcourt Brace Jovanovich, 1966.

———. *To the Lighthouse*. New York: Harcourt Brace Jovanovich, 1955.

———. *The Waves*. New York: Harcourt Brace Jovanovich, 1959.

———. *The Years*. New York: Harcourt Brace Jovanovich, 1965.

Zwerdling, Alex. *Virginia Woolf and the Real World*. Berkeley: University of California Press, 1986.

Index

187